Macmillan Computer Science Series

MW01178056

Consulting Editor: Professor F. H. Sumne

A. Abdellatif, J. Le Bihan and M. Limame, *Oracle – A User's guide*
S.T. Allworth and R.N. Zobel, *Introduction to Real-time Software Design, second edition*
Ian O. Angell, *High-resolution Computer Graphics Using C*
Ian O. Angell and Gareth Griffith, *High-resolution Computer Graphics Using FORTRAN 77*
Ian O. Angell and Gareth Griffith, *High-resolution Computer Graphics Using Pascal*
M. Azmoodeh, *Abstract Data Types and Algorithms, second edition*
C. Bamford and P. Curran, *Data Structures, Files and Databases, second edition*
Philip Barker, *Author Languages for CAL*
R.E. Berry, B.A.E. Meekings and M.D. Soren, *A Book on C, second edition*
P. Beynon-Davies, *Information Systems Development*
G.M. Birtwistle, *Discrete Event Modelling on Simula*
B.G. Blundell, C.N. Daskalakis, N.A.E. Heyes and T.P. Hopkins, *An Introductory Guide to Silvar Lisco and HILO Simulators*
Richard Bornat, *Understanding and Writing Compilers*
Linda E.M. Brackenbury, *Design of VLSI Systems – A Practical Introduction*
Alan Bradley, *Peripherals for Computer Systems*
G.R. Brookes and A.J. Stewart, *Introduction to occam 2 on the Transputer*
J.K. Buckle, *Software Configuration Management*
W.D. Burnham and A.R. Hall, *Prolog Programming and Applications*
P.C. Capon and P.J. Jinks, *Compiler Engineering Using Pascal*
J.C. Cluley, *Introduction to Low Level Programming for Microprocessors*
Robert Cole, *Computer Communications, second edition*
E. Davalo and P. Naïm, *Neural Networks*
S.M. Deen, *Principles and Practice of Database Systems*
C. Delannoy, *Turbo Pascal Programming*
Tim Denvir, *Introduction to Discrete Mathematics for Software Engineering*
D. England *et al.*, *A Sun User's Guide*
J.S. Florentin, *Microprogrammed Systems Design*
A.B. Fontaine and F. Barrand, *80286 and 80386 Microprocessors*
J.B. Gosling, *Design of Arithmetic Units for Digital Computers*
M.G. Hartley, M. Healey and P.G. Depledge, *Mini and Microcomputer Systems*
J.A. Hewitt and R.J. Frank, *Software Engineering in Modula-2 – An Object-oriented Approach*
Roger Hutty, *COBOL 85 Programming*
Roland N. Ibbett and Nigel P. Topham, *Architecture of High Performance Computers, Volume I*
Roland N. Ibbett and Nigel P. Topham, *Architecture of High Performance Computers, Volume II*
Patrick Jaulent, *The 68000 – Hardware and Software*
P. Jaulent, L. Baticle and P. Pillot, *68020–30 Microprocessors and their Coprocessors*
M.J. King and J.P. Pardoe, *Program Design Using JSP – A Practical Introduction, second edition*
V.P. Lane, *Security of Computer Based Information Systems*
M. Léonard, *Database Design Theory*
David Lightfoot, *Formal Specification Using Z*
A.M. Lister and R.D. Eager, *Fundamentals of Operating Systems, fourth edition*

Continued overleaf

Macmillan Computer Science Series (continued)

Elizabeth Lynch, *Understanding SQL*
Tom Manns and Michael Coleman, *Software Quality Assurance*
R.J. Mitchell, *Microcomputer Systems Using the STE Bus*
R.J. Mitchell, *Modula-2 Applied*
Y. Nishinuma and R. Espesser, *UNIX – First Contact*
Pham Thu Quang and C. Chartier-Kastler, *MERISE in Practice*
A.J. Pilavakis, *UNIX Workshop*
E.J. Redfern, *Introduction to Pascal for Computational Mathematics*
Gordon Reece, *Microcomputer Modelling by Finite Differences*
F. D. Rolland, *Programming with VDM*
W.P. Salman, O. Tisserand and B. Toulout, *FORTH*
L.E. Scales, *Introduction to Non-Linear Optimization*
A.G. Sutcliffe, *Human–Computer Interface Design*
Colin J. Theaker and Graham R. Brookes, *Concepts of Operating Systems, second edition*
M. Thorin, *Real-time Transaction Processing*
M.R. Tolhurst *et al.*, *Open Systems Interconnection*
A.J. Tyrrell, *COBOL from Pascal*
M.J. Usher, *Information Theory for Information Technologists*
I.R. Wilson and A.M. Addyman, *A Practical Introduction to Pascal – with BS6192, second edition*

Non-series

Roy Anderson, *Management, Information Systems and Computers*
I.O. Angell, *Advanced Graphics with the IBM Personal Computer*
J.E. Bingham and G.W.P. Davies, *Planning for Data Communications*
B.V. Cordingley and D. Chamund, *Advanced BASIC Scientific Subroutines*
N. Frude, *A Guide to SPSS/PC+*
Percy Mett, *Introduction to Computing*
Tony Royce, *COBOL – An Introduction*
Tony Royce, *Structured COBOL – An Introduction*
Barry Thomas, *A PostScript Cookbook*

Data Structures, Files and Databases

Carl Bamford

School of Computing and Mathematical Sciences
Liverpool John Moore's University

and Paul Curran

Quantec Image Processing Ltd

Second Edition

MACMILLAN

First published 1987 by
THE MACMILLAN PRESS LTD
Houndmills, Basingstoke, Hampshire RG21 2XS
and London
Companies and representatives
throughout the world

ISBN 0–333–56043–4

A catalogue record for this book is available from the British Library.

Printed in China

Reprinted 1993

Contents

Preface

The first edition of this text has been used successfully on introductory courses in data structures, file structures and databases for second-year undergraduates and HND students in computer studies. It covers a wide range of material appropriate to this level, and assumes the reader has completed a first course in programming, Pascal being used to illustrate the topics covered. Although it is intended for undergraduate/HND students, its practical approach makes it suitable for professional programming practitioners.

For the second edition, we have retained the same theme: that the design of structures for data and processes should be considered first at an abstract level and then developed using concrete representations which take account of efficiency. The changes we have made relate to databases, where we have added more details of the language SQL and discussed fourth generation languages, topics which are increasingly important.

Data structures are treated informally, with an abstract view of each structure examined separately from its concrete implementation, preparing the reader for a more formal study of abstraction at a later date. We have emphasised the use of procedures and functions to implement the operations on the structures, thus hiding the implementation details to some extent from the main program, an important technique which is used extensively in object-oriented programming.

Standard Pascal is used for the examples on data structures and serial files. In the discussions of random access files, an extended version is introduced which is typical of many implementations with built-in routines to handle such files.

The later chapters of the book provide an introduction to databases. A practical design method which produces a conceptual data model is discussed. Such a model provides an abstract view of the data before a logical model is derived for a particular implementation. Both network and relational database models are discussed as possible implementations. With the increasing importance of the relational model and the adoption of SQL as a standard language, we have provided a fuller account of SQL in a separate chapter. Fourth generation languages are discussed in the final chapter, contrasting their non-procedural features with the procedural style of third generation languages such as Pascal.

We should like to thank the people who have helped in the preparation of this text; in particular, the reviewers whose constructive comments led to improvements in the presentation of the material, and the readers who made valuable comments on the first edition.

1 Data Structures I

1.1 Introduction

Computers process information. The information is represented by data values held temporarily within the program's data area or recorded permanently on a file. Often there are relationships between different data values which the program needs to use. For example, when processing sales orders, the relationship may be to link the quantity of an item ordered with the corresponding quantity in stock. Another relationship may be to sequence the sales orders according to the required delivery date. Here each sales order is related to the next in sequence.

To enable programs to make use of these relationships, the data values must be organised to allow access to related items of data.

The organised collection of data is called a *data structure*. If the data is held on a file, we speak of the *file structure*, while for more elaborate file structures the term *database* can be employed.

The operations allowed on the data structure must be defined to specify how programs may access and process the data in the structure. We can use the 'equation'

DATA STRUCTURE = ORGANISED DATA + OPERATIONS

to express this fact.

The data structures have to reflect the required relationships between the data items and are designed for a specific application. Nevertheless there are some standard data structures which are often used in their own right and can form the basis of other special-purpose structures.

In order to keep implementation details out of the way when discussing data structures, we shall look at abstract views before mentioning concrete implementations. This approach should also be adopted when you design data structures for an application.

For each data structure, several points may be considered:

- Its abstract structure

that is a picture of the data fields and their relationships, without considering exactly how they may be implemented in a programming language or as a physical file.

- The concrete structures which might be used to implement it.

- The methods (algorithms) used to process the structure

for example, adding or deleting values, listing all the data items or finding a specific item.

- How the algorithms may be coded.
- Typical applications for the structure.

For a specific problem you need to consider the possible data structures which could be used and the processing requirements of the application in order to design the most appropriate structure for it.

Data structures are used to permit efficient storage of related data items and provide efficient access to that data. Often, simple structures will provide storage for and access to a collection of data items, but not efficiently enough. More complex data structures and more complex methods of processing are used to increase efficiency. In some cases the need is to reduce storage space and in others to increase processing speed.

1.2 Data types and conversions

Before studying data structures, the ways in which individual data items are stored and processed will be reviewed. A more detailed review is given in appendix A.

1.2.1 Simple data types

Programming languages like Pascal use constants and variables holding data values. The languages distinguish between different data items according to the type of value which can be stored. In Pascal a distinction is made between integer, real, character and boolean values, these being four simple data types available. Whenever a variable is declared its type must be specified.

The type specification defines what can be stored in the data item and what operations are allowed. We can say

DATA TYPE = PERMITTED DATA VALUES + OPERATIONS.

There are three reasons for distinguishing between data types. The first relates to storage. All data values are represented by some form of binary pattern inside the main memory of the computer. Different types of binary patterns are used for the different data types. The type specified in the data declaration is used to allocate the correct form of internal binary pattern.

The second reason relates to processing. Since the underlying binary representations differ, so do the operations on them. The addition of two integers requires different steps from those used for the addition of two reals. The specification of the type of the data allows the correct type of operations to be used. The internal representations and the ways they are processed are hidden from the programmer by the programming language.

The third and, from the user's point of view, perhaps the most important reason is to specify usage. The program designer can make it clear what values are allowed and what operations are to be used on the data item. This enhances error avoidance and enables error-checking to be carried out. Impossible operations, such as the addition of a character and an integer, can be detected as an error by the compiler using type-checking.

Type-checking follows strict rules concerning the operations allowed on data items of the various data types. Certain operations between differing types of data are forbidden but others are allowed. In particular, Pascal allows arithmetical expressions involving both integer and real values. The integers are automatically converted to a corresponding real format where necessary. Thus the assignment

$$x := y + 1$$

where x and y are reals, is acceptable. The value 1 is converted to a real value 1.0 before the addition is performed.

Conversion also takes place automatically when a real or integer value is typed in at the keyboard. The appropriate read statement might be

$$read(x);$$

while the value 2.43 typed in would be transmitted as a string of characters, "2", ".", "4", "3". The conversion from the character type to the internal real format is carried out as part of the read statement. Similar remarks apply to writing values to the screen or printer. The internal format is converted to a string of characters to be sent to the device.

Some functions are provided to establish correspondences between the different data types. The two standard functions TRUNC or ROUND are used to produce integers corresponding to real numbers, depending on whether you want to ignore the possible fractional part or to round up. Other functions like ORD and CHR are provided to establish a correspondence between character and integer types.

In summary, each data item is of a particular data type determining how it is stored and how it can be processed. Type-checking permits the detection of errors involving impossible operations on the data items. Certain permitted operations include automatic conversions of data, hidden from the programmer, while others require explicit use of standard functions to establish a correspondence between types.

1.2.2 Other scalar and structured data types

The simple data types can be used to build new scalar data types. In Pascal there are the subrange and enumeration types. A review of these is given in appendix A. The concept of an ordinal type, in which there is an underlying order with successor and predecessor functions, is identified as a property shared by several data types and is important in the definition of structured data types. In particular, only ordinal types can be subscript ranges of arrays.

Pascal provides three structures to enable data values to be organised: sets, arrays and records. These are also reviewed in appendix A.

A set is a collection of elements. The operations on a set include testing whether a particular element is in a set, combining two sets (set union) or removing one set of elements from another (set difference). These provide the facilities for adding an element to a set or deleting an element from a set as a special case. Sets are especially useful in the validation of input values.

A one-dimensional array is a collection of values of the same type, each identified by a subscript value. The items can be accessed individually, or the whole array can be treated as a unit. Higher-dimensional arrays need two or more subscripts to identify the individual elements.

A record is a group of fields which may be of different types. The fields have names to identify them and may be accessed individually, or may be treated as a block when the record is accessed as a unit.

1.3 Lists

Abstract and concrete representations

A list is a collection of data items, all of the same type, arranged in an arbitrary or logical order. It can be implemented as a one-dimensional array. The following examples will use a simple subrange of integers for the subscript range.

As an abstract data structure, a list can be regarded as a block of data values which may vary in size as items are added or deleted. Most programming languages support the view of the array as a block of data items, but require a fixed size. In implementing this structure it is often necessary to declare an array large enough to meet the worst case, and keep a separate data value to show the current size.

Processing a list: bubble sort

To illustrate the use of a list we shall consider the task of sorting the items into ascending order.

Assume the definition of the array is

> VAR a : ARRAY [1 . . maxsize] OF INTEGER;

and that the current size is specified in a variable declared:

> CurrentSize : 1 . . maxsize;

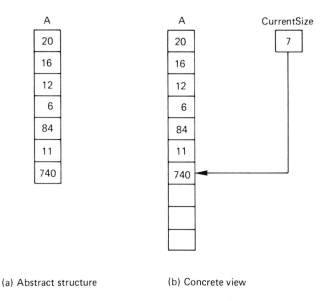

(a) Abstract structure   (b) Concrete view

The sort, known as the *bubble sort*, makes several passes down the list, comparing adjacent items. If the items are in the wrong order, they are swapped before the routine moves on to the next pair for comparison. On each pass a large item may be moved several places down the list, swapping with items smaller than itself. Since the small items are moved up at most one position on each pass, this routine may need a total of (Currentsize − 1) passes.

The algorithm is coded for the array implementation as shown in figure 1.1. It consists of an outer loop controlling the number of passes through the array, and an inner loop comparing adjacent items and swapping them if necessary.

Efficiency considerations

On the first pass through the array the largest item is placed at the end of the list. Each subsequent pass will move the next largest into position. The algorithm can be improved by shortening the inner loop to avoid comparing the large items already in place at the end of the array. This is done by replacing the inner loop

$$\text{FOR i} := 1 \text{ TO (CurrentSize} - 1) \text{ DO}$$

by the loop

$$\text{FOR i} := 1 \text{ TO (CurrentSize} - \text{pass) DO}$$

Surprisingly, this small change almost halves the effort involved in sorting the list. There are several other sorting methods which improve on this considerably. We shall see one such method in chapter 6.

```
PROCEDURE bubble;

(* sorts items in array a into ascending order *)
(* a is a global array of integers *)
(* Global variable CurrentSize specifies last
                entry used *)

VAR pass,i : 1..maxsize;
    c: INTEGER;

BEGIN
FOR pass := 1 TO (CurrentSize-1) DO
   FOR i:= 1 TO (CurrentSize-1) DO
      BEGIN
      IF a[i] > a[i+1] THEN
         BEGIN         (* swap items *)
         c:= a[i];     (* use c to save one value *)
         a[i]:=a[i+1];
         a[i+1]:=c
         END
      END
END;  (* procedure bubble *)
```

Figure 1.1 Bubble sort.

1.4 Hierarchical structures

The base types for the elements of an array, or the fields within a record, need not be simple data types. Indeed, they can be structured types as is shown by the way Pascal regards a two-dimensional array as a one-dimensional array of row vectors. Structures can be nested inside other structures in a hierarchical fashion. Thus a record may contain an array or another record as a field, and an array may have records or other arrays as its element base type.

Hierarchical record structures

A record may contain a field which is itself a record. Figure 1.2a shows a declaration of a credit card record where the field for the expiry date is itself made up of two fields. The record called card contains the field card.ExpiryDate which itself contains card.ExpiryDate.month and card.ExpiryDate.year. The abstract hierarchical structure is shown in figure 1.2b.

```
TYPE
date = RECORD
        month : 1 .. 12:
        year   : 70 .. 99
        END;


CardDetail = RECORD
             cardNo : PACKED ARRAY [1 .. 12] OF CHAR;
             ExpiryDate : date;
             CreditLimit : 0 .. 50000
             END;


VAR card: CardDetail;
```

(a)

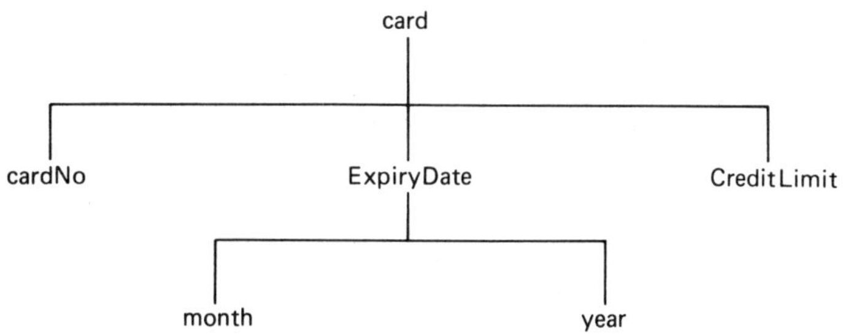

(b)

Figure 1.2 (a) Declaration of nested records. (b) Abstract view of nested records.

1.5 Tables

1.5.1 Abstract and concrete representations

A second example of a nested structure occurs when the elements of a list are themselves records. Such a structure is often called a table.

One typical application is for a stock list which shows the quantity in stock for each stock item and its location (bin no.) in the store. As is often the case, each item can be identified by a single field in the record, called the key field, which is the item no. in this example.

Item no.	Quantity in stock	Bin no.
X4207	84	201
Y6308	62	264
A4721	157	198
L8917	98	165
P6221	341	207
B6271	26	110
K7865	377	249
L9462	620	138
B6284	84	285
L9871	847	188

In Pascal, again using an array implementation, this could be declared as in figure 1.3

```
TYPE

   ItemCode = PACKED ARRAY [1 .. 5] OF CHAR;


   StockEntry = RECORD
                ItemNo : ItemCode;
                quantity : INTEGER;
                binNo : 100 .. 299
                END;


VAR StockList : ARRAY [1 .. maxsize] OF StockEntry;
```

Figure 1.3   Declaration of a table.

With this declaration, each element of the array StockList is a record with three fields. We can refer to the records as StockList[1], StockList[2], etc., or to the individual fields as StockList[1].ItemNo, StockList[1].quantity, StockList[1].binNo, and so on.

In contrast to a two-dimensional array, the rows of a table are records whose fields need not all be of the same type. The data items in each column are all of the same type, being the same field from different rows. In a two-dimensional array all the elements are of one type.

1.5.2 Processing a table

Using this example, we shall look at the methods of adding a new entry to the table, searching for an entry with a specific key or deleting an entry. A variable called CurrentSize will specify the current number of entries in the table.

(a) Processing an unordered table

Additions

If the entries in the table are in an arbitrary order, any new entry can be added to the end of the table, provided there is room. The value in CurrentSize is increased by 1 when an item is added.

Searching

Searching for an entry for a given item number requires each entry in the table to be examined in turn until the matching entry is found or until all the table has been examined. This search method is known as the *linear search*. In searching for an item we must cater for the possibility of there being no corresponding entry in the table. In figure 1.4 one possible coding of the linear search algorithm is given. The loop which examines the items in turn has two conditions controlling it: one for finding the item and one for detecting the end of the list.

```
PROCEDURE linearsearch (requiredItem : Itemcode;
                        VAR position : SubscriptRange;
                        VAR found    : BOOLEAN);

(* Version 1 *)
(* Searches through the table StockList for an entry
   with key requiredItem, using linear search *)
(* SubscriptRange is 1..maxsize *)

VAR i : 0..maxsize;

BEGIN
i:=0;
found:=FALSE;
WHILE (NOT found) AND (i< CurrentSize) DO
   BEGIN
   i:=i+1;
   found := (StockList[i].ItemNo = requiredItem)
   END;
IF found THEN position:=i
END; (* procedure linearsearch *)
```

Figure 1.4 Linear search routine.

Efficiency considerations

A second version of the linear search is given in figure 1.5. The method is modified slightly. This time the required item number is placed temporarily in an empty position at the end of the table. The search again examines the entries in turn, but this time must find a matching entry because the temporary value is in place to catch an unmatched item. A 'true' match is found if the loop stops before it reaches this temporary value.

```
PROCEDURE linearsearch (requiredItem : Itemcode;
                        VAR position : SubscriptRange;
                        VAR found    : BOOLEAN);

(* Version 2 *)
(* searches through the table StockList
   for an entry with key requiredItem,
   using a modified linear search *)
(* SubscriptRange is 1..maxsize *)

VAR i : 1..maxsizePlus1;

BEGIN
StockList[CurrentSize+1].ItemNo := requiredItem;
                                  (* temporary store *)
i:=1;
WHILE (StockList[i].ItemNo <> requiredItem) DO
   i:=i+1;
found := (i <> CurrentSize+1);
IF found THEN position:=i
END;   (* procedure linearsearch *)
```

Figure 1.5 Modified linear search routine.

To use the procedure of figure 1.5, we must declare the table with an extra position at the end:

StockList : ARRAY [1 . . maxsizePlus1] OF StockEntry;

This gives room to search the table even when all the items 1 . . maxsize are used.

Comparing these two versions, notice that the second version uses an extra storage position but gains some processing efficiency. Since both methods compare the same table entries, the gain in efficiency is achieved by simplifying the coding of the loop where most of the processing effort lies. The loop in the first version contains an extra assignment and uses an extra test as control.

Deletions

Deleting an entry from a specified position requires all the following entries to be moved up to fill the gap. The value in CurrentSize is altered to reflect the deletion. Figure 1.6 shows the coding for this process.

In some applications it may be preferred simply to mark entries as dead and avoid the shifting of the remainder of the table. In this case, the entries have to be given another field to mark them as live or dead. The algorithm for addition will remain the same. Searching needs to be modified to match only live records, while deletion merely alters the live entry to dead. Some method must be provided to remove dead items and move up all following entries so that the space can be recovered. This would only be used if there were no room to add a new item, or if the number of dead entries became excessive.

```
PROCEDURE delete (position : SubscriptRange);

(* Deletes the entry in table StockList
    by moving all following entries up *)
(* SubscriptRange is 1..maxsize *)

VAR i: 1..maxsize;

BEGIN
FOR i:= position TO CurrentSize-1 DO
    StockList[i] := StockList[i+1];
CurrentSize := CurrentSize-1
END; (* procedure delete *)
```

Figure 1.6 Deletion from a table.

(b) Processing a sorted table

If the entries in the stock list are held in ascending order of the item number, the methods of processing will be different.

Additions

Firstly, the addition of a new entry now requires it to be placed in its correct position in the sequence. All entries following it in sequence must be moved down one place to make room. In coding this algorithm (figure 1.7), an empty slot at the front of the table is used to simplfy the conditions controlling the loop. This requires an extra entry to be declared for position 0.

Searching

The linear search could be used in this case. The search routine would examine the entries in sequence, but could now use the fact that the items are sorted to detect a failure before reaching the end of the list. As soon as an entry is found with item number greater than or equal to the required value, no further comparisons are necessary.

```
PROCEDURE insert   (newentry : StockEntry);

(* inserts a new entry in an ordered table moving
   all following entries down to make room *)

VAR i: 0..maxsize;

BEGIN
StockList[0] := newentry; (* temporary store *)
i:= CurrentSize;
WHILE  StockList[i].ItemNo > newentry.ItemNo DO
    BEGIN
    StockList[i+1] := StockList[i];
    i:=i-1
    END;
StockList[i+1]:= newentry; (* new item put in place *)
CurrentSize := CurrentSize+1
END; (* procedure insert *)
```

Figure 1.7 Insertion into a sorted table.

The modifications to figure 1.5 would be to replace the loop by

WHILE (StockList[i].ItemNo < requiredItem) DO i: = i + 1;

and to replace the evaluation of the boolean found by

found: = (i < > CurrentSize + 1) AND (StockList[i].ItemNo = requiredItem) ;

Efficiency considerations

An alternative method, known as the *binary search* (or *binary chop*), makes fuller use of the sorted order. If you are looking for a specific item number and examine the entry nearest to the middle of the table, you can determine which half of the table the item must lie in (if it is there) by seeing whether the required item is less than or greater than the middle entry. Once you have determined which half to select, there is no need to look at entries in the other half. A comparison with the middle entry of the selected half will narrow the range to one-quarter. This continues until the match is found or the range reduces to a single entry.

Figure 1.8 shows an example where the StockList table is searched for the entry with item number K7865.

The range is initially the full table (positions 1-10). The middle position (5) is compared with K7865. The required value is less than the middle entry L8917, so the range reduces to the lower half of the table (positions 1-4). The middle position of this range (2) contains B6271 which is less than the required item, so the range is reduced to the upper half (positions 3-4). This time the

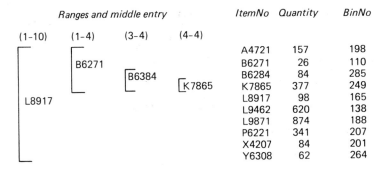

Ranges and middle entry				ItemNo	Quantity	BinNo

Figure 1.8 Example of binary search.

middle position (3) contains B6384 which is still less than K7865, so again the upper half is selected (position 4-4). The middle position (4) itself contains the key item and the correct position is found.

In implementing the binary search, the range under examination at each stage is specified by two subscripts, the lower and upper positions in the range. The middle position is determined from these two values. Each time the range halves, one of these values is altered.

There are several ways of coding the binary search. The version shown in figure 1.9 stops as soon as a match is found. Some other versions do not test for equality inside the loop but continue until the range reduces to a single entry. A single test after the loop has ended determines whether the item has been found.

One point to watch when coding the binary search is that the range must reduce in size at each iteration. If in the version of figure 1.9, we had written

$$low: = mid$$

instead of

$$low: = mid + 1$$

there are some cases in which the range would fail to reduce. Consider the case when low=3, high=4 and the required item is at position 4. The value of mid is also calculated as 3; the key is not in that position, so the assignment

$$low: = mid$$

is executed. However, this merely keeps low at its current value of 3. The loop never terminates.

The advantage of the binary search over the linear search is its efficiency. If we assume all the items are equally likely to be requested, we can estimate the average number of comparisons needed to find a key which is in the table. For the linear search this is $(n+1)/2$ where n is the number of items (Currentsize as

```
PROCEDURE binarysearch (requiredItem : Itemcode;
                        VAR position : SubscriptRange;
                        VAR found    : BOOLEAN);
(* Uses a binary chop technique to locate the
   requiredItem in the table StockList *)
(* Global variables used are CurrentSize
   and the array StockList *)
(* SubscriptRange is 1..maxsize, defined globally *)

VAR low : 1..maxsizePlus1;
    high : 0..maxsize;
    mid  : 1..maxsize;

BEGIN
low:=1;
high:=CurrentSize;
found:=FALSE;
WHILE (NOT found) AND (low<=high) DO
   BEGIN
   mid:=(low+high) DIV 2;
   IF (StockList[mid].ItemNo = requiredItem)
   THEN
       found:=TRUE
   ELSE
   IF (StockList[mid].ItemNo < requiredItem)
   THEN              (* select upper half *)
       low:=mid+1
   ELSE              (* select lower half *)
       high:=mid-1
   END;
IF found THEN position:=mid
END;  (* procedure binarysearch *)
```

Figure 1.9 Binary search routine.

we called it earlier). For the binary search the value is closer to log n (using logs to base 2), since each comparison halves the range to be examined. (In our version, each item is compared first for equality and then for the ordering, so we would expect the estimate to be 2log n.) This value is little different in the binary search for items not in the table, while the linear search needs $n+1$ comparisons for such items.

The following table compares the values of n, $(n+1)/2$ and log n for a few values showing the divergence between the values as n increases.

n	$(n+1)/2$	$\log n$
2	1.5	1
4	2.5	2
8	4.5	3
16	8.5	4
32	16.5	5
64	32.5	6
128	64.5	7
256	128.5	8
512	256.5	9
1024	512.5	10

1.6 Variant records

The record types considered so far have required every variable of that type to contain exactly the same fields. There are some occasions when a more flexible record structure is desirable. For example, in a program which allows updates to the stock list table, the transactions can be thought of as one record type. But a transaction to delete an item need only specify the item number, whereas one to add a new item must specify a quantity and a bin number as well as the item number. A transaction to remove a quantity of a particular item would specify the item number and the quantity removed.

In Pascal, a variant record can be defined specifying different fields for different variations within a record type. The distinction between the variants is made by a tag field.

```
TYPE
transactiontype = (addition, deletion, removal);

transaction =
    RECORD
    item      : itemcode;
    CASE tag : transactiontype OF
        addition : ( newquantity : 0 .. maxint;
                     bin         : 100 .. 299);
        deletion : ( ) ; (* no extra fields *)
        removal  : ( quantityRemoved : 0 .. maxint)
    END;
```

There can be any number of fields in common at the start of the record. The variation occurs at the end of the record within the CASE part.

Although these records appear to be of variable length, in practice each record of this type is allocated sufficient space to cater for the largest variant.

In this example, a deletion record uses the same space as an addition record even though the latter has extra fields.

In processing variant records, the tag field must be tested to determine which variant is being processed. Only the fields of the variant indicated should be accessed.

Variant records allow data items of alternative types to be packaged as a single type, with the tag field identifying to which of the alternatives any particular item belongs. This is especially useful when an array structure, for instance, is to hold data items of different types. Packaged as a variant record, they can be used as the base type of the array.

1.7 Summary

Data structures were defined as organised collections of data together with the operations allowed on them. They are an extension of the concept of data type. The basic structured types provided by Pascal can be nested in a hierarchical fashion to provide more complex structures and variant records can be used to package two or more types into a single type.

In studying data structures it is important to consider the abstract view before the concrete representation so that implementation details do not obscure the view of the structure.

The operational performance of an implementation can be assessed by analysing the complexity of the algorithms which implement the operations. An estimate of how the complexity depends upon the volume of data is used for this assessment.

Lists and tables were considered implemented as arrays and the relative efficiencies of the linear and binary search algorithms were discussed. The gain in efficiency in the search operation by using a sorted table is offset by a more complex algorithm to add a new item to the table.

In the next chapter we shall look at serial and sequential files and how the data in them is processed.

Exercises

1.1 The straight selection sort is one alternative to the bubble sort. Starting with an unordered list, it makes several passes through the list to sort the entries. The first pass starts at the first item in the list and finds the position of the smallest value. This item is then exchanged with the first item. The second pass starts at the second position and finds the smallest item in the rest of the list, which is then exchanged for the second item. The process repeats for the remaining positions.

(a) Code this algorithm as a procedure to sort a list of real values.

(b) Estimate the number of comparisons made by this procedure when sorting a list of *n* items.

1.2 Write a program to demonstrate the relative efficiencies of the linear and binary search routines as follows. Set up an ordered list of 1000 integer values in an array. (Use, for example, the even numbers 2 . . 2000 .) Read values from the terminal and, for each, search the list using both the linear and binary search routines. Write messages saying whether the value was found in the list, its position if found, and the number of comparisons made by each of the search routines in looking for the item.

1.3 Write a program to set up a table of company car allocations, containing field for

employee name, make of car, model, registration no.

The table should initially be unordered. The program should sort and print the table in

(a) employee name order,

(b) registration no. order.

1.4 Modify the program of exercise **1.3** to allow some table entries for employees with no car currently allocated, and some for cars which are not currently allocated to an employee, as well as the standard entries. When the table is printed in employee name order (a), the entries for employees with no car should be printed in their correct positions with an appropriate message. The entries for cars not allocated to anyone should not appear on this list.

When the table is printed in registration number order (b), the entries for unallocated cars should be in their correct positions with a suitable message, but the entries for employees with no cars should not be printed.

2 Serial and Sequential Data Files

2.1 Introduction

For permanent storage, data values can be held on a file on backing store (magnetic disc, tape etc.). By 'permanent', we mean that the values will remain until they are deliberately (or accidentally!) overwritten, and could be held indefinitely.

For data values held on a file to be processed by a program, they must first be copied into variables in the program's data area. This is done by a read operation which retrieves a single data item, or possibly a few items at a time. The opposite task of saving values on a file is done by a write operation.

In a *serial file* the data values are physically held in the order in which they were written to the file and can be accessed only in this order. A program reading the file must start with the first value and gradually work its way through the file.

Although there is a similarity between a serial file and an array, there are important differences:

- A value held on a file must be read before it can be processed: a value held in an array is already in main store.
- An array must have its size declared in the program; a file has a dynamic size.
- Values in an array can be accessed in any order using subscripts; values in a serial file can be processed only in physical order.
- There is an enormous difference in access time between reading a value from a file and retrieving a value from an array.

In data processing applications, the data values stored on a file are often grouped into records and it is the records which are accessed as units in the read and write operations. This is one abstract view of the file structure which can be supported directly in Pascal, as section 2.5 will show. But there are occasions when the read and write operations handle individual data fields or even characters within the fields. To cover all these possibilities, the term *component* is used to refer to the basic unit handled by the read and write operations.

A serial file can be viewed as a sequence of components accessed in physical order. Any program processing a serial file will keep track of its current position in the file. When a file is being created, each write operation places a new component on the file and moves the file position forward one component. When a file is being read, each read operation retrieves the next component and moves the file position forward one component.

When the last component on a serial file has been read the end-of-file condition is TRUE. Programs reading a serial file can use this condition to detect the end of the data.

With this view of a serial file it is possible to treat the data typed in at the terminal as a serial input file, and the data written to a terminal screen or to a printer as serial output files.

In Pascal, a file is identified by a variable name declared as a FILE of a particular component type. Procedures used to process the file use this variable name to identify the file involved. Two files, INPUT and OUTPUT, are pre-declared and are both text files.

2.2 Files of simple data types

Serial files whose components are integers can be created on disc or tape. In these files the data is represented by binary values in the same way that integers are stored in the main memory of the computer. Similarly, files of reals hold binary data in the format of real values.

When values are written to such files, no conversions take place. The files cannot be examined by editors because the data is not in character form, but they can be read by other programs.

In Pascal, files can be defined with component type real, integer, Boolean or character. For example

```
VAR intFile  : FILE OF INTEGER;
    realFile      : FILE OF REAL;
```

Such files are streams of values of the simple data type. There is no structuring into lines as is the case for text files discussed in the next section.

The Boolean function EOF can be used to detect the end-of-file condition, while the procedures READ and WRITE can be used to transfer values from and to the file.

Figure 2.1 illustrates this by showing a program which reads values from a file of integers, counts the number of values and calculates the sum of the values.

2.3 Text files

A text file is a serial file whose basic component type is character and which is structured into lines. Files created by an editor program are text files, as are the files associated with input and output at the terminal or to a printer. Appendix B contains a review of text files in Pascal.

```
PROGRAM addintegers (infile, OUTPUT);

(* reads values from a file of integers, counts them
   and sums them *)

VAR x, sum : INTEGER;
    infile : FILE OF INTEGER;
    count  : INTEGER;

BEGIN
RESET (infile);
sum := 0; count:= 0;
WHILE NOT EOF(infile) DO
   BEGIN
   READ( infile, x);
   count:=count+1;
   sum:=sum+x
   END;
WRITELN('Sum is ',sum,' Count is ',count)
END.
```

Figure 2.1 Processing values in a file of integers.

Although values stored in a text file are always held as character data, they could represent numeric values. The characters

"66 42.97 13.224 −207.6"

held on a text file would use 22 character components, but represent four numeric values separated by spaces. This demonstrates the difference between a logical view of the data and its physical representation. Programming languages provide ways of reading such data and converting them to the appropriate internal representation for numeric values.

In Pascal, the procedures READ, READLN, WRITE and WRITELN are used with text files for the read and write operations, and the Boolean functions EOF and EOLN are used to detect the end-of-file and end-of-line conditions.

When a Pascal program reads numeric values from a text file there is no need to test for the end-of-line conditions. A read statement

read(x);

where x is a real or integer variable, will skip all spaces or end-of-line markers in searching for the value of x. This succeeds in hiding from the programmer the fact that the data is really held in character form. However, problems can arise in detecting the end-of-file condition.

If, in the example of figure 2.1, the input file was instead a text file holding integer values, the file declaration would have to be replaced by

infile : TEXT;

If the remainder of figure 2.1 were unchanged, the program would not work correctly.

The program would successfully read the values one by one, no matter how many values are held on each line, but would fail to detect the end of file. If the last integer value were followed by an end-of-line marker (as it should be in a true TEXT file), the Boolean EOF would not be TRUE immediately after the last value was read.

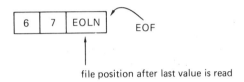

file position after last value is read

The WHILE loop would be executed one more time, and an attempt made to read another integer. This would skip any spaces or end-of-line markers and encounter the end-of-file. For standard Pascal, the result would be a run-time failure.

The problem has arisen because of the difference between the logical view of the data as integer values and the physical representation as characters. The extra separator characters cause no problem in the read operation, but prevent the end-of-file condition being detected as soon as the last logical data item has been read.

One way to overcome the problem is to insist that the data values are held one per line and replace the read statement in figure 2.1 by

READLN (infile, x);

This would first read the value of x, then skip all characters up to and including the next end-of-line marker. Since text files often have just one end-of-line marker before the end-of-file, in practice this would suffice. But the problem would return if a blank line were written at the end of the file.

Another method of solving the problem is to use a procedure to position the file at the next value or at the end of the file if the last value has been read. This makes use of the file buffer and will be introduced in the next section.

A common method used in data processing which overcomes the problem is to place an extra integer value after the last value, to be used as a terminator. This value must differ from all the permitted values in the file. If, for example, all the values were positive, a terminator of -1 could be used. Figure 2.2 shows a revised program to read the integers, count them and calculate their sum.

The terminator value is used to control the loop. Since a value must be read before it can be tested, the read-ahead technique is used. The first value is read before the loop starts, and the loop itself processes the current value before reading the next. The loop finishes when the terminator value has been read.

```
PROGRAM addintegers (infile, OUTPUT);

(* reads integers from a text file, counts them
   and sums them. Uses terminator value -1 *)

CONST  terminator = -1;

VAR x, sum : INTEGER;
    infile : TEXT;
    count  : INTEGER;

BEGIN
RESET (infile);
sum := 0; count:= 0;
READ (infile,x);        (* read first value *)
WHILE (x <> terminator) DO
   BEGIN
   count:=count+1;      (* process this value *)
   sum:=sum+x;
   READ( infile, x)     (* read next value *)
   END;
WRITELN('Sum is ',sum,' Count is ',count)
END.
```

Figure 2.2 Using a terminator value.

There is no longer a conflict between the logical data values and the method used to detect the end of file. The terminator is the logical marker for the end of file.

2.4 File buffers in Pascal

A value held on a file must be read into a program before it can be tested or processed. The read-ahead technique introduced above is commonly used to ensure values are read before any tests are performed on them.

The tests for end-of-file and end-of-line in Pascal appear to violate this rule. They test the next component on the file. But this is only apparent. Pascal uses its own read-ahead technique on the individual file components, using an area called the file buffer to store them.

For an input file using the file variable InFile, the file buffer is referred to as InFile↑. There is a procedure, GET, to retrieve the next component from the file and store it in the file buffer:

GET(InFile)

When the procedure RESET is used, it retrieves the first component and places it in the file buffer.

The end-of-file and end-of-line conditions are set when an attempt is made to move the next value into the buffer and the end of file or end of line is reached.

The procedures READ and READLN copy the content of the file buffer to a program variable before issuing another GET. Where compatible components are being used, a single READ may require several GET operations.

A file buffer is also used for output. The procedure call

PUT(OutFile)

will copy the component from the file buffer to the output file. WRITE and WRITELN work by copying values into the file buffer and using the PUT procedure.

The procedures GET and PUT can be used directly from a program and values can be moved from and into the file buffers. They could be used instead of the WRITE and READ procedures, except that they make no provision for converting data held in variables of a compatible type.

Figure 2.3 is an example which uses the file buffer and the GET operation on an input text file. It is a procedure which skips spaces and end-of-line markers in the text file to position the file at the next non-space character, or at the end of file. Note that the file buffer contains a space when the end-of-line condition is TRUE. This procedure can be used to provide a solution to the problem, mentioned in the previous section, of detecting the end of file for a text file containing integer values. If it is used once before the main loop of the modified figure 2.1, and after each READ(infile,x), it will position the file correctly for each read operation.

```
PROCEDURE skipspace (VAR filename : TEXT);

(* skips all spaces or end of lines to position the
   file at the next non-space character, or end of file *)

CONST space = ' ';

VAR SpaceFound : BOOLEAN;

BEGIN
SpaceFound := TRUE;

WHILE SpaceFound DO
   IF EOF( filename) THEN
      SpaceFound := FALSE
   ELSE IF (filename^ = space) THEN
      GET (filename)
   ELSE
      SpaceFound := FALSE;

END;
```

Figure 2.3 Procedure to position a text file at next non-space character or end of file.

24   *Data Structures, Files and Databases*

2.5 Files of records

Data values held on a file are often logically grouped into records. A stock file, for instance, may hold item numbers with their corresponding quantities in stock and bin number. Logically these are records with three fields. Using a text file, this could be organised by having the three fields on the same line. Reading a record is then equivalent to reading the three fields from a line.
The Pascal data declarations for the fields could be:

```
VAR
        itemNo : PACKED ARRAY [1 .. 5] OF CHAR;
        quantity : INTEGER;
        binNo : 100 .. 299;
```

Reading a single line is performed by the statements:

```
FOR i: = 1 TO 5 DO READ( itemNo[i] );
READLN (quantity, binNo);
```

Some non-standard implementations of Pascal permit character strings to be read from a text file, in which case the simpler statement

```
READLN (itemNo , quantity, binNo);
```

could be used.
The three fields are being processed individually, with conversions from character format being applied to each field as necessary. The logical view of the data differs from the physical representation.
An alternative way to store the data on a file is to use a file whose component type is a record. A whole record can be read from such a file or written to it as a unit. Within a program processing the data, each record can be treated as a unit, or the fields can be accessed individually, as discussed in appendix A.
These files are distinct from text files. They are not text files viewed in a different way.
The records held on the file are represented in a way similar to that in which records are stored in the main memory of the computer, that is as a block of fields each with its own internal representation. The data is not converted to character form when it is stored on the file.
The file is a stream of records. There is no structuring into lines as in text files.
Pascal programs refer to such files using a variable declared as a FILE of a record data type. The procedures RESET, REWRITE, READ and WRITE together with the Boolean function EOF apply to this type of file as well. Figure 2.4 illustrates their use in a program which reads stock details from a text file and creates a file of records from the data.
Both files in this case have the same abstract structure. In the input file, the concrete representation is a text file whose lines are equated to records. In

```
PROGRAM createStockFile (INPUT, stockFile);

(* reads stock details from a text file,
   creates records from them and
   writes them to the stockfile *)

TYPE
    ItemCode = PACKED ARRAY [1..5] OF CHAR;
    StockEntry = RECORD
                    ItemNo : ItemCode;
                    quantity : INTEGER;
                    binNo : 100..299;
                    END;

VAR
    StockRec : StockEntry;
    StockFile : FILE OF StockEntry;
    i : 1..5;

BEGIN
REWRITE (StockFile);   (* prepare for output *)
WHILE NOT EOF DO
    BEGIN
    WITH StockRec DO    (* read details into record *)
       BEGIN
       FOR i:=1 TO 5 DO READ ( ItemNo[i] );
       READLN ( quantity, binNo );
       END;
    (* write whole record to stock file *)
    WRITE( StockFile, StockRec)
    END;
END.
```

Figure 2.4 File of records.

the output file, the concrete representation uses Pascal records to match the abstract view more closely.

2.6 Sequential files and applications

2.6.1 Sequential files

A record is often used to hold data relating to the same entity and contains a key field used to identify that entity. In stock records, the key is the item number; in invoice records it is the invoice number; in bank transaction records it is the account number.

When a file holds records in ascending (or occasionally descending) order of a key field, it is called a *sequential file*. Processing the file sequentially accesses the records in key sequence.

2.6.2 Merging sequential files

Two sequential files (with the same component type and sequenced on the same key field) can be combined to produce a single file sequenced on the common key. This process is called *merging*. The records are not updated in the process, merely copied to the output file in the correct order.

The program must detect when either input file has finished and continue to process all remaining records on the other file. To accomplish this, it is simpler to introduce a dummy record for the completed file whose key value will act as a terminator. The terminator value must be higher than any permitted key value on the files. There is no need to place the dummy record on the files themselves. The end-of-file conditions can be used to detect when they should be created inside the program.

The process can be designed using a read procedure for the two input files, which detects the end-of-file condition and sets up the terminator value in the key field. One record from each input file is held and the one with the smaller key is chosen to be copied to the output file. The chosen record is replaced by the next record from its input file.

Figure 2.5a is an outline design of a merge program, while 2.5b and 2.5c are the read and select routines used in the merge.

2.6.3 Batch update systems

Sequential files form the basis of many data processing systems known as batch systems. The example of stock details can illustrate the main update of a batch system.

Current details of the items in stock are held on a sequential master file. Transaction records specifying changes to be applied to the master file data, such as receipts into stock, issues from stock, adding new stock items and deleting old items, are collected and placed on a serial transaction file. The aim of the batch update is to create a new version of the master file (called the carried-forward master) from the current version (called the brought-forward master) and the transaction records. Figure 2.6 shows the steps involved in this process.

The first step is to validate the transaction records, that is check each record for errors. Invalid records are rejected, their details being written to an exceptions report. Valid records are copied to a validated transaction file.

This file is still a serial file. The next step is to read the records from it, sort them into order and produce a sequential transaction file.

The final step is to run the main update program, which reads records from both the brought-forward master file and the sequential transaction file, matches the transactions against the master records, and produces the updated master file. Some transaction records will be rejected at this stage if they request

```
Read one record from each input file.
Move the input record with smaller key
          to the output record and
          replace the input record.
WHILE output record key <> terminator DO
    BEGIN
    write output record to output file
    move the input record with the smaller key
          to the output record and
          replace the input record.
    END
```

(a)

```
PROCEDURE ReadRec    (VAR Infile: FileType;
                      VAR Rec: RecType);

(* Reads next record into Rec from specified Infile.
   At end of file it sets key field of record to be
   the terminator *)
(* FileType and RecType are types of input
   file and record *)
(* terminator is a global constant *)

BEGIN
IF EOF(Infile) THEN
    Rec.key := terminator
ELSE
    Read (Infile, Rec)
END;   (* procedure ReadRec *)
```

(b)

```
PROCEDURE MoveAndReplace;

(* selects input record with smaller key
           moves it to the output record
           and reads the next input record *)
(* assumes global declarations of all variables used *)

BEGIN
IF (RecordA.key <= RecordB.key)
THEN
    BEGIN
    OutRec:=RecordA; (* copy RecordA to output record *)
    ReadRec (fileA, RecordA);  (* replace RecordA *)
    END
ELSE
    BEGIN
    OutRec:=RecordB; (* copy RecordB to output record *)
    ReadRec (fileB, RecordB);  (* replace RecordB *)
    END;
END;
```

(c)

Figure 2.5 (a) Outline design of merge program. (b) Read procedure for input
files. (c) Move routine for merge program.

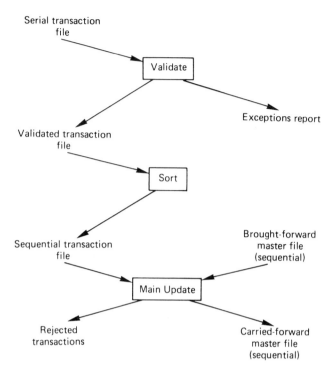

Figure 2.6 Batch update system.

impossible updates, such as issuing stock for an item number that does not exist on the master file.

The carried-forward master file becomes the brought-forward master file for the next batch run. The update runs are performed on a regular basis: daily, weekly, monthly etc., depending on the application.

The use of sequential as opposed to serial files is vital to the operation of the main update program. Its task involves matching the master file record with the transactions to be applied. There will be some items with several transactions for them, while others will have no updates and will be copied unchanged to the carried-forward file. The sequencing of the records on both input files is used to recognise when the master file record has no transactions for it, when transactions have no matching record on the master file and when a master record does have transactions to be applied.

The process of matching records is demonstrated in figure 2.7.

B/F Master File:

key	A4721	B6271	B6284	K7865	L8917	L9455
quantity	157	26	84	377	98	127
bin	198	110	285	249	165	206

Transaction file:

key	B6271	B6271	B6284	L4617	L8917	L8917
type	issue	receipt	issue	new	issue	delete
quantity	6	100	4	100	98	
bin				275		

C/F Master File:

key	A4721	B6271	B6284	K7865	L4617	L9455
quantity	157	120	80	377	100	127
bin	198	110	285	249	275	206

Figure 2.7 Master file update.

The first record from the brought-forward master file has no transactions for it and is copied to the carried-forward file.

The second record has two transactions which update the stock quantity. The third record has one transaction, while the fourth has none.

The transaction with key L4617 has no corresponding master file record and is used to create a new record on the carried-forward file.

The master file record with key L8917 has two transactions. The first reduces its quantity to 0, while the second deletes it.

The master file update problem is like an iceberg ready to sink an unwary programmer who rushes into it. As with all programs, before starting the design we must specify precisely what the program is to do. The precise details required in this problem will depend on the application. A typical informal specification is as follows.

The two input files are sequenced on the stock item number. The master file has at most one record for any key, while the transaction file may have several transactions on the same key.

There are four types of transactions: new-record, issue from stock, receipt into stock, and delete-record.

A master file record with no matching transactions should be written to the C/F (carried-forward) master file.

When a master file record has matching transactions, the action depends on the transaction type. A new-record transaction is rejected as invalid. Issues and receipts are valid and are used to adjust the quantity in stock. A delete-record transaction is valid only if the current quantity in stock is 0. Following a valid deletion, all further transactions on the same key are rejected.

```
CONST   terminator = 'ZZZZZ';

TYPE    Transactions =
                  (newRec, issue, receipt, deleteRec);
             (* names for types of transactions allowed *)

        ItemCode = PACKED ARRAY [1..5] OF CHAR;
        TransType =

             RECORD  (* variant record *)
             ItemNo : ItemCode;
             CASE tag : Transactions OF

                issue : ( quantityIssued : INTEGER);
              receipt : (quantityReceived : INTEGER);
            deleteRec : ();
               newRec : (quantity : INTEGER;
                                binNo : 100..299)

             END;

        MasterType = RECORD
                     ItemNo : ItemCode;
                     quantity : INTEGER;
                     binNo : 100..299
                     END;

VAR  BFMaster , CFMaster : FILE OF MasterType;
     TransFile : FILE OF TransType;
     MasterRec : MasterType;       (* record for B/F
                                      master file *)
     Workarea : MasterType;        (* new record for
                                      C/F master *)
     TransRec : TransType;         (* record for
                                      transaction file *)
     key : ItemCode;               (* stores value of
                                      key being processed *)
  (*----------------------------------------------------*)
```

(a)

```
PROCEDURE ReadTrans (VAR TransRec: TransType);

(* Reads next record from transaction file
   if there is one, otherwise sets key field
   of record to be terminator *)

BEGIN
IF EOF(TransFile) THEN
   TransRec.ItemNo := terminator
ELSE
   READ (TransFile, TransRec)
END; (*procedure ReadTrans *)
(*------------------------------------------------*)
```

```
PROCEDURE ReadMaster (VAR MasterRec: MasterType);

(* Reads next record from B/F masterfile
   if there is one, otherwise sets key field
   of record to be terminator *)

BEGIN
IF EOF(BFMaster) THEN
   MasterRec.ItemNo := terminator
ELSE
   READ (BFMaster, MasterRec)
END; (*procedure ReadMaster *)
(*-----------------------------------------------*)
```

(b)

Figure 2.8   (a) Data declarations for master file update. (b) Read procedures for two input files.

When a transaction has no matching B/F master file record, its transaction type again determines the action required. Any delete-record, issue or receipt is rejected. Only a new-record transaction is valid. Its data is used to create a new record in a work area. Following a valid new-record, only issues and receipts on the same key are valid and are used to update the quantity in stock in the new record. Any further new-record or delete-record transactions on the key are rejected. When all the transactions on the new record are completed, it is written to the C/F master file.

The design of a program to perform this update has to consider the end-of-file conditions as well. An approach similar to that used for the merge program can be employed. The read procedures for the two input files can be designed to detect the end-of-file condition and set up a dummy record inside the program with a key value set to a terminator higher than any expected key on the file.

With this approach, the program can hold one master record and one transaction record at a time and use them in the key-matching process. A dummy record is held when one file is finished, but its key can still be used while processing the remainder of the other input file.

Figure 2.8 shows the data declarations and read procedures for the update of the sequential stock file. The read procedures detect the end of file and set up the dummy records with the terminator as key.

An outline program body is given in figure 2.9 (a, b and c). The program consists of a main loop which continues until both input files are finished. Within the loop, three possibilities are catered for. A master record with no transaction is written to the output file. A master record with transaction has all its changes applied. A transaction with no master should be for a new record which is created in a work area. All valid transactions on the new record are applied before it is written to the output file.

```
(* outline code for master file update *)

(* allows existing master file records
   to be modified or deleted
   and new records to be added *)

read first transaction and master records

loop WHILE either of the files has
            unprocessed records
      BEGIN
      IF (B/F master key < Transaction key) THEN
         (* MASTER ALONE *)
         write B/F master rec to C/F file
         and read next B/F master record
      ELSE
      IF (B/F master key = Transaction key) THEN
         (* MATCHING KEYS *)
         Process all transactions on this key
      ELSE
      IF (B/F master key > Transaction key) THEN
         (* TRANSACTION ALONE *)
         Process all transactions with the same
            key as the transaction record
      END; (* main loop *)
```

(a)


```
MATCHING KEYS: processes all transactions matching
               one B/F master record

save current key value
loop WHILE the transaction is for this key
            and is not a valid deletion
      BEGIN
      IF the transaction is a new-record
            or invalid deletion
      THEN
         reject it and read the next transaction
      ELSE (* issue or receipt *)
         adjust value in B/F record
         read next transaction
      END; (* loop *)

IF the current transaction is a valid delete
            on this key
THEN
      read next B/F master (* overwiting deleted record *)
      read next transaction
      loop WHILE the transaction has the same key
            reject the transaction and read the next one

ELSE (* no deletion: all transactions on this
                     key processed *)
      write record to C/F file
      read next B/F master record.
```

(b)

```
TRANSACTION ALONE : processes all transactions with the
      same key as an unmatched transaction

save current key

loop WHILE the transaction has this key and is not
                    a new-record transaction
      reject this transaction and read the next one

IF the transaction is a new record transaction
                    on this key
THEN
      create the new record in the Workarea
      read the next transaction
      loop WHILE the transaction is for this key
            BEGIN
            IF it is a new-record or delete-record
                          transaction
            THEN
                  reject it and read the next transaction
            ELSE (* it is an issue or receipt *)
                  adjust the value in the Workarea record
                  read the next transaction
            END (* loop *)
      write Workarea record to C/F file.
```

(c)

Figure 2.9 (a) Outline program for master file update. (b) Processing matched records. (c) Processing unmatched transactions.

2.6.4 Merge sort

The technique used in merging two sequential files can also be used to sort the records from a serial file into sequential order. The sort algorithm, known as a *merge sort*, uses four workfiles.

Figure 2.10 shows an example of the record keys in a serial file which is to be sorted. The file contains some short sequences of records already in order. For instance, the first three records are in order, as are the next three.

32	37	49	21	28	50	33	69	20	17	12	19	26	88

Figure 2.10 Record keys in a serial file to be sorted.

These sequences are called strings of records. The end of each string is recognised by the fact that the following record has a lower key.

The process will first distribute the strings of records alternately on to two workfiles, as shown in figure 2.11.

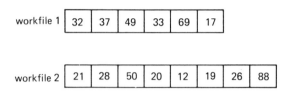

Figure 2.11 String of records distributed on to workfiles.

The two workfiles are then read serially. The first string from workfile 1 is merged with the first string from workfile 2, forming a longer string. This is written to the third workfile. The next pair of strings, one from each workfile, are merged to form the second output string. This is written to the fourth workfile. The process continues, merging strings from the two input workfiles to form longer strings which are written alternately to the two output workfiles, until all the strings from the input files have been read.

Figure 2.12a shows two strings merged to form the output string, while figure 2.12b shows the workfiles after the merge pass.

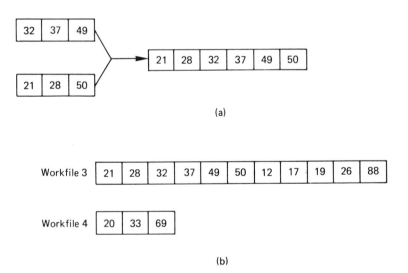

Figure 2.12 (a) Merging strings. (b) Workfile after one merge pass.

The process is repeated with the roles of the workfiles interchanged. Two workfiles act as input, two as output. Several merge passes may be needed before the merge produces a single string of records on to one of the workfiles. The records are then in sequential order.

In this example, two further merge passes are required. The results of each pass are shown in figure 2.13.

Results of next merge pass:

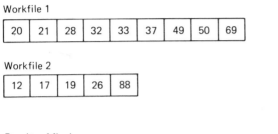

Workfile 1

| 20 | 21 | 28 | 32 | 33 | 37 | 49 | 50 | 69 |

Workfile 2

| 12 | 17 | 19 | 26 | 88 |

Results of final merge pass:

Workfile 3

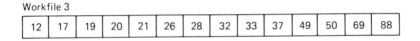

| 12 | 17 | 19 | 20 | 21 | 26 | 28 | 32 | 33 | 37 | 49 | 50 | 69 | 88 |

Figure 2.13   Final two merge passes.

In the general case, the original data file with n records could hold a single string (when the data is already in order) or as many as n strings (when it is in reverse order). If the data is randomly ordered, we can estimate the average length of the strings. Half of them should have length 1. A quarter should have length 2, an eighth length 3 and so on. This leads to the estimate of the average length as 2 which means that an average of $n/2$ strings is expected. Each merge pass will approximately halve the number of strings which leads to an estimate of log $n/2$ for the number of merge passes.

2.6.5 Multiple keys

When a sequential file contains several records with the same key value, a secondary key field can be used to order those records with the same (primary) key. In the batch update example of section 2.6.3, the transaction file was sequenced on the stock item number. The transaction type could be used as a secondary key to ensure that, for transactions with the same stock number, the records are arranged in the order: new-record, receipts, issues then delete-record.

Multiple keys are commonly needed for sequential files used to produce reports. A file of stock receipt details may hold records with fields for

delivery date, item code, quantity, supplier name.

A report of these details may require the records listed in date order within supplier name within item code. The item code would be the primary key, with supplier name as secondary key and delivery date as tertiary key. The report would produce results as illustrated in figure 2.14. The date field could not be treated as a character string but must be handled as a data type with comparison operators which look at the year, month and day to determine the correct order.

Item Code	Supplier	Date	Quantity
A1406			
	Jones Bros		
		10.10.86	200
		12.11.86	100
		7.12.86	300
	Kennedy Stores		
		6.09.86	300
		15.09.86	400
A6207			
	Jones Bros		
		10.10.86	500

Figure 2.14   Report using multiple keys.

2.6.6 File structures and program design

Sequencing the records on a file, particularly when multiple keys are used, imposes structures on the file. Records sharing the same key value are grouped together and the end of the group can be detected by a change of key value. These structures influence the design of programs which process the files.

One program design methodology suitable for some applications, known as *Jackson Structured Programming*, is based on examining the structures of the files being processed and deriving a program structure from them. A discussion of this methodology is beyond the scope of this text and the reader is referred to the bibliography (at the end of the book) for further reading.

2.7 Summary

Serial data files are streams of data values of a component type held externally to the program. The component type can be a simple data type or a structured type. Text files are a special case of files whose component type is character in which the components are structured into lines.

Pascal provides procedures and functions to handle serial files. They allow single components to be read from or written to a file, and in the case of text files, handle conversions between compatible data types and character representations.

In a sequential file the components are stored in sorted order of a key value. The structure resulting from this ordering is exploited in various applications. In this chapter the operation of merging sequential files was discussed, as were the batch update of a sequential master file and a merge sort.

Exercises

These exercises refer to the stock file example introduced in section 2.5.

2.1 Implement the CreateStockFile program of figure 2.4. Create two ordered input text files for this program, and run the program to produce two files of stock records sequenced on the stock item code (that is, make sure that your input files have the records in sequence).

2.2 Write a program to print a file of stock records to a text file. Run this program on the two files produced in exercise **2.1**.

2.3 Develop the merge program outlined in figure 2.5 for the stock file example. Merge the two files produced in exercise **2.1**, and use the program of exercise **2.2** to print the result.

2.4 Develop the merge sort program for the stock file example. Create a text file of stock records in arbitrary order, and use the CreateStockFile program of exercise **2.1** to produce an unordered stock file. Sort this file using the merge sort program and print the resulting file using the program of exercise **2.2**.

2.5 Develop the main batch update program for the stock file example. For this exercise, assume that the transaction file is a text file with each transaction on a separate line. Use the first character of the line to indicate the type of transaction, followed by the additional fields on the same line. Create suitable sequential transaction files to update the sequential stock files produced in the previous exercises.

3 Data Structures II

3.1 Pointers

In implementing data structures it is often convenient to use additional variables to point to the data items. Such variables are called *pointers*. In abstract, a pointer is a link to a data item.

In low-level languages, a pointer would hold the store address of the data item. Certain high-level languages, including Pascal, provide data types for pointer variables, as will be discussed in chapter 4.

Pointers can be implemented as subscripts. The data items are stored in an array or table, and a subscript is then a pointer to the item.

Pointers are needed when a data structure is dynamic, that is items are continually being added or deleted from the structure. They are also useful when the data items have several relationships between them; several pointers can be used to provide the access paths between related items.

3.2 Access vectors

An access vector is a list of pointers providing access to a set of data items. We shall look briefly at three applications of access vectors.

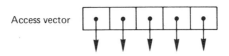

3.2.1 Sparse matrices, ragged arrays and access vectors

One application for access vectors is in reducing storage space for a sparse matrix, that is a two-dimensional array of which only a few entries are used.

In figure 3.1a, a 5 × 30 matrix uses only 7 entries. The remaining 143 are at present unused.

```
        Column
          1            2   ...  6...18 ...29   30
   Row ┌                                          ┐
    1  │  2.6                      3.8            │
    2  │                                     26.0 │
    3  │             0.2     4.9                  │
    4  │                           5.6            │
    5  └                                 12.0     ┘
```

Figure 3.1a   A 5 × 30 matrix with only 7 entries used.

A more economical way to store the data is as a ragged array (figure 3.1b), where only the first few entries in each row are used. Here the entries are records with two fields. One identifies the column of the sparse matrix while the other is the data item.

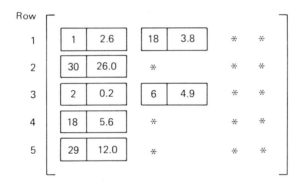

Figure 3.1b   Ragged array 5 × 4 of records with column no. and value.

The number of columns in the ragged array limits the number of entries allowed in any row of the original matrix. Allowing 4 columns reduces the storage space to 5 × 4 (20) records, each holding a subscript and a data value.

Further reduction in space is possible by introducing an access vector. The records from the ragged array are stored in a one-dimensional array. A separate access vector is used to show where each row begins (figure 3.1c). To find the entries from row 3, for instance, the 3rd and 4th entries in the access vector are needed. These show that row 3 begins in position 4, while row 4 begins in position 6. Row 3 thus uses positions 4 and 5.

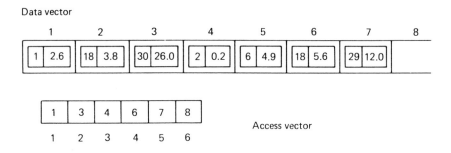

Figure 3.1c   Access vector.

Although there is no 6th row, a sixth element is needed in the access vector to determine where row 5 ends. Its value must be 1 above the last entry in row 5.

The access vector representation allows any number of entries in a row, removing the limitation imposed by the ragged array size. It does, however, limit the total number of entries allowed in the matrix.

The price paid for reducing the storage space is an increase in complexity, both in the structure and in the algorithms needed to process it. For example, inserting a new item requires other items to be moved down. It is one example of the space/time compromise, where we can trade-off space for processing time or vice versa.

3.2.2 Character strings in BASIC

Readers familiar with BASIC will know that string variables can be assigned string values of varying length. The BASIC assignments

N$="FRED"
T$="TOM, TOM, THE PIPER'S SON"

give string values to the variables N$ and T$ of lengths 4 and 25.

The way BASIC handles this is to hold all the string values in a list in memory called the string space. Each string variable name is held in a table, known as the symbol table, together with its current length and a pointer to the start position of its current value in string space (figure 3.2a).

The assignment

N$=T$

is implemented by copying the length and position from the symbol table entry for T$ to that for N$. Figure 3.2b shows the result.

Symbol table

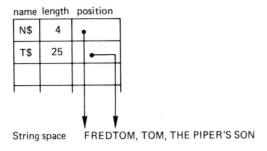

Figure 3.2a *Two strings held in variables N$ and T$.*

Symbol table

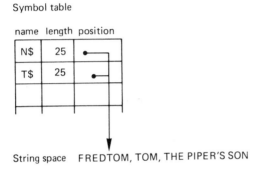

Figure 3.2b *String space after the assignment N$=T$.*

3.2.3 Indexes

A table holding details of customer names, towns and telephone numbers in ascending order of name, is shown in figure 3.3a.

	Name	Town	Tel. no.
1	Abbey	London	6342861
2	Ackers	Birmingham	2884166
3	Adams	Wolverhampton	6898413
4	Appleby	Liverpool	2201111
5	Aspinall	Manchester	4856261
6	Barwise	Taunton	1233660
7	Basnett	Exeter	8426290
8	Beattie	Edinburgh	1284355
9	Bently	Cardiff	4476928

Figure 3.3a *A table held in name order.*

Retrieval of the record for a given name can use the binary search, since the items are in name order. But retrieval of the record for a given telephone number would need a linear search: a slow process when the table is large. If an access vector is used for the telephone numbers, the process can be made much more efficient. The access vector (or index), shown in figure 3.3b, stores the telephone numbers in ascending order together with pointers to the record entries in the table. The binary search can be used on the index to find the index entry for a given telephone number. Its associated pointer gives immediate access to the corresponding table entry.

Tel. no.	Pointer
1233660	6
1284355	8
2201111	4
2884166	2
4476928	9
4856261	5
6342861	1
6898413	3
8426290	7

Figure 3.3b   Index (access vector) for telephone number field.

The index provides easy access to data stored in the table at the price of using more storage space. The structure has also made it much more difficult to add new items to the table. Not only would space have to be made in the middle of the table by moving entries, but this would affect all the pointer values in the index.

An alternative structure is to hold the data records in an arbitrary order and use an extra index for the name field as well as one for the telephone number field. The indexes provide efficient access to the records by name or telephone number. Addition of a new item needs entries in both indexes to be moved, but no longer needs pointer values to be altered since the new item can be placed at the end of the table. Deletions of items still require pointer values to be changed.

3.3 Stacks

3.3.1 Abstract and concrete representation

A stack is a dynamic data structure in which items are added and deleted on a last-in-first-out (LIFO) basis. This is like a stack of plates in a cafeteria: the plates added to the top of the stack are used before those already on the stack.

In computing, the stack is one of the most common data structures, particularly in system software.

The operations needed for a stack are:

- to initialise a stack as empty;
- to add an item to the top of the stack: this operation is called PUSH;
- to delete an item from the stack: this operation is called POP;
- to access the top element of the stack without removing it;
- to test if the stack is empty;
- to test if the stack is full (if the implementation limits the size of the stack).

If the elements of a one-dimensional array are used to hold the items on a stack, a pointer, called the Stack Pointer, is used to indicate the top of the stack. It holds the subscript of the last item placed on the stack. All the items on the stack are of the same type. It could be a simple data type like INTEGER or REAL, or a record or other structure.

The stack is empty when the Stack Pointer is 0, and full when it is the size of the array.

Figure 3.4 shows a stack containing three REAL values entered in the order: 62.7, 28.8, 146.1. The top of the stack is the last value entered, 146.1.

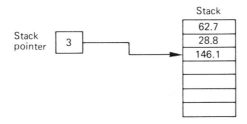

Figure 3.4   A stack of real numbers.

As further items are pushed on to this stack, more of the array is used and the Stack Pointer value is increased. In the diagram of figure 3.4 the stack appears to grow downwards.

As items are deleted from the stack, it reduces in size using less of the array: the Stack Pointer is decreased. Note that there is no need to clear the entries as they are popped from the stack.

Figure 3.5 gives Pascal declarations for a stack of real numbers implemented as an array. The routines needed to process the stack are also shown, except for the one to access the top item without removing it. This is left as an exercise.

```
(* declarations *)
VAR StackPointer : 0..maxsize;
    Stack : ARRAY [1..maxsize] OF REAL;

(* routines to process the stack *)
(*-------------------------------------------------*)
PROCEDURE clearStack;
(* initialise teh stack as empty *)

BEGIN
StackPointer := 0;
END;
(*-------------------------------------------------*)
FUNCTION StackFull : BOOLEAN;
(* test if the stack is full *)

BEGIN
StackFull := ( StackPointer=maxsize);
END;
(*-------------------------------------------------*)
FUNCTION StackEmpty : BOOLEAN;
(* test if the stack is empty *)

BEGIN
StackEmpty := (StackPointer=0);
END;
(*-------------------------------------------------*)
PROCEDURE push (X:REAL);
(* push X onto the stack *)

BEGIN
StackPointer:=StackPointer + 1;
Stack [StackPointer] := X;
END;
(*-------------------------------------------------*)
PROCEDURE pop (VAR X:REAL);
(* pop value from stack into X *)

BEGIN
X:= Stack [StackPointer];
StackPointer := StackPointer - 1;
END;
(*-------------------------------------------------*)
```

Figure 3.5   Stack declarations and processing routines.

Access to the values in the stack should be restricted to the use of the standard operations. This makes the implementation details transparent to the user and guards against improper use.

With the routines defined in figure 3.5, the user is responsible for testing whether the stack is full before trying to push a new value on to it, and similarly testing for empty before popping an item from the stack.

Stacks are used in situations where data items are dynamically stored and later retrieved in reverse order, looking at the most recent values first. The term 'backtracking' is often used in such cases.

3.3.2 Use of stacks in handling procedure calls

When high-level language programs are compiled, the procedures, functions and main routines generate separate blocks of low-level code. Where a procedure is called from the main routine, or from another procedure, the low-level code will jump to the start of the block of instructions for that procedure. At the end of the procedure, control must return to the statement after the call.

At low level, the jumps and returns are in terms of addresses in store. The start address of each procedure is fixed, but the return addresses vary from call to call.

Figure 3.6 shows a main routine calling procedure A, which in turn calls procedure B. There are two calls to procedure A from the main routine. The start addresses and addresses of the calls and returns are shown in the figure.

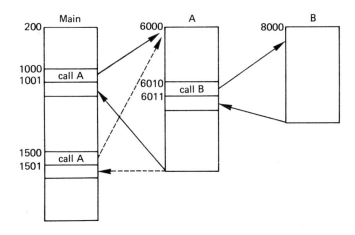

Figure 3.6 Procedure calls and returns.

When there is a chain of calls, such as when the main routine calls A which in turn calls B, the return addresses must be stored and later retrieved in reverse order. Procedure B returns to A which itself returns to the main routine.

A stack can be used to keep track of the return addresses. Each time a procedure is called, the return address is pushed on to the stack. When a procedure finishes, the return address is popped from the stack. Figure 3.7 illustrates the use of the stack in the example corresponding to figure 3.6.

Stack contents

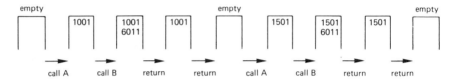

Procedure calls and returns

Figure 3.7 Use of stack for return addresses.

In practice, other data besides the return addresses is held on the stack. This includes the parameters of the procedure call and the local variables used by the routine.

Our description has been in terms of procedures, but functions are treated in the same way.

3.3.3 Use of stacks in evaluating arithmetic expressions

A second example shows how simple stacks can be used to tackle the complex problem of evaluating arithmetic expressions, as is done by language compilers and interpreters.

Arithmetic expressions involving values (operands) and operators are usually written in infix notation, where each operator is between the two operands. The expression

$$6 - 2 + 8$$

means that the values of 6 and 2 have to be subtracted, then the result added to 8. The rules for evaluating expressions give precedence to multiplication and division over addition and subtraction, so it is not possible to evaluate the expression working strictly from left to right. The expression

$$16 - 3 * 4$$

requires the 3 and 4 to be multiplied before subtraction from 16. Furthermore, brackets can be included in the expression to override the usual precedence rules.

An alternative notation, called Reverse Polish, writes expressions with the operators following the two operands. The Reverse Polish expression

$$6\ 2\ -$$

means subtract 2 from 6, while the expression

$$6\ 2\ -\ 8\ +$$

means subtract 2 from 6, then add 8. There are no precedence rules and no need for brackets. The operators appear in the order of evaluation, so the expressions can be evaluated working strictly from left to right. The expression

$$16\ 3\ 4\ *\ -$$

means multiply 3 by 4 then subtract from 16.

We shall describe in outline the tasks of converting an infix expression to Reverse Polish and of evaluating Reverse Polish expressions. As the latter is the easier to understand, it will be described first.

Evaluating Reverse Polish expressions

In evaluating the Reverse Polish expression 16 3 4 * −, we read from left to right past the operand values. When we meet the operator *, we backtrack to retrieve the last two values handled (3 and 4) and perform the multiplication, giving the value 12. This partial result is stored with the remaining value. When the operator − is reached, we backtrack to retrieve the previous two values (16 and 12) to be used in the subtraction. The result (4) is stored and as we have reached the end of the expression it is the final result.

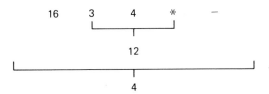

In the general case, a stack can be used to evaluate an expression in Reverse Polish form. It is used to hold the operand values of the expression and partial results. Initially, it is empty. The items from the Reverse Polish expression are examined one by one. An operand value is pushed on to the stack. For an operator, the last two values are popped from the stack and the operation used between them. The result is then pushed back on to the stack. At the end of the expression, the stack should contain a single value which is the final result. Figure 3.8 shows a stack used in evaluating the Reverse Polish expression

$$2\ 7 + 3 * 12\ 6 - 4 * - 4 *$$

which is equivalent to the infix expression

$$(\ (2 + 7) * 3 - (12 - 6) * 4) * 4$$

Reverse Polish expression :

2   7   +   3   *   12   6   −   4   *   −   4   *

Stack contents

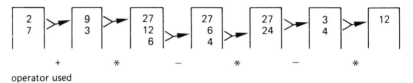

operator used

Figure 3.8   Evaluating a Reverse Polish expression.

Converting infix expressions to Reverse Polish form

When an infix expression is converted to Reverse Polish, the operand values appear in the same order in both expressions. The difficulty is to decide where the operators should be placed, taking account of brackets and operator precedence.

In converting the infix expression 5 + 6 − 3, the 5 can be placed in the Reverse Polish immediately, but the operator + must be stored until both of its operands are in the output string. The 6 is placed in the Reverse Polish, then the operator − is encountered. Because the + has the same precedence it will be performed first and can now be placed in the output string. The − is stored until after the 3 is processed. The resulting string is 5 6 + 3 −.

For the infix expression 5 + 6 * 3, the + is again held until the second operator (*) is reached. Because + has a lower precedence than *, it cannot be processed until after the *, so both operators are held. The 3 is placed in the output, then the * and + are added to the Reverse Polish to give the final result 5 6 3 * +.

These examples show that operand values can be placed directly into the Reverse Polish string, but operators must be held until another operator of lower or equal precedence is met, or until the end of the expression if no such operator follows.

In the general case, brackets must also be considered. Again a stack can be used. This time it holds the operators waiting to be placed into the Reverse Polish string, and open brackets waiting to be paired with closing brackets.

The process begins with an empty stack and an empty Reverse Polish string. The items in the infix expression are examined from left to right, and the action taken depends on the type of the item.

An operand is appended to the Reverse Polish string. An open bracket is pushed on to the operator stack.

For an operator, the procedure is more complicated. The operator is compared with the item at the top of the stack. If its precedence is less than or equal to that of the top item, the item is popped from the stack and placed into the Reverse Polish string. If, for example, the new operator is a + and the stack top is a *, the * is moved from the stack and appended to the Reverse Polish string. Further comparisons are then made, popping operators from the stack as necessary and adding them to the Reverse Polish string. In this process, the precedence of any open bracket on the stack is considered lower than that of the new operator, so that it will not be removed until the pairing close bracket is reached. Finally, the new operator is pushed on to the stack.

When a close bracket is encountered in the infix expression, the operators on the stack are popped from it and placed into the Reverse Polish string one by one until an open bracket is found on the stack. The open bracket is popped from the stack and discarded.

At the end of the expression, all operators remaining on the stack are popped from it and placed into the Reverse Polish string.

Infix expression :

((2 + 7) * 3 − (12 − 6) * 4) * 4

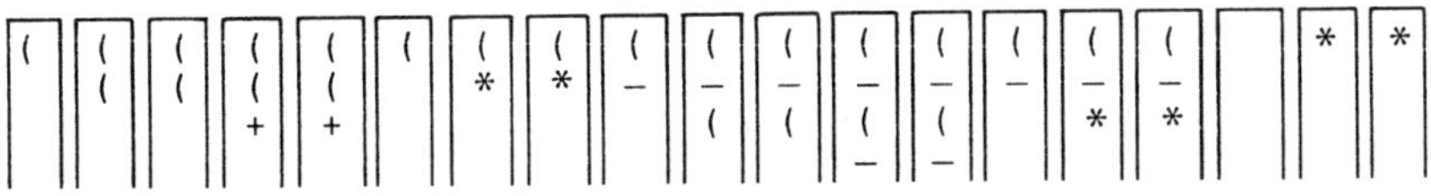

Stack contents

2   7   +   3   *   12   6   −   4   *   −   4   *

Reverse Polish

Figure 3.9   Converting infix to Reverse Polish.

Figure 3.9 illustrates the use of the stack in the conversion of the infix expression

$$((2 + 7) * 3 - (12 - 6) * 4) * 4$$

The outline algorithms just described have assumed all operators are binary operations, that is they act on two values. In some expressions unary operators are allowed which act on one value. In the expression

$$6 + (-3 * 7)$$

the minus is a unary operator acting only on the value 3. In the infix expression a unary minus can be recognised because it either follows a bracket or is the first item in the expression (as in $-7 * 85$). In the Reverse Polish form a unary minus must have a different operator symbol to the binary subtraction. The evaluation routine would have to be modified to check whether one or two values must be removed from the stack.

3.4 Queues

3.4.1 Abstract and concrete representation

A queue is a dynamic data structure in which the items are deleted in the same order as they were added — on a first-in-first-out (FIFO) basis.

The basic operations on a queue are:

- to initialise the queue to empty;
- to add an item to the tail of the queue;
- to delete an item from the head of the queue;
- to access the item at the head of the queue without removing it;
- to test if the queue is empty;
- to test if the queue is full (if the implementation limits the size).

A queue can be implemented using a one-dimensional array to hold the items. Although it would be possible to have the head of the queue in the first position in the array and following items in consecutive positions, this arrangement would require all the remaining items to be moved up each time an item is deleted. If, instead, two pointers are used, one for the tail of the queue and one for the head, there is no need to move items when one is deleted. The head pointer is updated so that it moves on to the next item in the queue.

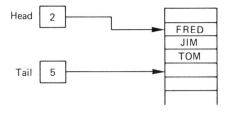

Figure 3.10   A queue with three items.

Figure 3.10 shows a queue with three items. The head pointer points to the first item in the queue. The remaining items are in consecutive positions with the tail pointer pointing to the next free location.

As items are added to the tail of the queue, the tail pointer moves towards the end of the array. As items are deleted from the head of the queue, the head pointer also moves towards the end of the array, freeing space at the front of the array. To make use of these entries, the tail pointer is cycled round to the beginning of the array once it reaches the end. Figure 3.11 shows a queue with five entries, where the tail pointer has cycled round to the start of the array.

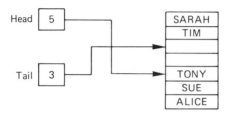

Figure 3.11   Queue in which the tail pointer has cycled round.

Similarly, when the head pointer reaches the end of the array and an item is removed, it is cycled round to the beginning.

The operations to test if the queue is full or if it is empty must compare the values of the head and tail pointers. In order to distinguish between being full and empty, it is necessary to leave one entry in the array unused. In figure 3.11, two spaces are left in the array, but only one more item can be added to the queue, leaving the final entry unused. With this stipulation, the queue is empty when

$$\text{Head} = \text{Tail}$$

and full when

$$\text{Head} = \text{Tail+1 (cycled round if necessary)}$$

The Pascal coding to declare a queue of names and define the routines to process it is given in figure 3.12. The MOD function is used to increment the Tail (or Head) pointer and cycle round to 1 if necessary. The expression

$$\text{Tail MOD maxsize}$$

will have the value of Tail if it is in the range 1 to (maxsize − 1), and a value 0 if Tail is maxsize. Adding 1 to this expression produces the desired results.

The procedures provide the basic operations for handling the structure. The user is expected to test for a full queue before attempting to add a new item,

```
TYPE
    QueueEntry = PACKED ARRAY [1..10] OF CHAR;

VAR Queue : ARRAY [1..maxsize] OF QueueEntry;
    Head, Tail :  1..maxsize;

(* routines to process the queue *)
(*----------------------------------------------*)

PROCEDURE clearQueue;
(* initialise the queue to empty *)

BEGIN
Head:=1;
Tail:=1;
END;

(*----------------------------------------------*)
FUNCTION QueueEmpty : BOOLEAN;
(* test if the queue is empty *)

BEGIN
QueueEmpty:= (Head=Tail);
END;

(*----------------------------------------------*)
FUNCTION QueueFull : BOOLEAN;
(* test if the queue is full *)

BEGIN
QueueFull := ( Head = Tail MOD maxsize + 1);
END;
(*----------------------------------------------*)
PROCEDURE addToQueue (X: QueueEntry);
(* adds item X to tail of queue *)

BEGIN
Queue [Tail] := X;
Tail := Tail MOD maxsize + 1;
END;

(*----------------------------------------------*)
PROCEDURE deleteFromQueue (VAR X: QueueEntry);
(* deletes item from head of queue *)

BEGIN
X:= Queue [Head];
Head := Head MOD maxsize + 1;
END;
```

Figure 3.12 Pascal declarations and operations for a queue.

and to test for an empty queue before attempting to delete an item. The routine to access the first item on the queue without removing it is left as an exercise for the reader.

3.4.2 Use of queues in system software

Queues are used in many circumstances in system software. In a multi-user system, for example, where several users share a printer, all the requests to print a file are held in a queue. Only one file can be printed at a time, the other requests waiting their turn.

A second example is when several programs are being run concurrently. Only one program can use the central processor at a time. The others are held in a queue.

There are many more examples where running programs are competing for system resources. The system software which monitors the state of the programs holds details of the resource requests in queues. When a resource becomes available it can be allocated to the first request on the queue.

3.4.3 Simulation

Computer simulation is the study of models of real-life systems on a computer. The real-life system might be a production plant, a proposed road network, a supermarket etc. The computer model would be designed to represent the essential details under study, but would not include all aspects of the real-life system. A model of a supermarket, for instance, might be concerned only with customers at the check-out tills, or it might include other features such as shelf-restocking.

Queues play a prominent role in simulation, representing items waiting to be processed at some part of the system. The simulation program has to monitor the arrival of new items into the system, the departure of items from the system and the movement of items between parts of the system.

Pseudo-random number generation routines are used to generate data values to provide control information, such as how frequently new items arrive in the system, and to supply the parameters for the items in the system. In a simple system with two queues, say, the parameters might specify which queue the item will join and the required service time (that is, the length of time it will remain at the head of the queue). More complex systems will use more parameters for each item.

Statistics can be gathered by the program as it runs. Typical examples include the average and maximum wait times in the queues and the number of items processed by the system. These can be displayed at regular intervals, or once when the program finishes after a fixed (simulated) time interval.

There are several computer simulation packages available which provide the outline framework for a simulation. The model is defined by commands to the package specifying the number of queues, how items are moved between queues, distribution parameters for generating the random numbers, required statistics, etc. These details are incorporated into the general framework giving a simulation program tailored to the specific model. The program can be run several times, varying the parameters to observe the results.

3.5 Summary

Pointers were introduced as simple data items which provide a link to other data values. In this chapter subscripts to array elements were used as pointers, and their application to access vectors and indexes described.

Stacks and queues were discussed in abstract as dynamic LIFO and FIFO list structures and implemented as arrays with subscripts as pointers. Outlines were given to show how these structures are applied to the backtracking problems of handling procedure calls and evaluating arithmetic expressions, and to computer simulation.

In the next chapter, an alternative implementation technique will be introduced and applied to these structures as well as others.

Exercises

3.1 For the access vector representation of a matrix of real values, write routines to:
  (a) sum the values in the ith row;
  (b) sum the values in the ith column.

3.2 Evaluate the following Reverse Polish expressions, showing how the stack is used (as in figure 3.8).
  (a) $6\ 5\ *\ 3\ 2 + 4\ 1\ -\ -\ /$
  (b) $5\ 4\ 2\ 8\ 6\ -\ +\ *\ +\ 2\ 4\ -\ +$
  (c) $8\ 4\ 6 + *\ 2\ 8\ 9 + -\ -$

3.3 Convert the following infix expressions to Reverse Polish, showing how the stack is used (as in figure 3.9).
  (a) $(\ (2{+}4)\ *\ 6)/9 + 4$
  (b) $(1\ -\ 2\ *\ 3)\ *\ (4{-}6/2{-}5)$
  (c) $1{+}(1{+}(14\ -\ 3)\ *\ (6{-}2){+}1{-}4){*}3$

3.4 Write a program to maintain the 3×3 board position of a game of noughts-and-crosses. The user should type in numbers (1 to 9, say) representing the square for the next move for O and X alternately, and after each move the board position should be displayed. If a value of -1 is entered instead of the next move, the program should backtrack to the board position before the previous move and display the board again. Repeated use of the input value − 1 should be allowed to backtrack through previous positions up to the initial empty board.

An input value of 900 can be used to terminate the program. Values other than those mentioned should be ignored.

3.5 A communication link from a computer to a printer is usually buffered. Characters sent to the printer are placed in the buffer which acts as a FIFO queue, the character at the front of the queue being printed when the device is ready.

If you have access to a pseudo-random number generation routine, write a program to simulate the operation of such a link with a buffer size of 10 characters. Have one procedure to place a character in the buffer, if there is room, and another to remove the front item from it. The program should use a string constant as the supply of characters, and when it reaches the end of the string it starts again at the beginning. The main routine should be a loop which uses the pseudo-random number routine to generate a real value between 0 and 1, and from this value decides whether to place a new item in the buffer or to remove one from the buffer. If the program tries to remove an item from an empty buffer, no error occurs, but if it tries to add to a full buffer, the new character is lost. Each time that the program adds or removes an item from the queue, it should display the current queue contents and, if a character has just been lost, an error message saying what the character was.

Run the program with the following decision criteria based on the value of the pseudo-random number, v:

(a) if $v \leqslant 0.5$, choose to add a new item to the buffer
  if $0.5 < v$, choose to remove an item from the buffer.

(b) if $v \leqslant 0.25$, choose to add a new item
  if $v > 0.25$, choose to remove an item.

(c) if $v \leqslant 0.75$, choose to add a new item
  if $v > 0.75$, choose to remove an item.

4 Dynamic Data Structures

4.1 Linked lists

In previous chapters, we have seen lists implemented using consecutive entries in an array. There are three problems with this. Firstly, if items are deleted from the middle of the list, all following items must be moved up to fill the gap. Secondly, if the items are held in a specified order, the addition of a new item to the middle of the list also requires other items to be moved. The third problem is that the size of the array limits the size of the list.

An alternative implementation, known as a *linked list*, overcomes the first two of these problems. This technique is discussed in section 4.1.1 The third problem can be overcome using Pascal's pointer data types and dynamic data structures to form linked lists. These are discussed in sections 4.1.3 and 4.1.4.

4.1.1 Linked implementation of lists

Instead of storing the list entries in consecutive locations, the order can be represented by pointers. Each data item has a pointer attached to it, linking it to the next item in the list. The last item has a null pointer to show that nothing follows it. One extra pointer, Head, is needed to show which item is the first in the list. This implementation is illustrated by the diagram:

This structure is a (one-way) linked list. Each entry is a record holding the data items and their associated Next pointer.

We shall consider how the basic list operations are implemented for a linked list. These are:

- to initialise the list as empty;
- to test if the list is empty;
- to access the items in order;
- to search for a specific item in the list;
- to insert a new item into the list;
- to delete an item from the list.

56

Initialising and testing

Initialising the list as empty is achieved by setting the Head pointer to null. The test for empty examines the Head pointer. The list is empty when its Head is null.

Accessing the list in order

The items can be accessed in order by following the links. The Head pointer is used to access the first item, then the Next pointer is used to access the second item, and so on until a null pointer is reached.

Searching

The search for an item with a specific key, X, uses the Head pointer to give the start position, compares this item's key with X and, if the keys differ, follows the Next pointer to the second item. Subsequent items are compared in turn until a match is found or the end of the list is reached. This is the same as the linear search described in chapter 1, except that here the Next pointer is used to access the successor of an item.

If the items are linked in ascending order of the search key, the search procedure can be shortened slightly. Instead of comparing for equality (X = item key), the items can be compared for the order relation $X \leqslant$ item key, and the search terminated as soon as an item with key greater than or equal to X is found.

The binary chop technique cannot be used because it relies on finding the mid-point of a range of items. There is no way of finding a mid-point value in a linked list without searching through the list.

Inserting

Inserting a new item, X, into the list has two separate cases: when the item is to be inserted in the middle (or at the end) of the list, and when the item is inserted at the front of the list. In both cases a record is created holding the new data values, and its Next pointer is set to link it to the item which is to follow it in the list.

If it is inserted into the middle or end of the list, the Next pointer of the item which is to precede it in the list must be modified to point to the new entry.

If it is inserted at the front of the list, there is no preceding item, and the value of the Head pointer must be modified.

Figure 4.1a illustrates an item added between two items in the list, while figure 4.1b shows an item inserted at the front of the list.

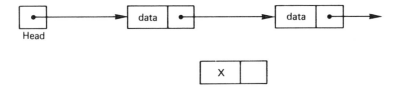

X is to be inserted between the first and second items on the list

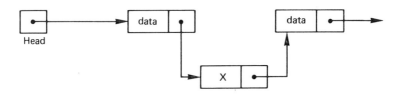

The list after X has been added

(a)

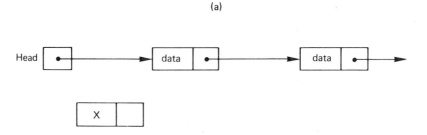

X is to be added at the front of the list

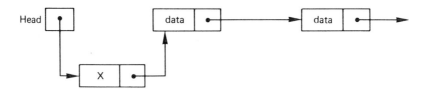

The list after X has been added

(b)

Figure 4.1 (a) Adding an item to the middle of the list. (b) Adding an item to the front of the list.

Deleting

Deleting an item from a list is achieved by altering pointers. Again there are two separate cases: deleting from the middle or end of the list, and deleting from the front of the list. In the first case, the Next pointer of the item immediately preceding the one to be deleted is altered. It is made to point to the item following the deleted item. Figure 4.2a illustrates a deletion from the middle of a list.

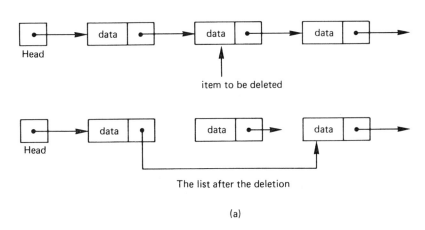

Figure 4.2a   Deleting an item from the middle of a list.

Deleting items from the front of the list requires the Head pointer to be altered to point to the second item in the list. Figure 4.2b illustrates this situation.

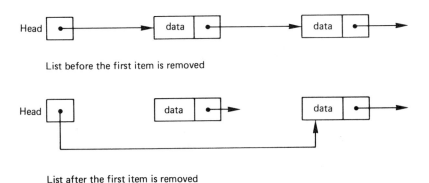

Figure 4.2b   Deleting an item from the front of a list.

Altering the pointers disconnects the item from the list and effectively deletes it. Further steps may be needed if its space is to be re-used for new items.

4.1.2 Array implementation of linked lists

Before studying how linked lists can be set up using Pascal's pointer data types, we shall mention briefly how an array can be used with subscript values as pointers.

A linked list can be implemented as a table with fields for the data items and Next pointers. An extra variable, Head, is used for the Head pointer.

A Pascal data declaration for a list of names held in alphabetical order could be as follows:

```
CONST
        null=0;


TYPE
        String10  = PACKED ARRAY [1 . . 10] OF CHAR;
        ItemType = RECORD
                        name  :   String10;
                        Next  :   0 . . maxsize;
                        END;


VAR
        List : ARRAY [1 . . maxsize] OF ItemType;
        Head : 0 . . maxsize;
```

With these declarations, the routine to initialise the list as empty would set the Head pointer to null. Testing for an empty list would be testing if Head = null.

Figure 4.3 gives a routine which accesses the items in order, writing them to

```
PROCEDURE PrintList;
(* Prints out all entries in the linked list
            in order *)

VAR i: 0..maxsize;

BEGIN
i:=Head;
WHILE (i <> null) DO
   BEGIN
   WRITELN( List[i].name );
   i:= List[i].Next;   (* follow pointer to next item *)
   END;
END;
```

Figure 4.3 PrintList routine.

the output file. This illustrates how the Next pointers are used to follow the chain. The Head pointer is used to specify the start position.

Suppose the list is set up with the entries as follows:

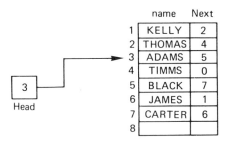

	name	Next
1	KELLY	2
2	THOMAS	4
3	ADAMS	5
4	TIMMS	0
5	BLACK	7
6	JAMES	1
7	CARTER	6
8		

The Print List procedure would start at position 3, as shown by the value of Head, then follow the Next pointers printing the names in positions

$$3, 5, 7, 6, 1, 2, 4.$$

Routines for the other list operations, such as searching for a given name, adding or deleting items, can be implemented for this structure. The details will not be given explicitly here, but can be derived from the similar routines discussed in section 4.1.4.

4.1.3 Pascal implementation of pointer data types

The concept of pointers was introduced in the previous chapter. It was stated that, at low level, pointers can be store addresses; but the examples given used subscripts as pointers with the data items held in arrays or tables.

There are two disadvantages of this implementation. Firstly, the size of the array must be declared in the program, which limits the number of data items allowed in the structure. Using a very large array to allow for the worst case wastes space in most cases. Secondly, the pointer values are likely to be integer subscripts which can be used erroneously in arithmetical assignments without being detected at compile-time. For example, instead of writing

i := List [i] .Next;

the erroneous statement

i:=i+1;

would be accepted by the compiler. The subscript data type does not truly reflect its usage.

Pascal provides an alternative implementation of pointers which overcomes these disadvantages. Variables can be declared as pointers, specifying the type of data item they can point to. In effect the pointer will hold the address of the data item and can be used to access its value. The type of the data item is usually a record, but could be a real, integer or even an array.

In figure 4.4 the data types IntPointer and cardPtr are declared as pointer types. Variables P and Q are pointers to INTEGER values, while First and Last are pointers to records of type CardRec.

```
                                              (* type declarations

TYPE
    IntPointer =  ^INTEGER;
    CardPtr    =  ^CardRec;

    CardRec = RECORD
                name : PACKED ARRAY [1..10] OF CHAR;
                membershipNo : INTEGER
                END;
(* variable declarations *)
VAR
   P,Q : IntPointer;
        (* Pointers to INTEGER values *)
   First, Last : CardPtr;
        (* Pointers to CardRec records *)
```

Figure 4.4 Declaring pointer types and variables.

The declarations allocate space for the pointers, but they do not assign any specific value to them, nor do they allocate space for the data items they might point to. There is a procedure, NEW, which is used to allocate the space for the data item and place its address in the pointer variable. The calls

NEW(P);
NEW(Last);

allocate space for an integer and a CardRec record, and place their addresses in P and Last.

Once the space has been allocated to the data item, a value can be given to it. The pointer must be used to refer to it, as in:

```
P^ := 20;
Last^.name := 'JOHN SMITH';
Last^.membershipNo := 26403;
WITH Last^ DO WRITELN ( name, blank:2, membershipNo);
```

The up-arrow, ↑, following the pointer name indicates that it is the data item which is being referenced. The result of the assignments is illustrated by the diagram:

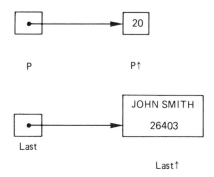

It is important to distinguish between the pointer values, P and Last, and the data values P↑ and Last↑. The ↑ makes all the difference.

The pointer value can be copied from one pointer to another as in

$$Q := P; (* \text{ copy P into Q } *)$$

but the two pointers must be of the same type (that is, point to the same type of data item). The assignment

$$\text{First} := P;$$

is not allowed because First should point to a CardRec record, while P points to an INTEGER.

There is a special constant NIL which is used to represent a null pointer value. It is compatible with all pointer types. The assignment

$$\text{First} := \text{NIL};$$

gives First a null value.

Pointers can be compared with other pointers of the same type for equality or inequality (but not the order relations Less Than etc.). The statement

$$\text{IF P=Q THEN} \dots$$

tests the values of the pointers, not the data values P↑ and Q↑.

The data values are accessed via the pointers and can be used in assignments and tests as any variable of their type. The statements

$$\text{NEW(First)};$$
$$\text{First}↑ := \text{Last}↑;$$

allocate space for a record with its address in the pointer First, then copy the data value from the record Last↑ into the new record.

When a data item is finished with, its space can be released by the DISPOSE procedure. The calls

$$\text{DISPOSE(P)};$$
$$\text{DISPOSE(Last)};$$

release the space occupied by the data items P↑ and Last↑. The pointers P and Last should not be used again until new values have been placed in them.

4.1.4 Linked lists using pointer types

Pointer data types can be used to form a linked list structure. Each item in the list is a record holding the required data fields and a Next pointer linking it into the list. With this implementation, the concrete structure closely mirrors the more abstract view.

In figure 4.5, a linked list of names is declared. The only space allocated by the declaration is a pointer. All entries in the list will be allocated dynamically by the procedure NEW as they are created.

```
(* declare types *)

TYPE
    String10 = PACKED ARRAY [1..10] OF CHAR;
    ItemPtr = ^ItemRec;
    ItemRec = RECORD
                name : String10;
                Next : ItemPtr
                END;

(* declare list *)

VAR
    List : ItemPtr; (* Pointer to list *)
```

Figure 4.5   Declaration of a linked list.

To demonstrate how pointer variables are used in this situation, we shall examine routines to set up and access the linked list. We shall assume that the names in the list are to be linked in alphabetic order.

Initialising and testing for empty

The routine to initialise the list as empty should set the list pointer to NIL.
    The list is empty when its List pointer is **NIL**.
    Figure 4.6 gives the Pascal routines to initialise the list and test it for empty.

```
PROCEDURE initialise;
(* sets up an empty list *)

BEGIN
List := NIL; (* List pointer NIL *)
END;
(*----------------------------------------*)

FUNCTION emptyList: BOOLEAN;
(*tests if list is empty *)

BEGIN
emptyList := (List=NIL)
END;
```

Figure 4.6 Routines to initialise the list and test for empty.

Accessing the list in order

A routine to print the entries of the list in order must start with the first entry given by the List pointer. The Next pointers are followed until a NIL value is found. The code is shown in figure 4.7.

```
PROCEDURE PrintList;
(* print items in list in order *)

VAR entry: ItemPtr;

BEGIN
entry:= List;   (* start position *)
WHILE (entry <> NIL) DO
    BEGIN
    WRITELN (entry^.name);   (* print this item *)
    entry := entry^.Next     (* move to next item *)
    END;  (* loop *)
END;
```

Figure 4.7 Printing items in order.

Inserting

Space for a new item is created by the NEW procedure using a pointer variable, entry, say, for the address. The data value can then be assigned to the field entry↑.name.

Linking it into the list between two entries indicated by pointers prior and successor is carried out by the LinkUp procedure of figure 4.8.

```
PROCEDURE LinkUp (entry, prior, successor : ItemPtr);
(* Links entry between prior and successor *)

BEGIN
entry^.Next := successor;
                   (* new entry points to successor *)
IF (successor = List)
THEN        (* link to front *)
    List := entry
ELSE        (* link to middle or end *)
    Prior^.Next := entry;
END;
```

Figure 4.8 Linking an entry into the linked list.

Linking a new entry to the front of the list must be treated as a separate case since it requires the List pointer to be modified.

Deleting

Deleting an item from the list is done by disconnecting the pointer links, then using the DISPOSE procedure to release the space. Figure 4.9 gives the code.

```
PROCEDURE delete (prior, entry : ItemPtr);
(* unlinks entry from list and releases
                         the items space *)

BEGIN
IF (entry = List)
THEN        (* delete from front *)
    List := entry^.Next
ELSE        (* delete from middle or end *)
    Prior^.Next := entry^.Next;
DISPOSE (entry)
END;
```

Figure 4.9 Deleting an entry from the list.

Again, deleting from the front of the list is treated as a separate case and involves modifying the List pointer.

The process of adding or deleting items from the list requires the position of the prior and successor entries to be found. A search routine, FindPosition, given in figure 4.10, can be used to find the positions for an item with key value X. It returns the pointers Prior and Entry, and a Boolean Found. If the item X is found in the list, Found is TRUE and Entry points to its position. If the item X is not in the list, Found is FALSE and Entry points to the successor position.

```
PROCEDURE FindPosition (X: String10;
                        VAR prior, entry : ItemPtr;
                        VAR found : BOOLEAN);

(* searches for the position for the key value X *)
(* if X is in the list, found is set TRUE,
       entry is its position,
       and prior the preceding item (if any) *)
 (* if X is not in the list, found is set FALSE,
       entry is the successor position
       and prior the preceding item (if any) *)

VAR searching : BOOLEAN;

BEGIN
prior:=NIL;
entry:= List;
searching:= TRUE;

WHILE searching AND (entry <> NIL) DO
    IF (entry^.name >= X) THEN
        searching := FALSE
    ELSE
        BEGIN
        prior:= entry;          (* save this as prior *)
        entry:= entry^.Next     (* move to next entry *)
        END;

IF entry = NIL THEN
    found := FALSE
ELSE
    found := (entry^.name = X)
END;
```

Figure 4.10   Routine to find the position for key value X.

4.2 Free storage lists

As items are deleted from a linked list, the spaces become free and could be re-used. With the array implementation the spaces from deleted items are scattered throughout the table, and it is necessary to keep track of their positions so that they can be re-used. With a list implemented using Pascal's dynamic data structures, the DISPOSE procedure will release the space to the system, but is not particularly efficient. It is often preferred to keep track of the free space and re-use it instead of using the procedure NEW for each addition.

This is done by linking deleted items into a separate linked list called the free storage list. A pointer, Free, is used to indicate the head of this chain. When an item is deleted from the data list, its entry is added to the front of the free storage list, as shown in figure 4.11. When a new item is to be added to the data

list, a space for it is provided from the front of the free storage list if this list is
not empty.

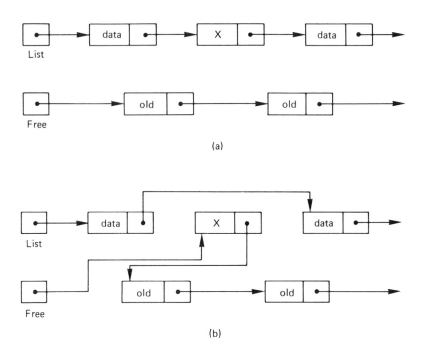

*Figure 4.11   (a) Linked list and free storage list before X is deleted. (b) Linked
list and free storage list after the deletion.*

The Pascal procedures LinkToFree, to link an entry to the free storage list,
and GetSpace, to provide a space for a new item, are shown in figure 4.12. They
are simpler than the general add and delete procedures for linked lists, since the
addition and deletion is always for the front of the list.

When an item is to be added to the data list, the free storage list is tested for
empty. If it is not empty, the procedure GetSpace is used to obtain the record
for the new entry. If the free list is empty, the procedure NEW is used to obtain
an entirely new entry.

The routines for the array implementation of a linked list are similar to figure
4.12. Initially, when the data list is set up as empty, the free storage list must be
set up containing all the table entries. Although it does not matter in which
order the spaces are linked, a simple way is to link each item to its physical
successor. The last entry has 0 in its Next pointer. When an item is added to the
data list, the space for it must be obtained from the free list. If the free list is
empty, the data list is full and no more entries can be added until something
is deleted.

```
PROCEDURE LinkToFree (entry : ItemPtr);
(* links entry record to free storage list *)

BEGIN
entry^.Next := Free;
Free := entry
END;

(*------------------------------------------------------*)
PROCEDURE GetSpace (VAR entry : ItemPtr);
(* gets first free space from free storage list *)

BEGIN
entry:= Free;
Free := Free^.Next    (* Unlink first entry *)
END;
(*------------------------------------------------------*)
```

Figure 4.12 Adding to and deleting from the free storage list.

4.3 Stacks and queues

A linked list structure can be used to implement abstract data structures such as a stack or a queue.

A stack is a LIFO list. If a linked list is used to implement it, additions and removals are always at the front of the list, so the Push and Pop operations are simpler than the general insertion and deletion routines for linked lists. In fact they are the same as the LinkToFree and GetSpace routines used for the free storage list of the previous section (figure 4.12).

In a queue, items are added to the tail and deleted from the head. A linked list can be used with a pointer to the head item and one to the tail. Each item has a Next pointer linking it to the next item in the queue. Strictly speaking, the tail pointer is not essential since the tail of the queue can be found by searching for the NIL pointer. But its use makes the task of adding a new item much simpler. The addition and deletion routines are further simplified if a dummy entry is kept at the tail of the queue as shown in the diagram:

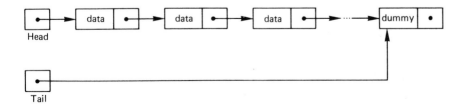

Creating an empty list must set up the dummy entry alone, with both Head and Tail pointing to it. The test for empty is if Head=Tail.

Adding an item to the queue is accomplished by the steps:

- place the new value in the dummy entry;
- create a new dummy space using the NEW procedure;
- link this to the end of the list;
- update the Tail pointer.

Deleting an item from the queue

Items are removed from the head of the queue by modifying the Head pointer:

```
entry := Head;
Head:= Head^.Next;
DISPOSE (entry);
```

There should be a test to see whether the queue is empty before any attempt to delete an item.

4.4 Dummy entries and circular chains

When a linked list is used in a situation where items are added and deleted from the front and middle of the list, a dummy entry can be used to simplify the routines. Both addition and deletion have to consider the cases where the item is in the middle or end of the list separately from the cases where it is at the front of the list. By including a dummy entry in front of the list, with its Next pointer showing the first true entry in the list, all additions and deletions appear to be in the middle of the list. The coding for these routines is simpler. The role played by the Head pointer is now played by the pointer List↑.Next. The last entry in the list points back to the dummy entry forming a circular chain as shown:

List

In this circular chain, the end of the list is identified when the Next pointer is the same as the List pointer.

The dummy entry serves two purposes. Firstly, it ensures that there is a prior entry for each addition or deletion. There is no need to treat the head of the list as a special case. Secondly, because the links are circular, the dummy entry can be used in a search routine to hold the search key temporarily. This simplifies the conditions used when searching for the position of the key.

A version of the FindPosition Pascal routine for this circular linked list with dummy entry is given in figure 4.13. Placing the search key value, X, in the dummy record ensures that the loop will find an entry with a value greater than or equal to X. The dummy entry traps the case when there is no such value in the other 'true' entries in the list, because it is linked in to the end of the search chain.

```
PROCEDURE FindPosition (X: String10;
                        VAR prior, entry : ItemPtr;
                        VAR found : BOOLEAN);

(* searches for the position for the key value X *)
(* if X is in the list, found is set TRUE,
        entry is its position,
        and prior the preceding item (if any) *)
  (* if X is not in the list, found is set FALSE,
        entry is the successor position
        and prior the preceding item (if any) *)

BEGIN
prior:=List;
entry:= List^.Next;
List^.name:=X;            (* temporary store *)

WHILE (entry^.name < X) DO
    BEGIN
    prior:= entry;        (* save this as prior *)
    entry:= entry^.Next   (* move to next entry *)
    END;

found := (entry^.name = X) AND (entry <> List)
END;
```

Figure 4.13 Findposition routine for circular chain with dummy entry.

The routines to initialise the list to empty and test for empty have to be modified to account for the dummy entry. The empty list will consist of the dummy entry alone, with its Next field pointing to itself, as in:

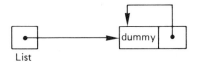

4.5 Sets

Pascal set types can be defined for sets with elements from an ordinal base type, but the implementation places restrictions on the range of the base type. For sets whose base type range is too large, an alternative implementation must be used. One possibility is to use a sorted linked list with a single entry for each element in the set. For example, the set of integers {2,−2,6,1} is represented by the list −2,1,2,6 implemented as a linked structure as in figure 4.14.

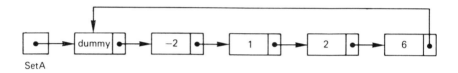

SetA

Figure 4.14   A set of integers represented by a sorted linked list.

The basic operations on sets include:

- setting up an empty set, and testing whether a set is empty;
- adding an element to a set, deleting an element from a set and testing whether an element belongs to a set;
- comparing two sets for equality or containment;
- forming the union, difference and intersection of two sets.

The empty set is represented by the empty list, so the operations of setting up an empty list and testing a list for empty apply directly.

Testing whether an element belongs to a set, adding and deleting elements are the same as the search, insert and delete routines for the linked structure. Items are inserted in sorted order and duplicates are not allowed. Using the linked structure with a dummy entry and a circular chain simplifies these routines.

Comparisons of two sets for equality or containment rely on the lists being sorted. The comparisons can be performed by routines which scan down the two lists comparing items. For equality, the two lists must have identical entries. For containment, each entry in the first list must be held in the second.

The operations of forming the union, difference and intersection of two sets can be performed by routines based on merging the two lists (similar to the merge of sequential files discussed in chapter 2, section 2.6.2) and filtering to remove unwanted items. The list for the union is formed by merging the two lists, detecting when an element appears in both lists and ensuring that only one entry is made for it in the union.

The intersection is formed in a similar way, except that entries are produced in the output only for those elements which appear in both sets.

The difference contains entries from the first list which do not appear in the second list as well.

For example, if the two lists hold the values $-2,1,2,6$ and $1,6,7$ the union operation forms the list $-2,1,2,6,7$. The difference operation forms the list $-2,2$ while the intersection forms $1,6$.

4.6 Priority queues

Many applications involving queues require priority queues rather than the simple FIFO lists discussed earlier. Each item has an associated priority value and the items on the queue are removed on a priority basis instead of using the order of arrival. For items with the same priority value, the FIFO order is used. The operations on a priority queue differ from those of the FIFO list in that the priority values must govern the order of deletions.

In a multi-user operating system, for instance, there will be several processes (programs) competing for use of the central processor at one time. The processes have a priority value assigned to them, and are held in a priority queue. The process with the highest priority is given first use of the central processor. This allows urgent jobs to take precedence over other processes.

A priority queue can be represented by a sorted list with the items in priority order. The first item on the list will have the highest priority, so a deletion will always choose the first item. Since items will be added to the middle of the list to maintain the priority order, a linked implementation is most suitable to avoid the movement of other items. Using a dummy entry and a circular chain will allow simpler implementations of the routines to find the position of an item and to add a new item.

In looking for the position for a new item with priority X, we must ensure that it is placed after any other entries with the same priority. The FindPosition routine of figure 4.13 will have to be modified to search for the first entry with a priority strictly greater than X, instead of greater than or equal to X. To aid the search the dummy entry can be used, but should now be given a temporary value strictly greater than X.

4.7 Circular chains and doubly linked lists

One problem with one-way linear linked lists is that from an item in the middle of the list there is no easy way to find another item which is earlier in the list. This does not seem much of a problem when only a single linked list is being used, but in more elaborate structures where several linked lists are in use, you may access an item without knowing which list it is linked into.

A possible solution, which has already been introduced, is to use a circular chain (with or without a dummy entry) where the last item points back to the first instead of holding a null pointer value, as illustrated in figure 4.15.

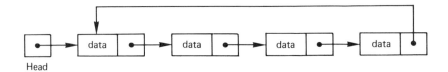

Figure 4.15   A circular chain.

From an item in the chain, all other items can be reached by following the pointers to the end of the chain and round to the beginning.

In certain situations, this provides access too slowly and additional pointers are used to link the list backwards. Each record in the list must hold both Next and Prior pointers, allowing access forwards or backwards through the list. It may also be required to keep a separate pointer Last to indicate the last entry on the list. Figure 4.16 illustrates this situation.

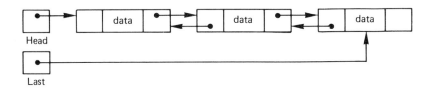

Figure 4.16   A doubly linked list.

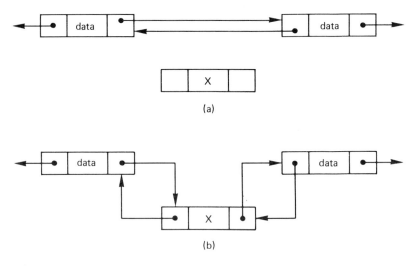

Figure 4.17   Inserting into a doubly linked list: (a) links before the insertion; (b) links after the insertion.

A structure of this form is called a two-way or doubly linked list.

The routine to insert a new item into this list must alter pointers in records on both sides of the new item. Figure 4.17 shows an insertion between two entries. Similar remarks apply to deletion. Insertion or deletion at either the front or end of the list must be treated as separate cases.

As was the case for a singly linked list, a dummy entry and a circular chain can be used to simplify the insert and delete routines. There is no need in this case to have both the Head and Last pointers. A single pointer to the dummy entry will allow access forwards or backwards through the circular chains (figure 4.18).

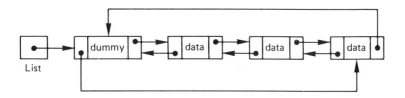

Figure 4.18 A doubly linked circular list with dummy entry.

Linked structures are used in some implementations of databases, as will be discussed in later chapters. There the items are stored on data files and the pointers are used to link related records. In a manufacturing database, for example, details of the assemblies made may be held as records on a database. Each assembly record may be associated with a number of component records specifying the quantity of a component used to make that particular assembly. The component records can be chained together in a linked list whose Head pointer is held in the assembly record. Circular chains are usually used and doubly linked chains are options.

4.8 Summary

The use of additional pointers with each data item permits lists to be represented as linked structures which support more efficient insertion and deletion operations from the middle of the list. Linked lists can be implemented using arrays and subscript pointers, but are still limited by the declared array size. Pascal pointer types give an alternative implementation which is free of this limitation.

Stacks and queues were shown implemented as singly linked lists, and the notion of a free storage list introduced to show how the space of deleted items can be re-used.

The use of a dummy entry and circular chain in the linked structure simplifies the search, insertion and deletion routines for applications such as sorted lists. These were applied to sets and priority queues.

Circular chains or doubly linked lists can be used when it is necessary to traverse the items in a list starting at some entry in the middle of the list. Such structures are used in some databases, as will be discussed in later chapters.

Exercises

4.1 Write a program to read characters from an input text file and write them to an output file with the characters on each line reversed. Use a linked representation of the stack to hold the characters until the end of line is reached.

4.2 Modify your program of exercise **4.1** to include a free storage list to re-use the space of deleted items.

4.3 Write procedures to implement the union, intersection and difference operators for sets of integers implemented as circular linked lists with dummy entries (as in section 4.5).

4.4 Modify the FindPosition procedure (figure 4.13) for the priority queue implemented as a linked structure as in section 4.6. Assume that the priority is in the range 1 . . 1000, with 1 as the highest priority.

4.5 A multi-set is a collection of elements, like a set except that elements may appear more than once. Thus the multi-set {1,2,1,3} is not the same as the multi-set {1,2,3}, since the element 1 appears twice in the first multi-set, but only once in the second.

(a) Design a data structure representation for multi-sets of integers, with operations analogous to those for sets.

(b) If the base range of the multi-sets is small (for example, the subrange 1 . . 10), how might an array implementation be used to provide a simpler implementation of multi-sets and their operations?

4.6 A set may be defined by specifying which elements are in it and which elements are not. A fuzzy set is defined by giving each element a probability of being in the fuzzy set. Elements not in the fuzzy set have a probability of 0. Elements definitely in the fuzzy set have a probability of 1. Other elements have probabilities between 0 and 1.

The union operation can be defined on two fuzzy sets by specifying the probability of an element being in the union as the maximum of the probabilities of the element being in the two sets. Similarly, for the intersection operation, you use the minimum of the two probabilities.

Modify the representation of sets of integers (section 4.5) to give a representation of fuzzy sets of integers with the operations defined above.

5 Non-serial File Access

5.1 Introduction

Files are important to the commercial computing world. File operations in standard Pascal are very elementary and rather restrictive. Many of the aspects of file design covered in this chapter are only supported by extensions to the Pascal language. The non-standard Pascal used here is Hewlett-Packard for HP1000 and HP9000 computers (HP Pascal), although most compiler writers are likely to provide similar facilities in their versions of Pascal.

The serial files examined in chapter 2 were updated on a batch basis. This process is acceptable provided that results are not required quickly. If only a few records in a file need to be altered (in computing terms the file has a low hit rate), then serial file processing would be inappropriate as all records have to be written out to a new file (see section 2.6.3).

To efficiently use files other than serial, the file storage medium has to provide direct access to data. The term *random access* is used to describe devices which can read blocks of data (likely to contain several records) which are uniquely addressed and directly accessible. Magnetic discs are the usual storage devices for non-serial files.

5.2 Direct files

The simplest form of a file on a random access device is the direct or relative file. Each record in the file is numbered, starting from 1 for the first record. If the relative position of a record in a file is known, it is possible to access it directly.

A serial file is either in read only mode (opened by RESET) or write only mode (opened by REWRITE). In the read only state, the next record available for reading from the file will be the one directly following the record just read. In a write only serial file, no record before the current position can be changed. To update a particular record, this file would have to be closed, re-opened by the function REWRITE (which destroys the existing file contents) and completely rewritten.

While a serial file can be in either a read only or write only state, a direct file can be both read from and written to without going through the process of

closing and re-opening. That is to say, a direct file is in a read/write state. There
is no limit on the number of records in a serial file. When creating a direct file
it is necessary to indicate a size, so there will be an upper limit on the number of
records which can be stored.

To initialise a file as being in a read/write state, HP Pascal uses the OPEN
statement

OPEN (filename)

The operating system gives a file, generated by the OPEN statement, a default
maximum size. If you wish to specify the size of the file, it is necessary to
create the file, using an operating system command, and the OPEN statement
within the Pascal program can then access this pre-defined file. In a serial file
the next record accessed, after the nth, is the $n+1$ record. In a direct file the
user can go to a position in the file before either reading or writing to the record
found there. The SEEK command is used to set the file pointer to the required
position in the random access file. It equates to the read/write heads of a magnetic disc unit being moved over the right track of the disc before actually
reading from or writing to the record held there. The form of the SEEK command
in HP Pascal is

SEEK (filename, position)

```
PROGRAM createDirectFile ( INPUT, DirectFile) ;
TYPE
   DirectEntry = RECORD
                    ItemNo : INTEGER ;
                    quantity : INTEGER ;
                    BinNo : 100..299
                    END;

VAR
   DirectRec : DirectEntry ;
   DirectFile : FILE OF DirectEntry;
BEGIN
   OPEN (DirectFile) ;
   WHILE NOT EOF DO
      BEGIN
         WITH DirectRec DO
               READLN (ItemNo,quantity,BinNo);
         SEEK (DirectFile, DirectRec.ItemNo );
         WRITE (DirectFile, DirectRec)
      END;
END.
```

Figure 5.1 Program to place records in a direct file.

Figure 5.1 shows a program, written in HP Pascal, which sets up a direct file, DirectFile. Records written to this file are positioned on the value of ItemNo they represent by means of the statement

SEEK (DirectFile, DirectRec. ItemNo)

In a serial file the process of reading, or writing, involves the file pointer in being moved forward one record. For a direct access file, the file pointer has to be moved by means of the SEEK command before reading or writing.

HP Pascal supports the commands GET and PUT, for a direct file, as described in section 2.4. GET (filename) places the value of the current component of the file in the file buffer and advances the file pointer to the next component, and PUT (filename) writes the value of filename↑ to the file and then advances the file pointer.

HP Pascal provides two standard functions for use with direct files. POSITION returns the current position of the file pointer. After the statement

SEEK (filename, i)

the POSITION (filename) function would return the value i. As stated earlier, when initially created there is a physical limit on the number of records which can be stored. The function MAXPOS (filename) returns the largest value the 'i' parameter in the SEEK command can take when addressing the file.

A physical record will always exist for a given key value. If, in our example of figure 5.1, a record accessed on a given item number is found to have an item number field, within the accessed record, of zero, this would imply that there is no entry for this particular item number. To delete a record, it is necessary to SEEK the correct file position, based on item number, and then write a null record to that record position, that is to set the item number field to zero.

In figure 5.1, the file DirectFile had a well-behaved key field ItemNo which was a suitable means of deciding where to store each record. In practice, few files have records with such convenient keys. A program which processes a random access file is likely to contain a routine to compute the address at which the file has to be accessed. The term *computed entry addressing* is applied to such a routine. The phrase 'key to address transformation' is used to describe the algorithm to convert a key field to a file address.

5.3 Hashed random files

Hash coding is often used for random access files. In hash coding, an algorithm is used to transform a key value into a file record position. Often there is no simple key which can be used to give a record position directly, so a direct file is inappropriate to store the information. If there will never be a need to access the records of the file in a pre-defined sequence, it is far better if a method which disperses the records throughout the file is used, as this will, on average, reduce the movement that the discs read/write head will have to make when 'seeking' the next record. Hash coding causes such dispersion.

There are several algorithms for hash coding, however the simplest is based on dividing the key field of a record by a prime number. The remainder of the division is then used to define the point in the file where the new record will be stored. It is likely that several keys will generate the same remainder, pointing to the same point within the file. When such a collision occurs, the file is accessed serially from that point until the first appropriate record is found. Therefore, hash coding consists of two phases. Firstly, a point is found in the file based on the hash coding of a record's key field. Secondly, from this point the file is searched serially until the required record is found.

Figure 5.2 shows a HP Pascal program which adds records to the file HashFile using a hashing algorithm which is based on the remainder after dividing the key field of the record by 101. Notice that every time a READ or WRITE to HashFile is performed it is preceded by SEEK. That is, it is necessary to move to the correct position in the file before accessing a record. The variable tablesize is set to the number of records in the file. If index exceeds this value, it is reset to 1 by the line

Index := (Index MOD Tablesize) + 1 ;

To find a particular record in a hashed random file follows a similar procedure to that for adding a record. A hashing function is used to find a particular position in the file and a sequential search is performed from that point until the actual record required is found.

A problem arises if there is no such record in the file. Because several records could give the same result via the hashing function, how do you know when to stop searching? A reasonable approach would be to decide to search until either a blank record is found or the end of file is reached. However, if this policy is employed, how do you then delete a record? Writing a null record to the file could well 'hide' other records with the same hashing result later in the file. If you move records up to fill the gap created by a deleted record, it is necessary to ensure that you do not move a later record, which represents the next hashing function point within the file. Care has to be taken when deleting a record from a hashed random file.

5.4 Indexes

In practice, the majority of random access files have records which can be ordered and use some form of index to allow for random access. The form of index used can vary. The simplest form of index relates to a file holding static information. Most files are dynamic, records being added while others are deleted.

```
    PROGRAM hashcoding (INPUT, OUTPUT, HashFile );
(*                                                  *)
(* Program to add new record to a random access *)
(* file using hash coding                        *)
TYPE
   HashEntry = RECORD
                   key : INTEGER ;
                   Temperature : REAL ;
                   Sensorid : INTEGER
                 END;

CONST  Prime = 101;
VAR
   Keyno, Sens, Index   : INTEGER;
   Tablesize            : INTEGER;
   Temp                 : REAL;
   HashRec              : HashEntry ;
   HashFile             : FILE OF HashEntry;
BEGIN
   OPEN (HashFile) ;
   Tablesize := MAXPOS(HashFile);
   WHILE NOT EOF DO
       BEGIN
          READLN (keyno, Temp, Sens);
(* Hash coding. remainder after dividing by Prime. *)
(* If over tablesize, restart at 1. Result is      *)
(* multiplied by Tablesize DIV Prime so hash start *)
(* points are spread through-out the file          *)

          Index := (keyno MOD Prime)
                    * Tablesize DIV Prime + 1;
(* Access record indicated by Index. If already    *)
(* used, do serial search                          *)

          SEEK (HashFile, Index );
          READ (HashFile, HashRec);
          WHILE (keyno <> HashRec.key) AND
                        (HashRec.key <> 0) DO
             BEGIN
               Index := ( Index MOD Tablesize) + 1;
               SEEK (HashFile, Index);
               READ (HashFile, HashRec)
             END;
(* Correct record position found, enter new values *)

          HashRec.key := keyno ;
          HashRec.Temperature := Temp ;
          HashRec.Sensorid := Sens;
          SEEK (HashFile, Index);
          WRITE (HashFile, HashRec);
       END;
END.
```

Figure 5.2 Program to add records to a direct file using hash coding.

5.4.1 Static indexed file

Such a file consists of two parts, the blocks containing the data records and
the index blocks. The data part of the file is set up by sorting the records
according to their key field value. They are then divided into blocks, with as
many records per block as will fit. Because the file is sorted, all that is required
to find a record is to know the key of the first and last record in each block. In
fact, only the value of the key of the last record is needed. An index to the file
consists of a list of key fields, each key being used to indicate which data block
to access. This index is equivalent to that discussed in chapter 3, section 3.2.3.

For example, if a file consisted of staff records, using surname as the key, a
typical block might hold all records with keys betweeen Little and Lynch.
Assuming that the index block consists of the last record key in the block, if
Little to Lynch was the 10th block of data, the 10th element of the corresponding index would be Lynch. If the record of Lucas was required, a serial
search of the index is performed until the record in the index is greater than
or equal to 'Lucas'. Figure 5.3 shows a routine index_search which performs
this procedure to find the correct data block position.

```
PROCEDURE Index_search (Index : Name_array;
                        Staff_name : Name;
                        VAR Position : INTEGER );

    BEGIN
      Position := 1;
      WHILE (Index [Position] < Staff_name) DO
         Position := Position + 1
    END;
```

Figure 5.3   Procedure to find a data block, assuming index holds the last name
             in the corresponding data block.

If the number of data blocks within a file is large, it takes time to do a serial
search through the index (there being one index record for each data block).
To reduce the search time a hierarchy of indexes could be used. Figure 5.4
shows a possible three-level index.

If we wished to find the record referring to an employee Lucas we would
first serially search the high level index. The index record Glass to Stowers
indicates the medium level index to examine. Within the medium level index
the record Jack to Mumford indicates the appropriate low level index. Finally,
one of the low level index records points to a data block which holds the
details of employees Lewis to Lynch. This data block would be serially searched
until the record for Lucas is found. Using the three-level index it is necessary to
do four short searches — that is, a search within each index level to find the
appropriate index record, and finally a search of a data block to access the

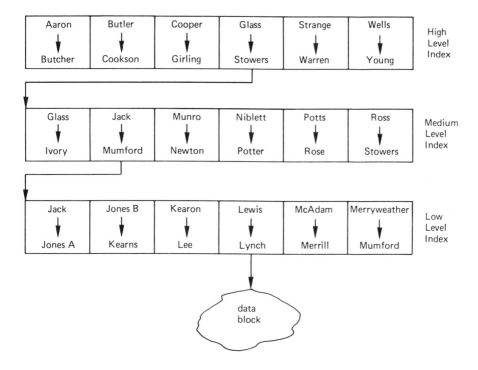

Figure 5.4 Three-level index of sample staff file.

```
index_search ( Index_high, Staff_name, Position);
index_search ( Index_med[Position], Staff_name,
                                          Position);
index_search ( Index_low[Position], Staff_name,
                                          Position);
```

Figure 5.5 Using Index_search, assuming Position is pre-defined, to search a three level index.

required data record. Figure 5.5 shows how using the routine of figure 5.3 it is possible to perform the index search for the three-level index. In this example the indexes are treated as one-dimensional arrays which are serially searched. However, these indexes would normally be in a direct access file.

5.4.2 Indexed sequential files

The majority of computer files are dynamic, in that is is necessary to insert and delete individual records. An indexed sequential file can hold dynamic data, allowing it to be processed in random order (by means of the index) or sequentially (without use of the index). Such a file consists of three essential elements: index blocks, data blocks and overflow areas.

The index blocks work in an identical manner to those described when discussing static indexed files. An index will point to a particular data block and indicate the key value of the last record to be found there.

The data blocks, also called data buckets, normally have space within them to allow for the insertion of new records. When a record is added the indexes are searched to see which data block or bucket it should be added to. The indexes are not changed in this process. If a particular part of the file has many new records added, some data blocks may have insufficient room to allow for the addition of any further new records. In such cases an overflow area will be used.

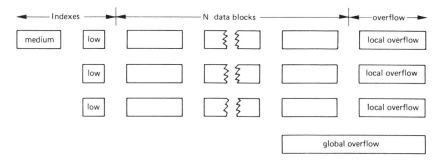

Figure 5.6   Index sequential file's overflow areas.

An overflow area can be shared by many or all of the data blocks. The normal practice is to have local and global overflow areas. Figure 5.6 shows how such a system could work.

A local overflow area is used by each group of *N* data blocks. If the local overflow area becomes full a large global overflow area, at the end of the file, is assigned and will now be used to hold the overflow records. When the global overflow is starting to be used, this normally indicates that it is time to restructure the file. Restructuring involves: placing the data records evenly throughout the data blocks (allowing space for additions within each block); and redefining the index so that its values reflect those of the new data blocks.

A pointer is normally used to link the data block to its local overflow area and, if necessary, the local overflow area to the global overflow. As index sequential files can be used to hold variable length records, within a data block pointers may be used to indicate the start of the next record. (Figure 5.7).

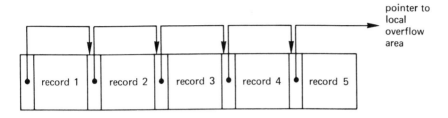

Figure 5.7 Use of pointers within a data block.

Unlike some commercially orientated computer programming languages, Pascal does not support index sequential files. However, by use of direct files, as described in section 5.2 of this chapter, it is possible to construct an index sequential file for any particular application. Figure 5.8 shows the block diagram for such a file.

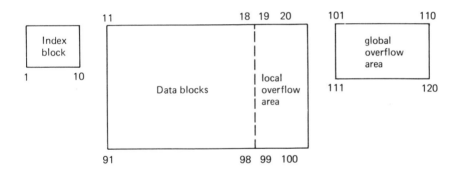

Figure 5.8 Example index sequential file structure.

The first ten blocks of the structure hold a single level index. Each index block holds eight entries of key field and data block position. In this way index block 1 references data blocks 11 to 18, index block 2 references data blocks 21 to 28, and so on. The key value, stored in the index block, indicates the highest key value to be found in the corresponding data block.

If all data blocks are the same size, then the index would not need to hold the data block position as it could be computed from the position of its index within the index block.

Each data block consists of up to four data records sorted by key field. If a data block is full, it is necessary to search the local overflow area. Each local overflow area is two blocks long, so it can hold 8 records. Finally, if the local overflow area is full, it is necessary to examine the global overflow area. Within both local and global overflow areas, the records are not sorted. Provided the record we require is in the data block area, access will be rapid.

Figure 5.9 shows possible declarations for this index sequential file. The logical file has been split into two physical files, indexfile and datafile. Using the variant form of record declaration, it is just as simple to declare a single index sequential file. Index blocks and data blocks are used for accessing the files instead of index and data records. If a block is physically accessed by the hardware, it is appropriate to use this as the logical addressing mechanism within the program.

```
CONST
    indexsize = 8;
    keysize = 20;
    record_count = 4;
TYPE
    keyfield = PACKED ARRAY [1..keysize] OF CHAR;
    otherdata = PACKED ARRAY [1..size] OF CHAR;
    indexrecord = RECORD
                    key : keyfield;
                    datapointer : INTEGER
                  END;
    indexblock = ARRAY [1..indexsize] OF indexrecord;
    datarecord = RECORD
                    key : keyfield;
                    data : otherdata;
                    entry : BOOLEAN
                  END;
    datablock = ARRAY [1..record_count] OF datarecord;
VAR
    indexpart : indexblock;
    indexfile : FILE OF indexblock;
    datapart  : datablock;
    datafile  : FILE OF datablock;
```

Figure 5.9 Index and data blocks declaration.

Figure 5.10 shows a routine to search the index. When my_key (the entry required) is found to be greater than or equal to the value held in the indexfile key field, the required data block has been found. Indexfile is serially accessed to find this data block.

Figure 5.11 shows a routine to search the data block within the datafile. It is possible that the record that we are attempting to find is not in the file. The Boolean noentry is set to true if this is the case.

Figure 5.12 is a routine to search the local overflow area. Unlike the data block, the records are not sorted so it is necessary to go through all the records

```
found := false;
block_no :=1;
WHILE (block_no <= 10) AND NOT found DO
    BEGIN
        SEEK (indexfile, block_no) ;
        READ (indexfile, indexpart);
        record_no := 1;
        WHILE (record_no <= indexsize) AND NOT found DO
            BEGIN
                IF (indexpart[record_no].key >= my_key)
                    THEN
                        BEGIN
                            pointer :=
                                    index[record_no].datapointer;
                            found := true
                        END
                    ELSE
                        record_no := record_no + 1;
            END;
        block_no := block_no + 1
    END;
```

Figure 5.10   Searching index blocks to find required data block.

```
found := false;
noentry := false;
SEEK (datafile, pointer);
READ (datafile, datapart);
record_no := 1;
WHILE (record_no <= record_count) AND NOT found
                                    AND NOT noentry DO
    BEGIN
        IF (datapart[record_no].key = my_key)
            THEN
                BEGIN
                    my_data :=  datapart[record_no].data;
                    found := true
                END
            ELSE IF (datapart[record_no] > my_key)
                    OR NOT  datapart[record_no].entry
                THEN noentry := true
            ELSE
                record_no := record_no + 1;
    END;
```

Figure 5.11   Searching the data block, assuming records are sorted.

until either the record is found, or there are no more records in the overflow area. If the local overflow area is full, and the record is still not found, it is then necessary to examine the global overflow area. The form of this search routine will be exactly the same as that for the local overflow area (figure 5.12) except

```
found := false;
noentry := false;
count := 1;
WHILE NOT found AND NOT noentry AND ( count<= 2) DO
   BEGIN
   SEEK (datafile, block_no);
   READ (datafile, datapart);
   record_no := 1;
   WHILE (record_no <= record_count) AND NOT found
                                    AND NOT noentry DO
      BEGIN
        IF (datapart[record_no].key = my_key)
           THEN
              BEGIN
                my_data :=
                      datapart[record_no].data;
                 found := true
              END
           ELSE IF  NOT  datapart[record_no].entry
              THEN noentry := true
           ELSE
              record_no := record_no + 1;
      END;
   count := count + 1;
   block_no:= block_no + 1
END;
```

Figure 5.12   Searching local overflow area.

that instead of two blocks being examined, the global overflow area has 20 (that is, count goes to 20).

This file does not take account of how a record would be deleted. Provided that the overflow areas have not been used by a particular data block, to delete a record is a comparatively simple matter. As the records in the data block are sorted, to delete a record involves moving records to fill in any gap that may have been caused. If the record to be deleted is the last record in the block, it is overwritten by a null record.

Once the overflow areas have been used, the deletion process becomes more involved. If the data block is full and a local overflow area has been used, to delete a record in the data block involves the following four steps. Firstly, the record to be deleted is removed, and the records in the data block are moved, leaving the last entry as a null record. Secondly, the local overflow area is searched to find a record which can go in the data block. Once found this record is moved to the last record entry in the data block. Thirdly, the gap left in the local overflow area is removed by moving forward the following records to put the gap at the end of the overflow area. If the local overflow area was full, the process has to be repeated by moving an appropriate record from the global to local overflow, and moving the records in the global overflow area to remove any gap. Finally, the records in the data block are resorted.

This process of deletion would be too time-consuming. The more normal practice is to use pointers to link records in the data block with the overflow areas. Once a record is deleted, by use of the pointers, following the appropriate chain will give access to any linked record in the local overflow area. The gap created in the overflow area could then be added to a free record list.

5.5 Inverted files

Often a data file will contain records which are to be accessed via more than one particular field. While a staff file might use employee number as a suitable key field for the employee record, processing the staff file could involve collecting details of all employees within a particular department. The same file might be used to find all employees on a particular salary grade.

Inverted files are a means of storing data so questions, such as who works in a given department or who are on a particular salary grade, can be quickly answered. In an inverted file the key fields of records with a common field value, such as same salary grade, are held together. A completely inverted file is one which stores the key fields associated with every value of every field. In figure 5.13, for example, the fields department code and salary grade are shown as inverted lists for a sample staff file.

A partially inverted file is more common than a fully inverted one. In a partially inverted file, only some of the fields have an inverted list associated with them. Therefore as it stands, figure 5.13 represents a file with a key field of employee number which is partially inverted.

The addition or deletion of a record from an inverted file requires that all associated inverted lists are also updated. For example, if Adams A was to be removed from the file of figure 5.13, the record 01143/Adams A/015/12 would be removed from part a. The entry 01143 would be removed from Dept Code 015 in part b. The entry 01143 would be removed from Salary Grade 12 in part c.

5.6 Summary

If non-serial file access is required, there are several alternative file structures which could be used. The appropriate structure will depend on whether the data is static or dynamic and whether there is any order to the records within the file. If it is necessary to access a file in several different sequences, the use of inverted lists may be appropriate. Standard Pascal does not easily support non-serial file access, it being the commercial languages, such as COBOL, which are strong in this area.

Employee #	Employee Name	Dept Code	Salary Grade
01143	Adams A	015	12
01235	Bamford C	004	11
01446	Brown D	004	12
01532	Edge R	004	12
01654	France P	015	13
01691	Jones E	004	11
01857	Jones W	015	12
02121	Lomax W	010	11
02245	Morris J	010	13
02314	Nolan S	015	11
02400	Skinner V	015	13

(a)

Dept Code	Employee #
004	01235
	01446
	01532
	01691
010	02121
	02245
015	01143
	01654
	01857
	02314
	02400

Salary Grade	Employee #
11	01235
	01691
	02121
	02314
12	01143
	01446
	01532
	01857
13	01654
	02400

(b)   (c)

Figure 5.13 (a) Staff file. (b) Dept Code inverted list. (c) Salary Grade inverted list.

Exercises

5.1 In this chapter we have examined HP Pascal extensions to manipulate direct access files. Examine the equivalent facilities available on a computer to which you have access.

5.2 Figure 5.2 shows the HP Pascal direct file equivalent to the stock file of chapter 2 (figure 2.4). Write a createDirectFile program, equivalent to that of figure 5.2, using the direct access facilities of your Pascal system.

5.3 Outline a program to re-create an index sequential file. Assume that the original file has too many overflow records and a new version of the file is required which eliminates all overflow.

6 Recursion and Trees

6.1 Recursion

Procedures and functions are both used in programs to perform specific tasks. The concept of recursion applies to them equally, so we shall use the term *subprogram* to refer to them both.

A subprogram can be called from several places in a program, from the main routine or from other procedures or functions, and can call other subprograms. When it calls itself, it is said to be *recursive*. A subprogram is also recursive if it contains a circular chain of calls, where it calls a second subprogram which in turn calls a third and so on until the first is called again.

Not all programming languages support recursive subprograms, but Pascal does. You can write Pascal subprograms which call themselves directly or indirectly.

Using recursion to solve a programming problem requires an approach entirely different from that used in non-recursive solutions. If step-wise refinement is used to reach a non-recursive solution, each step breaks the task into different smaller subtasks, identifying how the control structures of sequence, selection and iteration are used to combine the solutions of the subtasks to form a solution of the task. The refinements continue until subtasks are reached which are readily solved. For a recursive solution, you make use of a parameter of the problem to identify different cases. For some cases the solution will be simple. For the others, you must define how the solution to one or more simpler cases of the same problem can be combined to provide the desired result.

As an example, consider the problem of evaluating the factorial function for a positive integer n, defined as

$$\text{factorial}(n) = 1 \times 2 \times 3 \times \ldots \times n \quad \text{for } n \geqslant 1$$

The function has values factorial(1)=1, factorial(2)=2, factorial(3)=6, factorial(4)=24 etc.

A non-recursive solution would use a loop to calculate the value of the factorial, as shown in figure 6.1.

A recursive solution would be based on a recursive definition of the function, such as

$$\text{factorial}(1) = 1$$
$$\text{factorial}(n) = n \times \text{factorial}(n-1) \quad \text{for } n=2,3,4,\ldots$$

```
FUNCTION factorial (n:INTEGER): INTEGER;
(* non-recursive version of factorial function *)

VAR f: INTEGER;
    i: INTEGER;

BEGIN
f:=1;
FOR i:=2 TO n DO
    f:=f*i;
factorial := f
END;
```

Figure 6.1 Non-recursive version of factorial function.

This definition has one case (*n*=1) where the value is known, and another case (*n*=2,3,4 . .) where the value is defined using a recursive call to a simpler case. The call to factorial(*n*−1) is regarded as a simpler case because it is a step nearer to the case *n*=1 whose result is known.

The definition can be used directly to design a recursive version of the function, as in figure 6.2.

```
FUNCTION factorial (n:INTEGER): INTEGER;
(* Recursive version of factorial function *)

BEGIN
IF (n=1) THEN
    factorial:=1
ELSE
    factorial := n * factorial(n-1)
END;
```

Figure 6.2 Recursive version of factorial function.

The recursive version of the function treats the case *n*=1 separately and only makes a recursive call in the other case.

In general, all good recursive definitions must have the following two properties:

● at least one case has a known result;
● all recursive calls are to simpler cases which lead towards one of the known results.

Although the equation

$$\text{factorial}(n) = \text{factorial}(n+1)/(n+1)$$

is true, it cannot be used in a recursive definition because the recursive call to factorial(*n*+1) is not closer to the known case with *n*=1.

The recursive calls in the factorial function have replaced the loop needed in the non-recursive version. When the program calls the recursive function, the function calls itself repeatedly until it reaches the special case of $n=1$. The results are then combined back up the chain to provide the final result. The statement

WRITELN (factorial(4));

would call factorial with parameter 4. Because its parameter is not 1, it delegates the task to a call with parameter 3, setting the result to be 4 × factorial(3). This in turn calls factorial(2), which calls factorial(1). The case with parameter 1 is known to be 1, so the recursive calls stop and the result is passed back:

factorial(1)=1,
factorial(2)=2 × factorial(1) = 2
factorial(3)=3 × factorial(2) = 6
factorial(4)=4 × factorial(3) = 24

The value 24 is then printed by the **WRITELN** statement.

A second example, for a function to evaluate Fibonacci numbers, shows how more than one recursive call can be used.

Fibonacci numbers form a sequence:

1 1 2 3 5 8 13 21 . . .

where each number is the sum of the two preceding numbers. To start the sequence, the first two numbers are specified as 1.

The recursive definition of the function is

Fib(1) = 1
Fib(2) = 1
Fib(n) = Fib($n-1$) + Fib($n-2$)   for n=3,4,5, . .

This time there are two cases with known value: Fib(1) and Fib(2). The recursive calls in the third case, to Fib($n-1$) and Fib($n-2$), are simpler cases since they lead to one or other of the known cases. The coding for the function, given in figure 6.3, follows directly from the definition.

```
FUNCTION Fib (n:INTEGER): INTEGER;
(* Evaluates nth fibonacci number *)

BEGIN
IF (n=1) OR (n=2) THEN
    Fib:=1
ELSE
    Fib := Fib(n-1) + Fib(n-2)
END;
```

Figure 6.3 Recursive function for Fibonacci numbers.

The statement

WRITELN(Fib(4));

makes a call on the function Fib with parameter 4. This calls both Fib(3) and Fib(2), setting the result to the sum Fib(3)+Fib(2). The call to Fib(2) returns a result of 1, while the call to Fib(3) itself makes two calls to the function with parameters 2 and 1, whose values are returned as 1. The call sequence is illustrated by the diagram:

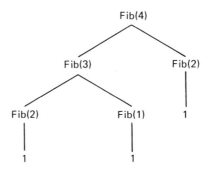

The final result is found by backing up the values:

$$Fib(3) = 1+1 = 2$$
$$Fib(4) = 2+1 = 3$$

The expansion of the function calls and the backing-up of the results is handled at run-time and is transparent to the programmer. Current computers use an underlying stack. As each call is made, its return address, parameters and local variables are pushed on to the stack. These form the data area for this particular call of the routine. As each routine terminates, its result value is passed back to the calling routine and its own data area popped from the stack. Eventually, the first (highest-level) routine will terminate, returning the final result.

Recursion is a powerful technique which can be used instead of iteration. Any iterative routine can be rewritten as a recursive routine and vice versa. However, the recursive version implemented using an underlying stack can be inefficient. There are two main reasons for this. Firstly, some values are pushed on to and popped from the stack unnecessarily. In the factorial function, for example, the recursive version will keep the values $n, n-1, n-2$ etc. on the stack, so that they can be restored and used as the value is eventually calculated. The iterative version shows that the values need not be stored since they are simply consecutive numbers.

Secondly, a recursive routine may evaluate the same partial result several times. In evaluating Fib(5), for example, the recursive routine calls Fib(4) and Fib(3). But Fib(4) also calls Fib(3). The routine evaluates Fib(3) for a second time instead of re-using the value determined earlier.

A well-designed iterative routine can overcome these problems and increase efficiency. But in certain cases the iterative routine is much harder to design than the recursive version, and if the loss of efficiency is not significant, the recursive version is preferable.

For neither the factorial nor the Fibonacci functions shown as examples above would recursion be preferred. The factorial wastes space on the stack, while the Fibonacci function also wastes an enormous amount of time recalculating results. The call to Fib(20), for instance, makes almost 14 000 procedure calls. The iterative versions of both are easy to write and more efficient.

In the future, computers using parallel processors may make recursive solutions far more efficient. The idea is to do the recursive calls as parallel steps in a solution, instead of using an underlying stack to derive a sequential process. At present, such an approach is still experimental.

Recursive definitions of data structures

Many data structures are inherently recursive and are defined in terms of themselves. Even simple list structures can be defined recursively. Recursive definitions can be used directly to design recursive procedures to process the structures.

To illustrate this, we shall look again at a linked list and the procedure to print the entries in order. These were introduced in chapter 4, with the declaration shown in figure 4.5 and the iterative version of the print routine in figure 4.7.

One recursive definition of a linked list is: a linked list is either empty or it contains a single item followed by a linked list.

This definition is used directly to design a recursive version of the print procedure whose code is given in figure 6.4. It checks for the special case when the list is empty, when it does nothing. For the other cases, it writes the first item and makes a recursive call to print the list shown in figure 6.4.

In this example, the definition contains just one self-reference and it occurs at the end. Such a situation is called *tail recursion*. It is generally a simple matter to design non-recursive procedures to process such a structure, as was shown for this example (figure 4.7).

For recursive definitions which contain multiple self-references, it is usually not such an easy matter: recursive routines are much the easier to design in these cases. However, they are also potentially the most inefficient, as was the case for the Fibonacci function.

To decide whether recursion is appropriate, you must examine how, for typical calls of the procedure, the recursion will be expanded at run-time. If the

```
PROCEDURE print (Listentry: ItemPtr);
(* prints the items from a linked list *)

BEGIN
IF (Listentry <> NIL) THEN    (* list is not empty *)
    BEGIN
    WRITELN (Listentry^.name); (* print this item *)
    print (Listentry^.Next)
                    (* print the following list *)
    END;
END;
```

Figure 6.4 Recursive procedure to print a linked list.

expansion shows that there are many unnecessary evaluations of the same case, the use of recursion will be inefficient. If the expansion proves to be essentially linear, an alternative iterative solution should be easy to design. In other cases, recursion may well be the most appropriate solution.

The choice of whether to use recursion or not is really an implementation consideration. For recursively defined data structures, it is natural to use recursion at the early stages of design, and perhaps reconsider the choice when the routine is to be implemented.

6.2 Indirect recursion in Pascal

Direct recursion is where a subprogram calls itself. Indirect recursion is where there is a circular chain of subprograms, one calling a second which calls a third and so on until the first is called again.

In Pascal, there is a rule that a subprogram must be declared before it is called. It is imposed to allow the compiler easily to check that each call has parameters which match those of the declaration. The rule ensures that the declaration is known before the subprogram call is made.

This rule causes problems with indirect recursion. Suppose that procedure A calls procedure B, which calls A again. Which should be declared first, A or B? This is a chicken-and-egg problem which breaks the rule whichever way you try to declare them.

Fortunately, Pascal provides a way round the problem. A subprogram can have its parameters declared separately from its body in what is called a FORWARD declaration. The subprogram can then be called in a second subprogram following the FORWARD declaration. The simple example of the two procedures A and B above could be declared as follows:

```
PROCEDURE A( parameter-list);
    FORWARD;

PROCEDURE B( parameter-list);
BEGIN
(* body of procedure B*)
(* including calls to procedure A*)
.
.
END;
PROCEDURE A;
(* local declarations, if any *)
BEGIN
(* body of procedure A*)
(* including calls to procedure B*)
.
.
END;
```

Notice that when the body of procedure A is declared, the parameters of A are not specified again. If local variables are used, they are declared along with the body of the procedure.

6.3 Trees

Abstract view

The dynamic data structures considered so far — stacks, queues and lists — have all been linear or one-dimensional. Their recursive definitions can all be expressed using single tail recursion. A *tree* is a dynamic structure which is essentially two-dimensional. Its recursive definition requires two self-references, as will be shown below. Its entries, called *nodes*, form a hierarchical structure. If a tree is not empty, it has a single root node with branches stemming from it, linking it to nodes at level 1 of the tree. There may be further branches linking the level 1 nodes to nodes at level 2, and so on. The diagram of figure 6.5 illustrates this abstract view of a tree.

Nodes with no further branches are called *leaves* (or leaf nodes).

Unlike real-life trees, these have the root at the top and the branches stemming downwards. But this is just the way we picture them, similar to the way family trees are drawn in genealogy. Because of the latter similarity, the terminology of family trees is often applied: parent, child, descendant, etc.

The recursive definition of a tree is based on the fact that each level 1 node is the root node of a subtree. Each branch from the root node links it to a

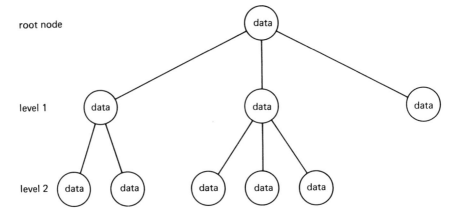

root node

level 1

level 2

Figure 6.5   Abstract view of a tree structure.

subtree. Thus, the tree is either empty or it consists of a single node (its root) linked to a set of subtrees. This definition will be useful when recursive procedures are required to process the tree.

6.3.1 Binary trees: abstract view

In the general case, there is no limit to the number of branches allowed from any node of a tree, nor is there any particular order to the branches from a node. A special case, in which the number of branches from a node is limited to two and in which the branches are ordered, is called a *binary tree*. We can use the ordering to distinguish between the Left and Right branches from any node and this distinction will be used in the applications of the binary tree.

The following diagram is a picture of a binary tree.

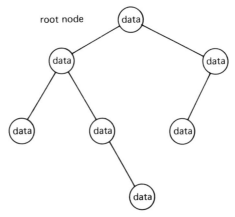

Abstract view of a binary tree.

6.3.2 Binary tree: concrete representation

One possible implementation of a binary tree is to use a record for each node containing the data items and two pointers, Left and Right, linking it to its descendants on the left and right branches. A separate pointer, Root, indicates which node is the root of the tree and will have a null value when the tree is empty. Nodes with no left or right branch will have a null value in the corresponding pointer.

This is a generalisation of the linked list implementation and is illustrated below:

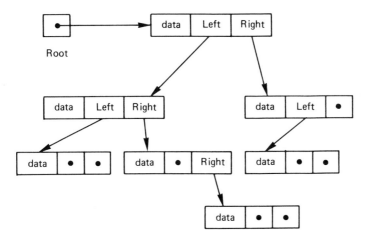

A binary tree as a linked structure.

The Pascal data declaration for this structure using dynamic data structures has to declare the pointer type and the record type for the nodes. The only variable declared would be a pointer, Root. Figure 6.6 shows the coding for the case where each node holds an integer data value.

```
TYPE
     NodePtr =  ^ NodeRec;
     NodeRec = RECORD
                 value : INTEGER;
                 Left,
                 Right : NodePtr
                 END;

VAR
     Root : NodePtr;
```

Figure 6.6 Declaration of a binary tree.

6.3.3 Operations on binary trees

The general operations on a binary tree include:

- setting up the tree as empty;
- testing if it is empty;
- adding a new node;
- deleting an existing node;
- searching for a node with a specific key value;
- accessing the nodes in a specific order;
- testing if the tree is full (if the implementation limits the size).

The general operations allow more flexibility than many applications of the binary tree require. For example, a new node can be added anywhere in the tree structure. Applications will make use of the ordering of the branches for some specific relationship between data values held at the nodes, which may put some restriction on where new nodes can be added and how they are linked into the tree. Similarly, it may affect the operations for deletion, searching and accessing items.

To discuss these possibilities, we shall consider the operations needed for some particular applications.

6.3.4 Binary tree sort

The first application that we shall examine is the use of the binary tree to sort a set of data values. Suppose that the integer values

$$20\ 84\ 16\ 50\ 36\ 99\ 6\ 12$$

are to be sorted into increasing order. A binary tree containing these values can be built up in the following way.

The first value, 20, is placed at the root of the tree. The next value, 84, is compared with the value at the root and, because it is greater than the 20, is placed as the right descendant of the root. The third value is less than the root value, so is placed as the left descendant of the root. Since the fourth value, 50, is greater than the root, it should be placed on the right branch. But there is already a value there, so the 50 is compared with the 84. It is less than 84 and is therefore placed as its left descendant.

The tree built up so far is shown below:

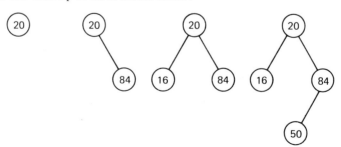

The process continues adding the values to the tree one by one. Each new value is compared with values already in the tree, starting at the root node. If the new value is less than the node value, the left branch is chosen. If it is greater than or equal to the node value, the right branch is chosen. The comparisons continue down the tree, choosing the branches, left or right, until an empty branch is chosen. The new value is then placed as a new leaf node on this branch.

When all the values above have been added to the tree, it will look as follows:

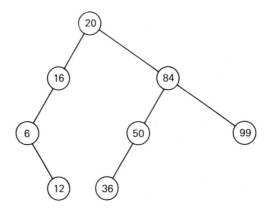

The choice of Left or Right branch is determined by the relations 'Less Than' or 'Greater Than or Equal To'. The tree has the property that all the values on the left branch from any node are less than the value at the node; all those on the right branch are greater than or equal to the node's value. To print out the values in ascending order, we must ensure that, for each node, all the values on its left branch are printed first, then the value at the node, then the values from the right branch.

These ideas can be stated more precisely as procedures to add a new item to the tree and to print the tree in order. Considering first the add routine, we shall develop an iterative version.

The add routine is given as two procedures. One creates a new node record and sets up its data value and pointer values. The pointers will be null as for a leaf node. It then calls the second procedure which finds the position in the tree where the node should be placed and links it into the tree. Figure 6.7 gives the coding for these procedures, assuming the declarations as in figure 6.6.

These iterative versions are fairly easy to design because the algorithm to locate the link position is essentially linear. In traversing the path from the root node to the link position, there is a well-defined decision procedure to determine which branch to take from each node.

```
PROCEDURE LinkToTree (newentry : NodePtr);
(* Links the node at newentry into the binary tree *)

VAR entry, branch : NodePtr;

BEGIN
IF root=NIL THEN    (*add at root *)
   root := newentry
ELSE
   BEGIN
   branch:= Root; (* start at Root *)
   REPEAT
      entry:=branch;
      IF (newentry^.value < entry^.value)
         THEN
            branch:=entry^.Left    (* look left *)
         ELSE
            branch:=entry^.Right   (* look right *)
   UNTIL (branch = NIL);

   IF (newentry^.value < entry^.value)
   THEN    (* place on left branch *)
      entry^.Left := newentry
   ELSE    (* place on right branch *)
      entry^.Right := newentry
   END
END;
(*-------------------------------------------------*)

PROCEDURE AddToTree (x:INTEGER);
(* adds value X into the binary tree *)

VAR newentry : NodePtr;

BEGIN
NEW(newentry);
WITH newentry^ DO
   BEGIN
   value := x;
   Left:=NIL;
   Right:=NIL
   END;
LinkToTree (newentry)
END;
```

Figure 6.7 Procedures to add an item to the binary tree.

A recursive version of the procedure LinkToTree can be derived from a recursive definition of a binary tree: a binary tree is either empty or it consists of a single node (its root) and two (binary) subtrees (Left and Right). The procedure uses an extra parameter, startnode, which indicates the root of the tree or subtree and is a **VAR** parameter so that its value can be changed. The coding is shown in figure 6.8.

```
PROCEDURE LinkToTree (newentry : NodePtr;
                           VAR startnode : NodePtr);
(* Links the node at newentry into the binary tree *)
(* recursive version *)

BEGIN
IF (startnode=NIL) THEN     (* subtree is empty *)
   startnode:= newentry     (* place new node *)
ELSE
   IF (newentry^.value < startnode^.value)
   THEN
     (* put in left subtree *)
     LinkToTree (newentry, startnode^.Left)
   ELSE
     (* put in right subtree*)
     LinkToTree (newentry, startnode^.Right);

END;
```

Figure 6.8 Recursive version of the link procedure.

The procedure to add an item to the tree must be changed if the recursive version of LinkToTree is to be used, to provide the extra parameter. The call would become

LinkToTree (newentry, Root);

As the procedure runs, the recursive calls will be made with the value in the parameter startnode varying as the routine makes its way from the root node down through the subtrees. When an empty subtree is reached, the new item is placed as a new node in this subtree by changing the value of the current parameter startnode.

Once the tree has been constructed, the values can be printed out in ascending order using the recursive procedure given in figure 6.9. The call to this routine must specify the Root as the startnode. The procedure will make recursive calls with different parameters to delegate the printing of the left and right subtrees.

```
PROCEDURE PrintTree (startnode : NodePtr);

BEGIN
IF (startnode <> NIL) THEN
   BEGIN
                          (* print left subtree *)
   PrintTree (startnode^.Left);
                          (* print this node value *)
   WRITELN (startnode^.value);
                          (* print right subtree *)
   PrintTree (startnode^.Right)

   END
END;
```

Figure 6.9 Recursive procedure to print the binary tree.

The recursive version of PrintTree just given is much easier to design than an iterative version. This is because there is no continuous linear path which traverses the whole tree. The path followed selects the left branch first but needs to backtrack to include the right branches from each node. Recursion takes care of the backtracking at run-time.

Efficiency of the binary tree sort

The efficiency of the sort depends on the effort required to find the position for each new item placed into the tree. The more levels the tree has, the more comparisons are needed in working down to the leaf nodes to place the new items. The initial ordering of the values affects the number of levels. If, for example, the values are already in order, as in the list

6 10 12 18 24

the tree built up would be completely unbalanced, having no left branches:

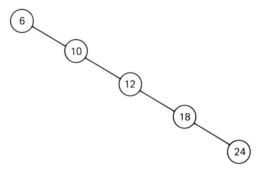

If the same values were entered in the order

12 6 18 24 10

the tree would be more balanced, with a maximum depth of two levels:

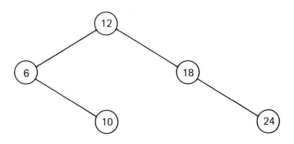

The figures for the number of comparisons in sorting a set of *n* items are approximately proportional to $n * n$ for the unbalanced case and $n\log n$ for the balanced case. These represent the worst and best cases, with the average between the two.

The table below gives values for $n\log n$ and $n * n$ for a few values of *n*, and shows how the figures diverge as *n* increases.

n	*n*log *n*	*n* * *n*
8	24	64
16	64	256
32	160	1024
64	384	4096
128	896	16384
256	2048	65536
512	4608	262144
1024	10240	1048576

6.3.5 Binary search tree

In the previous section, we showed how the binary tree can be used to sort a list of values. The operations to add a new item to the tree and to print the items in order were examined. The binary tree can also be used to store data values and permit fairly efficient operations for retrieval, addition and deletion. The tree is built up as for the sort tree, with new items added in place as they arrive. In this section, we shall examine the operations of searching for a specific item and deleting an item from the tree.

Searching

The routine to search for a specific item, X, starts at the root node and compares the node values with X. If the node value is not X, the procedure follows either the left or right branch depending on whether X is less than the node value or not. The process stops when the item is found, or when an empty branch is selected. Figure 6.10 gives the Pascal code for this procedure.

Deleting

Deletion is a more complex operation because, when a node is removed from the tree, its descendants must be linked back into the tree in the appropriate position. To delete an item we must find its parent node, so that we can unlink the item, and decide how to link the descendants back into the tree.

```
PROCEDURE SearchTree (X: INTEGER; VAR entry:NodePtr;
                            VAR found:BOOLEAN);
(* searches the binary tree for the value X *)

BEGIN
found := FALSE;
entry := Root;              (* start at root *)

WHILE (NOT found) AND (entry <> NIL) DO
   BEGIN
   IF (entry^.value = X ) THEN found := TRUE
   ELSE
      BEGIN
      IF (X < entry^.value)
      THEN                    (* go left *)
         entry:= entry^.Left
      ELSE                    (* go right *)
         entry:= entry^.Right
      END
   END
END;
```

Figure 6.10   Searching a binary tree for a specific item.

```
PROCEDURE FindPosition (X: INTEGER; VAR entry:NodePtr;
                            VAR Parent: NodePtr;
                            VAR found:BOOLEAN);
(* searches the binary tree for the value X *)
(* if X is found, entry points to its node. *)
(*      and parent points to its parent node *)

BEGIN
found := FALSE;
entry := Root;              (* start at root *)
Parent:= NIL;               (* root has no parent *)

WHILE (NOT found) AND (entry <> NIL) DO
   BEGIN
   IF (entry^.value = X ) THEN found := TRUE
   ELSE
      BEGIN
      Parent:=entry;        (*save as parent pointer*)
      IF (X < entry^.value)
      THEN                    (* go left *)
         entry:= entry^.Left
      ELSE                    (* go right *)
         entry:= entry^.Right
      END
   END
END;
```

Figure 6.11   Finding the position of the value X and its parent node.

The first step, then, in deleting an item X from the tree is to find its position in the tree and the position of its parent node. The procedure SearchTree can be modified to keep track of the parent node and return it as a parameter (Parent) together with the position of the value X (entry). The modified procedure, called FindPosition, is given in figure 6.11.

Once the item is found, some of the pointers in the tree are adjusted to remove the item X but reconnect its descendants. There are three separate cases to consider. In the two simplest cases, the removal of the item X is performed by altering the Left or Right pointer in the Parent node. (If there is no parent node, the Root pointer will be altered.) The new value for the child pointer is chosen to ensure that the descendants of X are still linked into the tree properly.

In the first case, if the node for deletion has no descendants, the value NIL is used for the new child pointer. This is the case of deleting a leaf node as shown in figure 6.12.

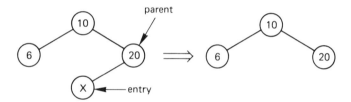

Figure 6.12 Deleting a leaf node.

Secondly, if the node for deletion has only one branch, the parent node is made to point to this branch. Figure 6.13 shows one such case where only the right branch exists. A similar situation arises when only the left branch exists.

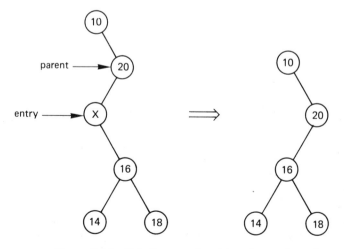

Figure 6.13 Deleting a node with only one branch.

The final case, where there are both left and right descendants for the deleted node, requires more alterations to the tree than the other cases. The basic idea is to find a suitable descendant of X which can be removed from the tree and then used to replace the value of X. There is no need in this case to unlink the node for X, since it can be re-used for the value of the promoted descendant.

Consider the example of figure 6.14, where the node Entry is to be removed and its two branches retained. Our task is to select a suitable descendant to be promoted to the node Entry, yet preserve the order relationship associated with the Left and Right branches. A suitable choice is the inorder successor of X, that is the node on the right branch whose value is closest to X. This is marked as successor in the figure.

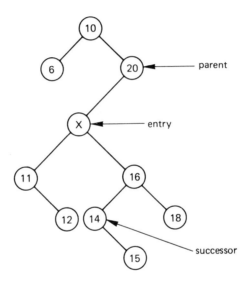

Figure 6.14   Successor of a node with two branches.

The successor node can be found by taking one step down the right branch and then going left as far as possible. It may itself have right descendants, but cannot have left descendants.

When the successor is found it can be removed from the tree in a manner similar to the second case described above. It is unlinked from its own parent, and its first descendant takes its place. In this example, the node for 15 is connected as the left descendant of 16.

The successor node is now free and its value can replace the value X, keeping the left and right branches of that node. The resulting transition is shown in figure 6.15.

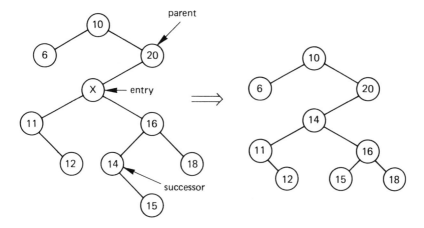

Figure 6.15 Deletion of a node with two branches.

The Pascal procedures for the deletion operation are given in figure 6.16. It is assumed that the FindPosition procedure of figure 6.11 has already been called and found the required item, setting the pointers Entry and Parent for use as parameters to this operation. The procedure DeleteEntry determines which of the three cases applies, and calls either the procedure AlterParent, to reset the pointer in the parent node (for the first two cases), or the procedure PromoteSuccessor, to find the successor node and promote it to replace the deleted item (for the third case).

```
PROCEDURE DeleteEntry (VAR Entry, Parent : NodePtr);

(* deletes the node specified by entry, whose parent
    is specified by Parent *)

VAR newchild : NodePtr;

BEGIN
IF (entry^.Left = NIL)
THEN                                  (* no branch *)
    BEGIN                             (* or just right branch *)
    newchild:= entry^.Right;
    AlterParent (Parent, Entry, newchild)
    END
ELSE IF (entry^.Right= NIL)
THEN                                  (* just left branch *)
    BEGIN
    newchild:= entry^.Left;
    AlterParent (Parent, Entry, newchild)
    END
ELSE                                  (* both branches exist *)
    PromoteSuccessor (Entry)
END;
```

(a)

```
PROCEDURE AlterParent (VAR Parent : NodePtr;
                            Entry, Newchild : NodePtr);

(* Sets the left or right pointer in node Parent
                          to the newchild value *)
(* if the Parent is NIL, the root pointer is altered *)

BEGIN
IF (Parent = NIL) THEN
   Root:= newchild
ELSE
IF (Parent^.Left = entry) THEN
   Parent^.Left:= newchild
ELSE
   Parent^.Right:= newchild
END;
```

(b)

```
PROCEDURE PromoteSuccessor (VAR  Entry: NodePtr);

(* Finds the successor of node Entry, and promotes it
   to take the place of Entry *)

VAR successor, succParent : NodePtr;

BEGIN
(* finds the successor node and its parent *)
successor:= entry^.Right;  (* take one step right *)
succParent:=entry;

WHILE (successor^.Left <> NIL) DO
   BEGIN                  (* go left as far as possible *)
   succParent:= successor;
   successor:= successor^.Left
   END;

(* remove successor from tree *)
IF (succParent = entry ) THEN
   entry^.Right:= successor^.Right
ELSE
   succParent^.Left := successor^.Right;

(* now use successor to replace entry *)
entry^.value := successor^.value
END;
```

(c)

*Figure 6.16 (a) Deleting an entry from a binary tree. (b) Altering the parent
          node pointer. (c) Procedure to find successor and promote it.*

Efficiency of the binary tree search

The binary tree search is most efficient when the tree is completely balanced. Indeed, the remarks about balanced trees made in the previous section apply equally to this case. The figures for the number of comparisons made to search for an item in a tree with n nodes is approximately proportional to $\log n$ in the best case, and to n in the worst case. The best-case figures are similar to those obtained for the binary chop technique introduced in chapter 1, which required the items to be stored in sequence in an array. The binary tree permits values to be added and deleted without the excessive overheads of shuffling values needed when the items are held in sequence.

The operations of addition and deletion described above make no attempt to keep the tree balanced. The order in which items are added and deleted will affect the balance and hence the efficiency of the processing.

In situations where it is desirable to maintain efficiency, more complicated algorithms can be used for addition and deletion which keep the tree 'nearly balanced'. The binary trees which are 'nearly balanced' are known as AVL-trees, named after Adelson–Velskii and Landis, and are properly defined in terms of the relative depths of their left and right subtrees. All the algorithms processing them ensure that the resulting tree is an AVL-tree, and thus maintain operating efficiency close to the maximum. For further details, see the references in the bibliography at the end of the book.

6.3.6 Representing arithmetic expressions

A binary tree can be used to represent arithmetic expressions if the node values can be either operators or operand values and are such that:

- each operator node has exactly two branches;
- each operand value node has no branches.

For example, the simple expression 12 + 16 would be represented by the tree:

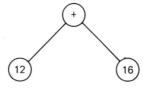

The branches from an operator node link it to the two values that it is to be applied to. These could be operand values, as in the example above, or they could be subtrees for other expressions. The expression

$$12 + 16 * 4$$

would be represented by the tree:

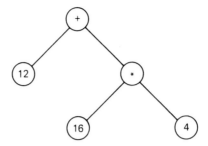

Notice that the leaf nodes appear in the same order (reading left to right) as in the original expression, and the operators at the lower levels must be applied before those nearer the root. In the above tree, the * is applied before the +.

An expression involving constants, operators and brackets can be represented as a tree in only one way when the precedence of the operators is taken into account.

For example, the expression

$$12 + 47 - 3 * (26 + 4) / 7$$

gives the tree:

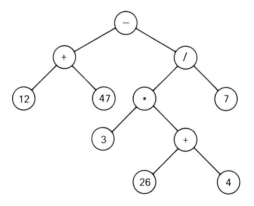

The brackets are used in the expression to imply that the 26 + 4 is carried out before the multiplication. In the tree, this is shown by having the addition at a lower level than the multiplication. The multiply operates on the value 3 and the result of the subtree:

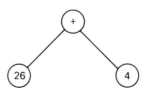

To convert an infix expression by hand into its expression tree, you should look for the operator which is performed last. This becomes the root of the tree and will split the original expression into two subexpressions.

Consider the example

$$12 - 6 * (3 + 8) - 4 * 12$$

The last operator to be used is the second subtraction, since operators of equal precedence are evaluated in a left-to-right order. This becomes the root of the tree. Its left subtree corresponds to the expression 12−6 * (3+8), while its right subtree corresponds to the expression 4 * 12. We can draw the tree so far with empty leaf nodes which need expanding:

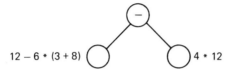

Repeating the process for the two subexpressions in turn will fill in the leaf nodes and add further branches. In the expression for the left branch, the minus is the last operator to be performed, so it becomes the root of its subtree and is entered in the empty leaf node:

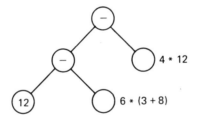

Continuing with the subexpressions until operand values are reached, results in the tree:

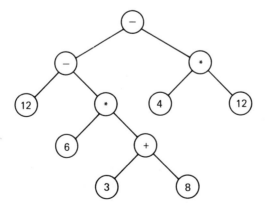

The brackets in the infix expression were needed only to indicate precedence, and are not needed in the expression tree. The structure of the tree indicates the precedence of the operators.

Operations on expression trees

The operations considered in this section are based on a recursive definition of an expression tree: it is either a single node with an operand value or it is a node with an operator and two (expression) subtrees, Left and Right. Note that the empty tree is not allowed.

Evaluation

The operation to evaluate an expression tree can be based on the recursive definition given above. It returns the node value if it is a single operand value node, and makes recursive calls in the other case. The recursive calls evaluate the two branches which are then combined by applying the operator to give the final result. The routine is outlined in figure 6.17.

```
FUNCTION eval (startnode : NodePtr) : INTEGER;

(* outline code to evaluate a binary expression tree *)

VAR result1, result2 : INTEGER;

BEGIN
IF startnode holds a data value
THEN eval:= node data value
ELSE
   BEGIN
   result1 := eval (startnode^.Left);
   result2 := eval (startnode^.Right);
   CASE startnode^.operator OF
     plus : eval := result1 + result2;
    minus : eval := result1 - result2;
    mult  : eval := result1 * result2;
    divide: eval := result1 DIV result2;
   END;
   END;
END;
```

Figure 6.17   Outline function to evaluate an expression tree.

Printing the tree

If a print routine similar to that used in the binary tree sort is used, the operator value will be printed between the left and right operands. This is the usual infix notation, except that the operator precedence is ignored.

An alternative is to print the operator after its two operands, producing Reverse Polish notation. This is sometimes called postfix notation. An algorithm to print the tree in this order can be based on the recursive definition. It must print the left branch, then the right branch and finally the operator value at the node. An outline is given in figure 6.18.

```
PROCEDURE postfix (startnode: NodePtr);

(* Outline code to print expression tree
        in postfix form *)
BEGIN
IF startnode holds a data value THEN
   WRITE this value
ELSE
   BEGIN
   postfix (startnode^.Left);
   postfix (startnode^.Right);
   WRITE this node's operator
   END;
END;
```

Figure 6.18   Outline procedure for postfix form.

A third possibility is to print each operator before its two operands. This is known as prefix notation.

Although the three possibilities have been described for expression trees, the ideas of accessing the items in infix, prefix or postfix orders apply to binary trees in general. The names usually applied for the general binary tree are the inorder, preorder and postorder traversal routines. The algorithms can be based on recursive definitions of the binary tree and just vary the order of processing the node value, the left and the right subtrees.

6.4 General trees

A general tree has no limit to the number of branches from a node, nor need it have any specific order to the branches. Applications include game trees used by game-playing programs to investigate possible moves. In chess programs, for instance, each node would be a board position with branches representing possible moves from that position to a new position (the child node). Branches from the next level of nodes would represent possible countermoves, and so on. The following diagram illustrates this situation:

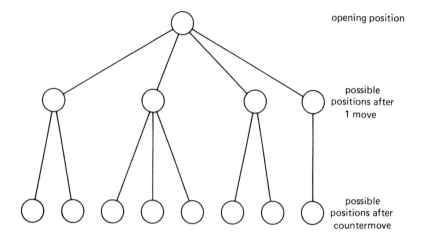

A general tree can be represented by a linked structure where each node has two pointers, one to its first child, and one to its next sibling. The structure is shown in figure 6.19.

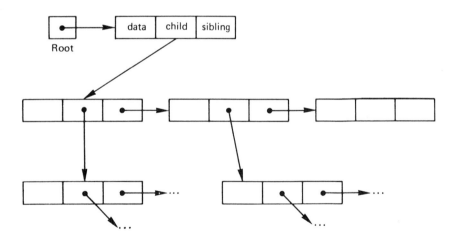

Figure 6.19   A linked structure for a general tree.

The child pointer leads down to the first descendant of the node, while the sibling leads across to the next branch.

Although the use of the two pointers in this case differs from the use of the two pointers in the binary tree, there is a correspondence between the two cases. The child pointer can correspond to the Left pointer, while the Sibling pointer can correspond to the Right pointer. Using these correspondences, the algorithms developed for binary tree traversal can be used for the general tree.

Figure 6.20 shows an example of a general tree. The reader should check that the order of accessing the nodes for the preorder traversal are

a b e j k l f c g m n d h i o p

and for the postorder traversal

l k j f e n m g p o i h d c b a

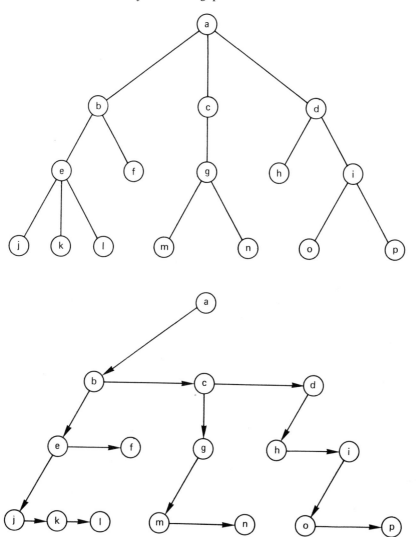

Figure 6.20   Example general tree and its linked representation.

6.5 Multi-way trees

In a binary tree, each node holds a single value and has at most two branches. These were used in the binary search tree to split the descendants into two groups. Those on the left branch had values less than the node value, while those on the right branch had values greater than the node value.

This idea can be generalised by allowing more values at each node and more branches to split the descendants into several groups. For example, with up to two values in each node, and up to three branches, the descendants are split into three groups. The first branch is used for values less than the first node value, the second branch for values between the two node values, and the last branch for values greater than the second node value. We can picture the node values as being between the branch pointers in the node, as shown below.

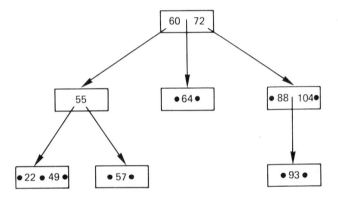

Notice that the values at each node are in order, but the nodes need not all be full. Some nodes hold only one value, in which case only the first two branches can hold values. Entries cannot be placed on their third branch until after the second value is placed in the node. This is because the value is used to determine the split between branches 2 and 3.

This structure is called a *multi-way tree*. A general multi-way tree can be defined in terms of its properties. For an integer m, an m-way tree is an ordered tree where, if a node has k branches, then it holds $k-1$ values and $k \leqslant m$.

A binary search tree is a two-way tree, while the example above is a three-way tree.

The motivation for having more than one value at each node is the use of multi-way trees with external files. Disc files commonly store data in fixed-size blocks which are the units of data transfer between the computer and the device. If the node records are made to correspond to the disc blocks, the pointers can be relative block numbers and each node access corresponds to a physical disc transfer. By allowing several data values at each node, full use can be made of the space within the disc block.

6.6 B-trees

When a linked tree structure is held in main store, it takes only a few micro-
seconds at most to follow a pointer to a node. When the structure is held on a
disc, the time to access another disc block is a factor of at least a thousand
times longer. It is important to minimise the number of accesses needed when
searching for an entry, and this is related to the number of levels in the tree.

A B-tree is a balanced multi-way tree. These are useful as index structures for
data held on external files. They can be defined in terms of their properties,
but are best explained by examining how they are used.

Consider a B-tree of degree 5, that is a balanced five-way tree where each node
can hold four data values and have five branches. Suppose the following values
are to be added to it:

    10   50   6   29   64   11   13   18   19   72   88   17   77   102   98

The first value, 10, is placed in a new node which has room for three other
values. The 50 is placed in the same node. So are the 6 and 29, but the values
are always kept in order as shown below:

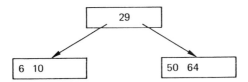

When the fifth value, 64, is to be added, there is no room in the node. Of
the five values, 29 is the median. The node is split into two separate leaf nodes,
with a new parent node holding the 29:

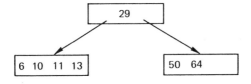

The following item, 11, is to be placed in a leaf node. Because the tree now
has more than one node, a search is needed to determine which leaf the value
is to be in. Both the 11 and the 13 are placed in the left leaf node:

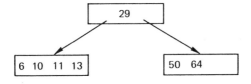

The 18 should also go into this leaf node, but it is full. Again the median value, 11, is chosen and this time moved up to the parent node. The value 29 and its adjacent pointer move along to make room for the 11. The left leaf node splits into two to provide the first two branches:

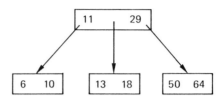

The items following are added to the B-tree in a similar way. Each is added to a leaf node, but when the 77 is added the leaf node must be split again to make room. The final result is the tree:

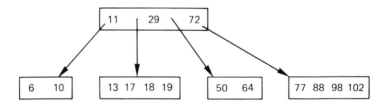

If two further items, 26 and 100, are to be added, the 26 should be placed in the second leaf node. Since there is no room, the node splits, adding a new value into the root.

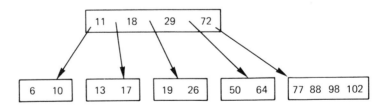

The value 100 again splits its leaf node, since there is no room there for it. The median value, 98, is moved up to be added to the parent node. But there is no room there, so the parent node splits to give a new root node:

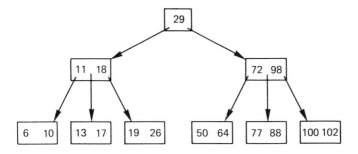

The leaf nodes now have more space available. If the values 20, 66, 70 are added, they are all placed in leaf nodes, as in figure 6.21.

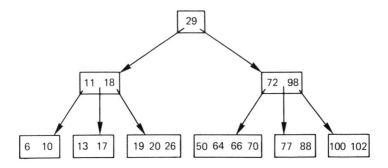

Figure 6.21   A B-tree of degree 5.

Notice that the tree built up in this manner is balanced, having all of its leaf nodes at one level.

The addition procedure uses a search routine to look for the position of the new item. This search routine is similar to the one used in the binary search tree except that there are more values to be checked at each node and more branches to select from.

Each new item is placed in a leaf node if there is room. If not, the leaf node splits into two and the median value moves up to the parent node. If there is no room there, it too splits with the (new) median value moving up. The tree appears to grow at its root, rather than at its leaves as was the case for the unbalanced binary tree.

A property of the B-tree of degree m is that, except for the root node, all the nodes hold at least $(m-1)$ DIV 2 values. This is because only the root node is created for a single value; all internal nodes are created by splitting a full node into two. Specifying the minimum number as a defining property of a B-tree, and ensuring that it is preserved by all operations, helps to keep down the number of levels of the structure and maintain balance. In particular, the deletion routine must maintain the property of the minimal number of values.

The simplest case of deletion is where the value is in a leaf node and its removal still leaves at least the minimal number of values. In figure 6.21, the value 19 is in this category. The leaf node is left with the two values 20 and 26.

If the value is not in a leaf node, its immediate successor (or predecessor) must be, and this can be brought up to replace the value to be deleted. For example, deleting the value 72 from figure 6.21 can be performed by bringing the value 70 from the leaf node to replace the 72. Figure 6.22 shows the B-tree after these deletions.

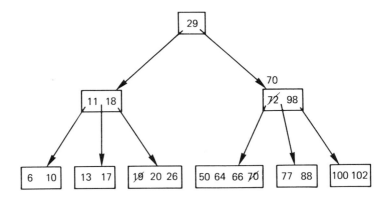

Figure 6.22   The B-tree after deleting 19 and 72.

If the value 88 is to be deleted, it is in a leaf node, but would leave only one value there if removed. However, one of its neighbouring leaf nodes has more than the minimal number, so we can bring down the value 70 from the parent node to replace the 88 and promote the 66 to the parent.

If the value 13 is to be deleted, its node and the neighbouring leaf nodes have only the minimal number of values. The method used here is to combine the leaf node with one of its neighbours and the value from the parent node to form a single leaf node. This is the opposite to the splitting of a leaf which occurs during insertions. The new leaf node will hold the values:

$$6 \quad 10 \quad 11 \quad 17$$

The 11 is removed from the parent. If the parent had held more values, the task would have been completed, but the removal of the 11 leaves the parent with too few entries. This is remedied by combining higher-level nodes in a similar fashion. The parent needs another value. An attempt to transfer a value from a neighbour at the same level fails because the neighbour has only two values. Instead, the neighbour must be combined with a value from the root yielding a new node containing the values

18 29 66 98

which becomes the new root:

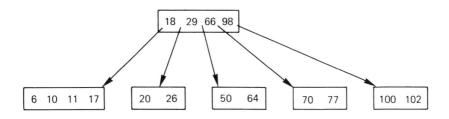

It is clear from the descriptions of the operations on a B-tree that alterations may affect several levels of the tree. The branch pointers let the procedures move down the tree, but moving back up is a backtracking problem. Recursion provides a way of solving this. A recursive view of a B-tree is that it is either empty or consists of a single node holding $k-1$ values and k pointers to B-subtrees, for some $k \leqslant m$. This view can be used to design recursive procedures for the search, addition and deletion routines.

Application of B-trees

A B-tree can be used as an index to a data file held on disc, providing direct access to the records through their key values. As an alternative to the indexed sequential file, the B-tree is a more complex structure requiring more complex processing, but it does not suffer from the overflow problems. When a large number of records with keys close together are added to the indexed sequential file, all the free spaces in the home block are used up and records are placed into overflow blocks. Retrieval of these records will require a sequential search through the home and overflow blocks, with a deterioration in access time (see chapter 5, section 5.4.2). In the B-tree, as records with keys close together are added, the leaf nodes split to provide more room for further additions.

When used as an index, each entry in the B-tree is a key value and an associated pointer to the data record. These entries (key + record pointer) play the role of the (integer) values used in the examples discussed above. The branch pointers are held in the nodes as well and provide the links to the branch nodes in the index tree structure. Figure 6.23 illustrates this for a data file holding seven records with key values 10, 50, 6, 29, 84, 11 and 13, and a B-tree of order 5. The entries 29/4 etc. mean key value 29 at data record 4.

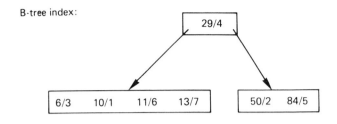

Figure 6.23   B-tree index to data file.

A variation on the B-tree index called the B^+-tree index (due to Knuth) provides an index for direct access by key and a simpler method for sequential access. The B^+-tree is divided into two parts. One is a tree structured index set corresponding to the non-leaf nodes of a B-tree whose entries are the key values (without the associated data record pointers). The other is a sequence set which holds key values and data record pointers for all the entries in the file. This corresponds to the values normally found in the leaf nodes of the B-tree together with entries for values held higher up the tree. Within each block the entries are stored in sequence, and the individual blocks of the sequence set are linked together in order. Figure 6.24 shows an example of a B^+-tree index.

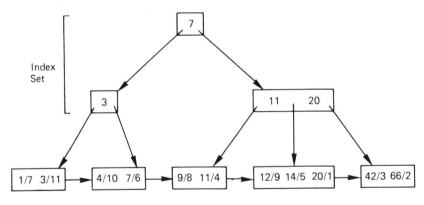

Data records held in the order:

20 66 42 11 14 7 1 9 12 4 3

Figure 6.24   A B^+-tree of degree 3 for a file of eleven records.

The operation of searching for a specific key is similar to that for the B-tree. Starting at the root node, the key is compared with values in the nodes to determine which branch to follow to find the appropriate sequence set block. A search through the items there will find the key and its record pointer which can be used to retrieve the data record. Sequential processing of the records is achieved by working through the sequence set, retrieving the data records via their pointers.

6.7 Summary

Recursion was introduced as a programming technique and as a means of defining data structures. It was shown how a recursive definition of a structure can be used to derive recursive routines to process the structure as an alternative to iterative routines. These concepts were then applied in the study of trees.

Binary trees were defined and their applications to sorting, searching and representing arithmetic expressions were discussed.

General trees represented as linked structures were mentioned and the correspondence with binary trees noted.

The concept of the binary tree was extended to multi-way trees and B-trees, and their application to file structures as alternatives to indexed sequential files was described.

Exercises

6.1 For the recursive Fibonacci function (section 6.1), count the number of recursive calls made in evaluating Fib(n) for $n=1,2,3,4,5$.
(Include the call to Fib(n) in the count in each case.)
What is the general formula for this count?

6.2 Write a recursive function to evaluate the binomial coefficient $C(n.m)$, defined for integers $n \geqslant m \geqslant 0$, by the equations

$$C(n,0) = 1 \text{ for } n \geqslant 0,$$
$$C(n,n) = 1 \text{ for } n \geqslant 0,$$
$$C(n,m) = C(n-1, m-1) + C(n-1, m) \text{ for } n > m > 0.$$

6.3 Write a recursive version of the binary search routine introduced in chapter 1.

6.4 Construct binary sort trees for the following lists of numbers:
(a) 22, 35, 11, 64, 65, 66, 2, 30, 13, 15, 12
(b) 2, 4, 5, 7, 1, 3, 9, 67, 68, 69
(c) 88, 77, 11, 89, 60, 55, 54, 22, 48, 46, 30
Comment on how well-balanced each of these trees is.

6.5 Write a program to read real values from a text file (held one per line), to construct a binary sort tree for them and to print them to an output text file in

(a) ascending order

(b) descending order.

6.6 Draw expression trees for the following expressions:

(a) $(12 + 3 * 2 * 4) * 2 - (3 + 4)$

(b) $1 + (2 + 3) + 4 * 5 + 6$

(c) $6 + 12/(3+1) * 2 - 4$.

6.7 Write a program to set up a table of bank account records holding fields for

account no., customer name, balance

The records are to be held in an arbitrary order in the table. The program should set up a B-tree index of degree 3 for the account number field, and use it to support enquiries in which the user enters the account number and has the details of the corresponding record displayed at the terminal.

7 Graphs, Networks and Relations

7.1 Graphs and networks

7.1.1 Abstract view of graphs and networks

A *graph* is a more general structure than a tree, consisting of a set of nodes and a set of edges connecting the nodes. Sometimes the term vertex is used instead of node, and arc instead of edge.

In an undirected graph there is at most one edge between any two nodes, and there is no direction associated with it. In a directed graph (digraph), each edge has a direction associated with it so that it goes out from one node and into the second. There is at most one edge in each direction between two nodes. Figure 7.1a shows examples of directed and undirected graphs. Arrow-heads are shown on the edges of the directed graph to indicate the direction of the edge.

An edge provides a simple path from a node to an adjacent node. A sequence of edges from one node to a second, then to a third and so on, is called a *path*. In a directed graph, the edges in the sequence must be followed in the correct direction. Thus, in figure 7.1a, there is a path from A to B, but not from B to A.

As can be seen from this figure, a graph may contain nodes which are not connected to other nodes, and it may have nodes with several edges. There may be several paths between two nodes, and even paths from a node to itself. It is thus more general than a tree, which has only one path from its root to any other node, but it will contain subgraphs which are trees. For example, the graph of figure 7.1a contains the subtree shown in figure 7.1b.

The nodes of a graph can hold data values. In certain cases, the edges also have data values associated with them, and the structure is called a *network* or *weighted graph*, the data values of the edges being the *weights*. The term 'network' is sometimes used in a wider context, as in 'communication network' or 'network database'. (Network databases are the subject of chapter 11.) In this chapter, a 'network' will mean a 'weighted graph'.

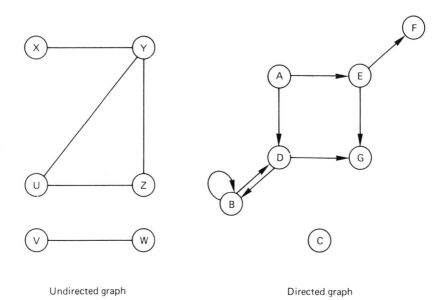

Undirected graph   Directed graph

Figure 7.1a   Example undirected and directed graphs.

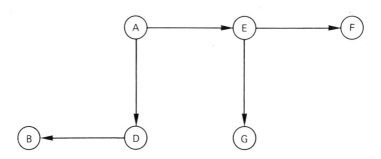

Figure 7.1b   A subtree of the directed graph.

7.1.2 Operations on graphs

The primitive operations on a graph include:

- creating an empty graph;
- testing if a graph is empty;
- adding a new node (without connecting it to other nodes);
- adding an edge between two existing nodes (possibly directed, weighted);
- removing an edge;

- removing an unconnected node;
- testing if two nodes are adjacent;
- traversing the nodes of the graph (needed, for example, in searching for a specific node, or finding a path between two nodes).

From an abstract point of view all the operations, except the last, are straightforward. The algorithms required simply depend on the concrete implementation of the structure. The last one can be considered at this abstract level. It is an operation which systematically visits the nodes in the graph.

7.1.3 Graph traversal

There are two widely-used methods of traversing the nodes of a graph. One is called the *depth-first search*, the other the *breadth-first search*. The former is analogous to the preorder traversal in a tree, while the latter is analogous to a tree search which visits the level 1 nodes, then all level 2 nodes and so on down the tree. Both traversal methods visit every node in the graph just once. In the implementation of these operations, the nodes must be marked as visited as the procedure reaches them, so that they are not visited again.

Both methods start with an unvisited node and traverse a subtree from this start node. When no further nodes can be reached as part of this subtree, another unvisited node is selected to start a new subtree. The process repeats until all the nodes have been visited. Both methods will have an outer procedure to select the start nodes, and an inner procedure to traverse the tree from the start node. The methods differ in the way that the subtree is traversed.

Depth-first search

A recursive algorithm for this is outlined in figure 7.2. The outer procedure is a loop which chooses an unvisited node and calls the recursive procedure to start from this node. The recursive procedure marks its start node as visited, then loops while there are unvisited adjacent nodes, selects one and calls itself to start from the adjacent node.

For each choice of start node in the outer procedure, the recursive routine will find a tree of unvisited nodes. The set of trees produced in this way is called a (*depth-first*) *spanning forest*. Every node of the graph must belong to just one of the trees in this forest.

The order of choosing nodes in the outer procedure, and the order of choosing adjacent nodes in the recursive routine, affect the resulting spanning forest. You could end up with several trees, or just one tree. Figure 7.3 shows a directed graph and the two spanning forests obtained by choosing the nodes in ascending order of node number, and in descending order.

```
Outer-level:
 mark all nodes as unvisited;
 WHILE there are unvisited nodes DO
     BEGIN
     select a node as the startnode
     TraverseTree (startnode)
     END;

Inner-level procedure TraverseTree (startnode):

   BEGIN
   mark the startnode as visited;
   WHILE there are unvisited adjacent nodes DO
       BEGIN
       select one as a startnode
       TraverseTree (startnode)
       END
   END
```

Figure 7.2   Outline of depth-first graph search.

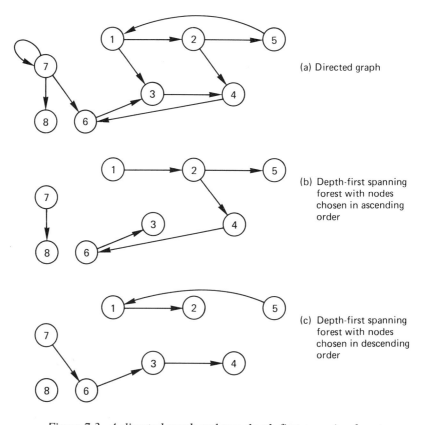

(a) Directed graph

(b) Depth-first spanning
    forest with nodes
    chosen in ascending
    order

(c) Depth-first spanning
    forest with nodes
    chosen in descending
    order

Figure 7.3   A directed graph and two depth-first spanning forests.

Breadth-first search

The breadth-first search visits a node, then all of its adjacent nodes, then all the nodes adjacent to these, and so on. The simplest way to define this algorithm is to use a queue for the order of visiting the nodes. Again the algorithm is structured at two levels. The outer level is a loop which continues while there are unvisited nodes, selects one of them and places it in the queue. The inner level finds a tree starting at the node at the front of the queue. It performs a loop which removes the items from the queue one at a time. If the item has not already been visited, it is now marked as visited, and all of its adjacent nodes are placed in the queue. Figure 7.4 is an outline algorithm for this operation.

```
Outer-level:
  mark all nodes as unvisited;
  WHILE there are unvisited nodes DO
      BEGIN
      select a node as the startnode and add to queue
      TraverseTree
      END;

Inner-level procedure TraverseTree :

  BEGIN
  WHILE the queue is not empty DO
      BEGIN
      remove the front item from the queue
      IF it is not already visited
      THEN
          mark it as visited
          place all of its adjacent nodes on the queue
      END
  END
```

Figure 7.4 Outline of breadth-first graph search.

The result of this search is a set of trees which contain every node just once. It is called a (*breadth-first*) *spanning forest*. Again, the order of selecting the nodes affects the resulting forest. Figure 7.5 shows a graph and two spanning forests obtained from selecting the nodes in ascending and descending orders.

7.1.4 Cycles

A graph is said to be cyclic if there is a path from some node to itself, and acyclic if there is no such path. A tree is a directed graph with the edges joining a node to its child nodes and is thus acyclic, but not all acyclic graphs are trees, as figure 7.6 shows.

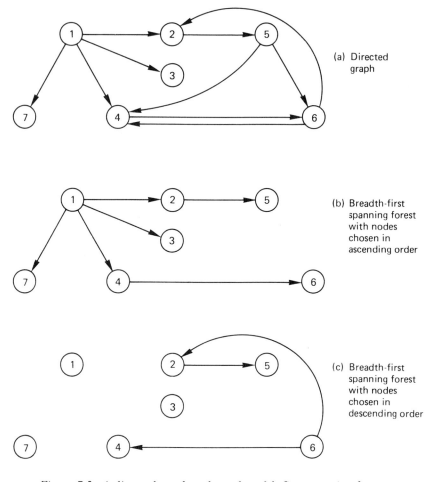

Figure 7.5   A directed graph and two breadth-first spanning forests.

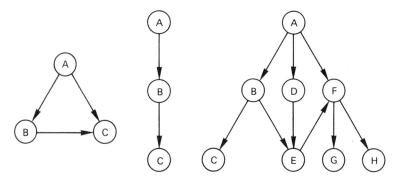

Figure 7.6   Sample acyclic graphs.

The depth-first search method can be modified to detect whether a graph has any cycles. As it traverses a subtree, the procedure will be examining nodes which can be included in the subtree at the next level down. If it finds a node which can be linked in, but has already been visited as an ancestor of the current node, then there is a cycle in the graph. Furthermore, every cycle will show itself in this way. On the other hand, finding a link from the current node to one which has been visited as part of a different branch, or indeed as part of a different subtree, is not a cycle. The visited node must be an ancestor in the same subtree for it to indicate a cycle. In the graph of figure 7.3, for example, the depth-first search which selects the nodes in ascending order (figure 7.3b), will visit the nodes

$$1, 2, 4, 6, 3$$

and can then detect a link from 3 to 4. Because 4 is an ancestor in this subtree, there is a cycle. Another cycle is found when node 5 has been included in the tree and the link from 5 to 1 is detected, since 1 is an ancestor of 5 in this subtree. But the link from 1 to 3 does not indicate a cycle, because 3 is not an ancestor of 1.

The modified routine must keep track of the ancestor nodes visited on the path from the chosen root to the current node. A LIFO list is needed for this, with nodes added to the list as the routine moves down the tree, and removed from the list as it returns up a level. Whenever a visited node is encountered, the list is searched to see whether it contains the node.

7.2 Applications of graphs

7.2.1 Resource allocation

A computer operating system which allows several users to run processes at the same time must cater for the processes competing for unsharable resources like printers, plotters and disc files. Since each process may be allocated some resources, then later request another resource, there is a possibility of deadlock. This is where one process holds a resource needed by a second process which itself holds a resource needed by the first process. Neither can continue. More generally, a circular chain of processes, where each holds a resource needed by the next and the last holds the resource needed by the first, is deadlock.

To detect if deadlock has occurred, it is possible to use a directed graph with a node for each resource and an edge from one node to a second if there is a process which holds the first resource and needs the second. Figure 7.7 illustrates such a graph. Deadlock has occurred if the graph contains any cycles.

The detection of cycles in the graph can be done by the search algorithm mentioned in the previous section.

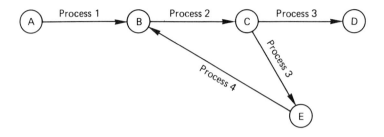

Resources A, B, C, D, E and Processes 1, 2, 3, 4

Figure 7.7　Resource allocation graph.

7.2.2 Project planning

A large project is often split into a number of well-defined tasks, some of which cannot be started until others have been completed. On the other hand, some tasks can be done independently. For instance, in building a house, laying the foundations, building the walls, plastering the walls, tiling the roof are a few of the tasks required. Clearly, a wall cannot be plastered before it is built, but the roof could be tiled before the wall is plastered.

A directed graph can be used to represent the tasks and their dependencies. A node is used for each task, and an arc joins one node to a second if the first task must be finished before the second is begun. The result is an acyclic graph which shows the tasks and how they depend on the other tasks. Figure 7.8 shows an example of a graph for a project.

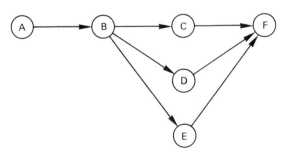

Tasks in a simple building project:
A — Lay foundations
B — Build external walls
C — Lay floors and ceilings
D — Build roof
E — Finish internal walls
F — Final inspection

Figure 7.8　Graph representing project tasks.

In this graph, we have shown only some of the dependencies as arcs and left out those which can be derived from longer paths. For instance, task A, to lay the foundations, must be completed before any other task is begun, but we have not included an arc from A to every other node. However, a path does exist from A to each other node. We can deduce that A must be completed before D because there is a path from A via B to D. In this context, an arc from A to D is redundant.

If the graph had included several redundant arcs, it would not have been as easy to determine the order in which the tasks should be performed. Indeed, the layout of the graph in figure 7.8 is chosen to make the order clear. This order is called *topological order*. It amounts to numbering the nodes in such a way that if there is an arc from node X to node Y, say, then X is given a lower number than Y. Our choice of names A to F for the nodes follows this rule.

The topological order for the nodes of an acyclic graph can be determined by choosing as the first node one for which no arc leads to it. Such a node must exist for a finite acyclic graph. If this node, and all the arcs which leave it, are removed from the graph, the whole process can be repeated to select the second node. Removing this node with its associated arcs and continuing in this way results in the topological order of the nodes.

7.3 Implementations of graphs

7.3.1 Adjacency matrix for directed graphs

One implementation of a directed graph, suitable if there are only a small number of fixed nodes, is as a matrix of Boolean values. The matrix has one row and one column for each node, and the Boolean element at position (i, j) is TRUE if and only if there is an arc from node i to node j. Such a matrix is called an *adjacency matrix*. Figure 7.9 shows a directed graph and its adjacency matrix.

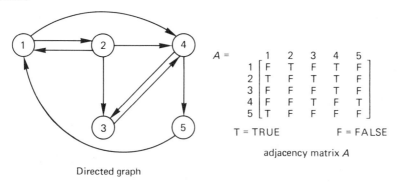

$$A = \begin{array}{c|ccccc} & 1 & 2 & 3 & 4 & 5 \\ \hline 1 & F & T & F & T & F \\ 2 & T & F & T & T & F \\ 3 & F & F & F & T & F \\ 4 & F & F & T & F & T \\ 5 & T & F & F & F & F \end{array}$$

T = TRUE   F = FALSE

adjacency matrix *A*

Directed graph

Figure 7.9 Directed graph and its adjacency matrix.

The operations of adding or deleting an arc from the graph are easily implemented by modifying the value of the element of the adjacency matrix. Changing the element (5,3) of the matrix of figure 7.9 to TRUE adds an arc from node 5 to node 3.

Testing whether two nodes are connected by an arc is simply a matter of examining the corresponding matrix element.

Testing whether there is a path between two nodes requires a more complicated routine. In our example, the graph has five nodes, and the adjacency matrix is called A, so for two nodes i, j there is a path of length 2 from i to j if the expression

$$(A[i, 1] \text{ AND } A[1, j]) \text{ OR } (A[i, 2] \text{ AND } A[2, j]) \text{ OR} \dots$$

$$\text{OR } (A[i, 5] \text{ AND } A[5, j])$$

is TRUE. This expression effectively checks if there is a path of length 2 via node 1 OR node 2 OR . . . OR node 5.

Readers familiar with matrix multiplication will realise that this expression is the (i, j)th element of the matrix product $A * A$. The Boolean operators AND and OR play the roles of multiplication and addition used in matrix multiplications for numerical matrices.

Evaluating the expression for all pairs (i, j) results in a matrix $A2$ whose elements indicate whether there is a path of length 2 between any two nodes. It is possible to apply this technique to derive matrices $A3, A4, A5$ for paths of length 3, 4 and 5. For paths of length 3, for example, the expression

$$(A[i, 1] \text{ AND } A2[1, j]) \text{ OR } (A[i, 2] \text{ AND } A2[2, j]) \text{ OR} \dots$$

$$\text{OR } (A[i, 5) \text{ AND } A2[5, j])$$

is used. Here we are looking for an arc from node i to node 1 and a path of length 2 from node 1 to node j, OR an arc from i to 2 and a path of length 2 from 2 to j, OR a similar path through one of the other nodes.

Since the example has only five nodes, there is no need to look for paths of length greater than 5; for a path of greater length must visit a node more than once, and there would be a shorter path between the two end-points obtained by omitting the cyclical path.

To determine whether there is a path of any length between nodes i and j, we can evaluate the Boolean expression

$$A[i, j] \text{ OR } A2[i, j] \text{ OR } A3[i, j] \text{ OR } A4[i, j] \text{ OR } A5[i, j]$$

The matrix which results when the expression is evaluated for all pairs (i, j) of nodes is called the *transitive closure* of the original adjacency matrix. It corresponds to a graph with the same nodes as the original, but with an arc between two nodes wherever there was a path between the nodes of the original graph.

Our discussion has concentrated on the example with five nodes. In the general case of a graph with n nodes, the expressions for the elements of the matrices $A2, A3$, etc., would involve terms for each of the graph nodes $1, 2, \ldots, n$, and all the matrices $A, A2, A3, \ldots, An$ would be required for the transitive closure of the adjacency matrix A.

There is a more efficient way of evaluating the transitive closure of an adjacency matrix than the construction of the matrices $A2, A3$, and so on. The method, known as *Warshall's algorithm*, starts with the adjacency matrix, then adds to it entries which correspond to paths through node 1 but no other intermediate node. If we call the resulting matrix $TC1$, the entry $TC1[i,j]$ can be computed as

$$A[i,j] \text{ OR } (A[i, 1] \text{ AND } A[1,j])$$

The matrix $TC1$ can now be modified to include paths between two nodes which pass through node 1 or node 2 (or both) but no other intermediate node. Calling the result $TC2$, the entry $TC2[i,j]$ is computed as

$$TC1[i,j] \text{ OR } (TC1[i, 2] \text{ AND } TC1[2,j])$$

This technique is repeated for paths which pass through the first three nodes, resulting in the matrix $TC3$ derived from $TC2$, and so on until all the nodes have been included. The final result is the transitive closure of the original adjacency matrix.

In the implementation, there is no need to keep separate matrices for $TC1$, $TC2$, etc., but the values can be built up in a single matrix, as shown in figure 7.10.

```
PROCEDURE Warshall( A: BoolMatrix; VAR TC: BoolMatrix);

(**** Warshall's algorithm to calculate the transitive
      closure TC of an adjacency matrix A.
      The matrix type is called BoolMatrix
      NoOfNodes is a global specifying number of
                                    graph nodes ****)

VAR i,j,k : 1..NoOfNodes; (* subscripts for nodes *)

BEGIN
TC := A;
FOR k:= 1 TO NoOfNodes DO
    FOR i:= 1 TO NoOfNodes DO
        FOR j:= 1 TO NoOfNodes DO
            TC [i,j] := TC[i,j] OR (TC[i,k] AND TC[k,j])
END;
```

Figure 7.10   Warshall's algorithm to compute the transitive closure.

7.3.2 Adjacency matrices for networks (weighted graphs)

The adjacency matrix representation can be extended to allow data to be stored on each arc by the use of a record as the matrix element type. The record would hold a Boolean field as before (called Linked, say), together with a field (called Weight, say) for the data stored on the arc. An arc from i to j with weight w would then be represented by a value TRUE in $A[i,j]$.Linked and a value w in $A[i,j]$.Weight, where A is the extended adjacency matrix.

To illustrate how the weights may be used in processing the network, we shall consider two further operations which apply to networks whose arc weights are positive numbers. Both operations are given a start node and examine paths in the network. We shall assume that there is a path from the start node to every other node in the network. (In the more general network where this assumption is invalid, the operations would apply only to the subgraph of nodes connected by a path from the start node, and the assumption would be valid for this sub-graph.) Under this assumption, the graph traversal routines find spanning forests of the network which consist of a single tree. Such a tree is called a *spanning tree*.

Minimal spanning tree

The graph traversal algorithms take no account of the weights of the arcs of a network in finding a spanning tree. From the specified start node, it may be desirable to find a spanning tree for which the overall sum of the arc weights is minimal. This is called a *minimal spanning tree*. If, for example, the graph represents a communication network and each arc weight represents the cost of providing a direct link between its two nodes, then the minimal spanning tree would represent the cheapest way of linking the start node to every other node.

Consider the graph in figure 7.11a. From the start node A, several spanning trees may be produced, as shown in figure 7.11b. The minimal spanning tree is shown in figure 7.11c and has a sum of arc weights of 32.

An algorithm to find the minimal spanning tree starts with the specified node and builds up the tree, adding one arc at a time, choosing an arc with minimal weight which joins a node in the tree to a node not yet included. To implement this a set can be used for the nodes included in the tree so far. Initially this holds just the start node. The procedure executes a loop in which the next arc is chosen and added to the tree, with the new node being added to the set of included nodes. Figure 7.12 gives the algorithm in outline. It relies on a step to choose the next arc for inclusion. This step must search through all arcs joining a node in the set to one not in the set, and select an arc after considering possible paths between the endpoints of these arcs.

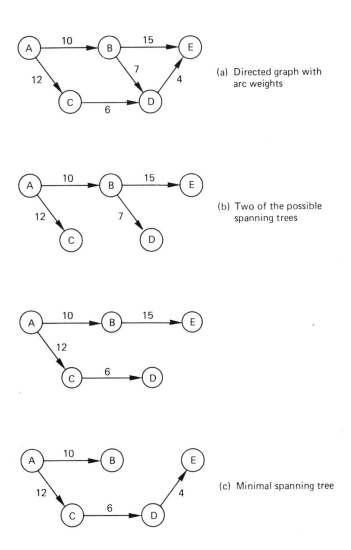

Figure 7.11 A directed network and some spanning trees.

In the example of the graph of figure 7.11a, the minimal spanning tree would be constructed by adding the edges in the following order:

(A,B), (A,C), (C,D), (D,E)

```
(* Start node is s *)
(* included is the set of nodes in the tree so far *)
included := [s];
```

REPEAT

```
    Choose minimal edge (i,j) with i IN included,
                         and j NOT IN included;

    Add arc (i,j) to the tree

    Included := included + [j];
```

UNTIL included contains all nodes

Figure 7.12   Outline algorithm for minimal spanning tree.

Shortest path between two nodes

If we regard an arc weight as a 'distance' between two nodes, the 'distance' along a path will be the sum of the arc weights in the path. We can introduce the concept of the shortest path between two nodes, defined as the path whose sum of arc weights is minimal. (Note, it is the sum of arc weights, not the number of arcs, which is minimal.)

The minimal spanning tree selects a tree with minimal overall sum of arc weights. This does not guarantee that the path between the given start node and any other node will be the shortest path. For example, the path from A to D in figure 7.11c has a path sum of 18. In the original graph, the path from A to D via B is shorter, having a path sum of 17.

An algorithm (due to Dijkstra) to find the shortest path between the start node and any other node follows an outline similar to the algorithm for the minimal spanning tree, but needs a different criterion in choosing the arc to be added to the tree each time. Whereas the minimal spanning tree algorithm examines the weights of arcs between any node included in the tree already and a new node, for the shortest path it is the distance from the start node which must be examined. A vector, Distance, is defined with the element Distance$[i]$ holding the shortest distance from the start node to i known so far. Initially, the start node, s, has Distance$[s]$ set to 0; each node k for which there is an arc from s to k has Distance$[k]$ defined as the weight of the arc (s, k). For all other values of k, Distance$[k]$ is defined as MAXINT, so that it is larger than any other possible value.

The arc chosen at each stage is one whose end-point has the smallest value of Distance. If this has end-point k, the node k is added to the set of included nodes, and the Distance values are updated as follows. For each arc (k, j) joining the new node k to a node j not in the included set, the element Distance$[j]$ is redefined to be the smaller of its current value and the sum

$$\text{Distance}[k] + A[k, j].\text{Weight}$$

This value allows for a path from the start node to j passing through the newly added node k. Should this path have a smaller distance value than the current smallest, it becomes the new value for Distance$[j]$.

Further data must be kept to determine which arc is being added to the tree each time. The Distance vector will say what the end-point is, but we need to record to which node currently in the tree the new node is linked. This can be done by maintaining another vector LinkNode such that the entry LinkNode$[k]$ identifies the node to which k is currently linked.

Initially, LinkNode$[j]$ is defined as node s for all nodes j with an arc from s to j, and undefined for all other nodes. Whenever a new node k is added to the tree, those nodes j which have the Distance value redefined also have the value of LinkNode$[j]$ defined to be node k.

An outline of this algorithm is given in figure 7.13.

Working through the example of figure 7.11a with start node A, we have the Distance vector defined initially as

$$\text{Distance}[A] = 0, \text{Distance}[B] = 10, \text{Distance}[C] = 12$$
$$\text{Distance}[D] = \text{MAXINT}, \text{Distance}[E] = \text{MAXINT}$$

and the vector elements LinkNode$[B]$ = A and LinkNode$[C]$ = A.

The node A is initially the only entry in the set Included. Since B has the smallest value of Distance, it is the next node added to the set, and redefines the values of Distance for the nodes D and E. The values become

$$\text{Distance}[D] = 17, \text{Distance}[E] = 25$$

while the elements Linknode$[D]$ and LinkNode$[E]$ become B.

The next node chosen is C, since its Distance value is 12. Because the value of the expression

$$\text{Distance}[C] + A[C, D].\text{weight}$$

is greater than the current value of Distance$[D]$, no alteration is made to the vectors Distance or LinkNode.

The node D is chosen next, and alters the values of Distance$[E]$ to 17+4=21, and LinkNode$[E]$ to D. Once the last node E is included, the tree is complete. Figure 7.14 shows the chosen tree, and the resulting values of Distance and LinkNode.

The shortest path from A to any node k can be derived in reverse order from the entries in LinkNode. For k=D, the value of LinkNode$[D]$ is B, and LinkNode$[B]$ is A, so the shortest path must be A to B to D.

```
(* Start node is s *)
(* included is the set of nodes in the tree so far *)
(* A is the extended adjacency matrix, in which     *)
(* Weight is the arc weight value, assumed INTEGER *)
(* Distance is the vector of the currently known
                              shortest distance *)
(* LinkNode is the vector defining to which node of
              the tree each new node should currently
              be connected                          *)


included := [s];

For all arcs (s,j),  initialise:

    Distance[j] := A[s,j].Weight
    LinkNode[j] := s

For all other nodes j, initialise

    Distance[j] := MAXINT     (* assuming INTEGER *)


REPEAT

    Choose node k not in included with least value
                          of Distance[k];

    Included := included + [k];

    For all arcs (k,j) DO

        IF (Distance[k] + A[k,j].Weight < Distance[j])
        THEN
            Distance[j] := Distance[k] + A[k,j].Weight
            LinkNode[j] := k

UNTIL included contains all nodes.
```

Figure 7.13   Outline algorithm for shortest path.

7.3.3 Linked implementations of graphs

The adjacency matrix representation is unsuitable in situations where the
number of nodes of the graph is not known beforehand or changes dynamically.
The operations of adding or deleting nodes from the graph require the adjacency
matrix to alter in size. Each new node requires an extra row and column to be
added to the matrix. The matrix would have to be declared large enough to cater

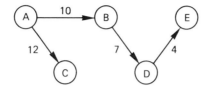

Node	Distance	LinkNode
A	0	—
B	10	A
C	12	A
D	17	B
E	21	D

Figure 7.14 Result of shortest path algorithm for graph of figure 7.11a.

for the maximum number of nodes expected and be expanded and contracted as nodes are added or removed dynamically. It is also very wasteful of space for sparse graphs.

A linked structure can be used to overcome these problems. The nodes are represented as records chained together in a linked list, each record holding the node data, a pointer linking it to the next node in the chain and an arc pointer. Figure 7.15 shows a node list for a graph with four nodes (A,B,C,D).

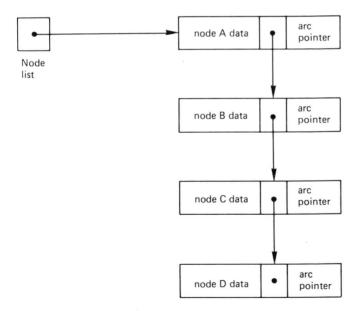

Figure 7.15 Node list for a graph.

The arcs of the graph are represented by records chained into separate linked lists, with the arcs from node A chained into one linked list, while those from node B are chained into a separate linked list, and so on for each node. The arc pointer in the node list record acts as a head pointer for the list of arcs from that particular node. Each arc record contains a pointer to its end-point node and a field to chain it into the linked list. For a weighted graph, the arc weight is also held in this record.

Figure 7.16 shows a directed graph and its linked representation. In the arc records, the node pointers are shown by the node name in brackets. Thus (B) means a pointer to the node record for B.

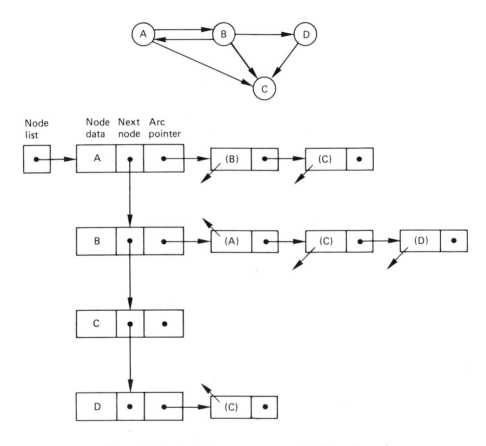

Figure 7.16   Linked representation of a directed graph.

The arc records for arcs (A,B) and (A,C) are held in a linked list from the node record for A. The three arc records for (B,A), (B,C), (B,D) form the linked list for node B, while C has an empty arc list and D has a list with just the one entry for arc (D,C).

The corresponding Pascal data declarations for this implementation are given in figure 7.17. Pointer data types have been used for the links in both the node records and the arc records. In this example, a single character is held as the node data in the node record. There could of course be data of any type at the nodes. The arc records are shown with just the two pointer fields, but if the graph is weighted, the arc weights would be stored there as additional fields.

```
TYPE
      NodePtr = ^ NodeRec;
      ArcPtr  = ^ ArcRec;

      NodeRec = RECORD
                   NodeData   : CHAR;
                   NextNode   : NodePtr;
                   FirstArc   : ArcPtr
                END;

      ArcRec  = RECORD
                   EndNode    : NodePtr;
                   NextArc    : ArcPtr
                END;
VAR

      NodeList : NodePtr;
```

Figure 7.17 Pascal data declarations for a graph.

7.4 Relations

7.4.1 Binary relations

An important concept in the study of databases is that of a *relation*. A manufacturing company, for example, will be concerned with, among other things, selling goods to its customers. There will be a relation between an individual customer and the sales orders that he has made. There will be another relation between a sales order and the goods ordered, and yet another between the goods and the components used to make them. A relation, then, is a way of linking pairs of items of the same or different types: a customer and a sales order, an item and a component, and so forth. Because we are considering pairs of items, we call these *binary relations*, and a natural way to represent such a relation is as a graph.

Binary relations have been studied in mathematics and given an abstract definition in terms of sets of objects or elements. A relation on a set is defined by specifying which (ordered) pairs of elements are related. For example, in the set of positive integers, the relation 'is a prime factor of' is defined by specifying all the pairs of elements, such as (2,4), (5,10), (3,12), for which the first number is a prime factor of the second. In this way a relation is identified as a collection of ordered pairs of elements of the set. A pair (x, y) is in the collection if and only if x is related to y. Notice that the pair (y, x) is not the same as the pair (x, y), which is what we mean by 'ordered' pair.

A relation between two sets A and B can be defined similarly. It is identified with a collection of pairs (x, y) of elements with x from the set A, and y from B. In the example of the sales orders, the set A is the set of all customers and the set B the set of all current sales orders. The relation 'has ordered' is identified with a collection of pairs of elements (x, y) where x is a customer and y is an order that he has made.

A directed graph can be used to represent a relation between two sets. The graph has a node for each element of the two sets, and an arc from node x to node y if x is related to y. Figure 7.18 shows a graph for the customer order example where the firm has just six customers and four current orders.

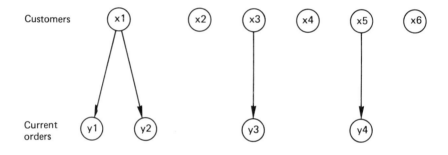

Figure 7.18   Graph of customer–sales order relation.

In this example, each current order is linked to just one customer, yet a customer may be linked to none, one or several current orders. We call this a (1:many) relation.

The relation 'is a prime factor of' discussed above is a (many:many) relation because each prime is a factor of many other numbers, while a number may have many prime factors.

7.4.2 n-ary relations

The concept of a binary relation can be extended to an n-ary relation, where n is greater than 2, by identifying it as a collection of ordered n-tuples of elements. Thus, when $n=3$, a collection of ordered triples (x, y, z) of elements of a set defines a ternary relation on the set. A triple (x, y, z) is in the collection if and only if the relation holds between the three elements x, y, z. Such a relation can be represented as a table with n columns. Each row of the table is one of the ordered n-tuples in the collection.

As an example, consider a ternary relation defined between the set of component parts bought by a firm, the set of all suppliers and the set of unit prices. The relation is defined by saying that (x, y, z) is in the relation if part number x is supplied by supplier y at a unit price of z. This relation can be represented as a table with columns for Part, Supplier and Unit Cost. Figure 7.19 shows some entries in this table.

Part	Supplier	Unit Cost
1234A	T.K. Jones	59.44
1235B	T.K. Jones	33.50
1234A	A.B. Thomas	57.60
1254A	Smith and Sons	22.30
1234A	Smith and Sons	57.90

Figure 7.19   A ternary relation represented as a table.

For a binary relation, the table has two columns, and it is possible to view this as a graph. For an n-ary relation, the tabular form does not translate simply into a graph. It is, however, possible to view a single n-ary relation as a binary relation between two smaller relations. If, for example, a 4-ary relation contains the 4-tuple (w, x, y, z), this could be viewed as a link from (w, x) to (y, z). Alternatively, it could be viewed as a link from (w, z) to (x, y), or as a link from x to (w, y, z). Figure 7.20 shows an example of such a relation viewed as a single table and as a graph between smaller relations. Notice that splitting the relation can reduce the number of times that a particular value is stored. The pair $(6,3)$ appears four times in the original table, but only once in the graph representation.

When relations are used in databases, it is desirable to split large relations into a number of smaller tables (relations) linked by binary relations. This reduces the amount of data redundancy and provides a better model of the data structure. A fuller discussion of this topic is given in chapter 10.

Table of 4-tuples (w, x, y, z):

w	x	y	z
6	3	12	4.7
3	9	7	12.6
6	3	10	55.8
2	6	11	22.9
6	3	12	5.1
3	9	10	55.8
2	6	5	8.9
6	3	5	8.9

Graph for pairs (w,x) to (y,z)

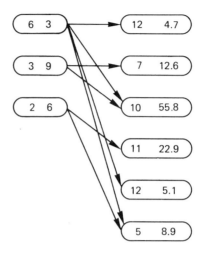

Figure 7.20   A relation and a view as a graph.

7.5 Summary

This chapter has introduced graphs and networks as data structures and examined typical operations on them. They are more general than trees and methods of finding spanning trees or forests have been described. Two implementations, as adjacency matrices and as linked structures, have been discussed.

The correspondence between graphs and binary relations has been established, and the concept of a relation extended to n-ary relations. These concepts will be developed further in the following chapters on databases.

Exercises

7.1 Write a program to read in details of a directed graph from a text file, as follows:

> the first line specifies the number of graph nodes:
> each subsequent line contains the numbers of the start
> and end nodes of an edge in the graph.

From these details, create and print the adjacency matrix and its transitive closure. (Allow a maximum of ten nodes in the graph, say.)

7.2 Modify the program of exercise **7.1** to:
   (a) determine whether the graph is fully connected (that is, whether there is a path from every node to every other node);
   (b) list all the nodes, if any, from which there is a path to every other node in the graph.

7.3 Write a program to read details of a connected, directed network from a text file, as in exercise **7.1**, except that the weight is also specified for each edge. The program should then accept pairs of node numbers from the user and print out the shortest path between them.

8 Design Considerations

In the preceding chapters we have discussed various data and file structures and examined some of their applications. In this chapter we shall look at a complementary question: given an application problem, how do you design a data structure for it? There is no simple answer to this, but some general guidelines can be discussed.

8.1 Problem analysis

An application problem is usually first described in a vague informal way. The application will be concerned with specific pieces of data and relationships between them. One task is to analyse the problem to identify the data and the relevant relationships, leading to a model of the data structure inherent in the application.

The operations required on the data structure must also be identified. Indeed, they will be needed to determine which of the numerous possible relationships between the data items are relevant to the application. Only when the inherent data structure and its required operations have been identified will a more precise specification of the problem emerge.

At this stage we are concerned only with abstract views of the data structure, not implementation details. The task is to determine *what* is required rather than *how* it will be provided.

8.2 Abstract data types and formal specifications

Throughout this book, the difference between abstract and concrete structures has been stressed. But our approach has been informal, with abstract structures shown in terms of pictures. In a formal approach, an abstract structure is defined as a mathematical object called an *abstract data type*. The primitive operations are specified in the definition of the abstract data type: some are actually used to define the structure.

Consider, for example, a stack of integer items. To define this as an abstract data type, we need an empty stack, Empty, as a given stack constant, and an operator Push to add a new item on to a stack. If x is an integer and s a stack,

Push(x,s) is the stack obtained by adding x on to s. In this notation, the stack holding the values 1,2,3 with 3 on top would be written as

$$Push(3, Push(2, Push(1, Empty)))$$

The removal operator Pop can be regarded as producing a stack as its result. The relationship between Push and Pop is established by the equation

$$Pop (Push(x,s)) = s \text{ for all integers x, stacks s}$$

which serves to define Pop. This essentially says that Pop removes the item entered last, which distinguishes a LIFO list.

A further operator, Top, to return a copy of the top element of the stack can be defined as

$$Top (Push(x,s)) = x \text{ for all integers x, stacks s}$$

Notice that the operators Pop and Top cannot be used with an empty stack: they are only defined for stacks of the form Push(x,s). Notice also the difference between the operator Pop defined here and that discussed in chapter 3. Here Pop discards the top element to give the resulting stack. In our earlier discussion we used the operator to return a copy of the top element as well as to reduce the stack. At this formal abstract level, it is neater to have Pop and Top as separate operators.

The advantage of a formal definition is its precision. Ambiguities which abound in informal specifications are much less likely in a formal definition. Furthermore, a formal definition of the data structures and their operations will lead to a formal specification of the problem. The program or programs needed for the application can be regarded as possibly complex operations on the data structures, and can thus be defined formally in terms of the primitive operators of the structures.

The formal definition helps to show where errors may occur. In the example of the stack, errors occur if the operators Pop or Top are applied to an empty stack. Identifying error conditions at an early stage means that they can be included in the specification and not left to *ad hoc* decisions during implementation.

In chapter 3 we gave a Pascal procedure to implement the stack operator Pop and there assumed that the stack was not empty. We stated that the user of the procedure was responsible for ensuring that it was not applied to an empty stack. Only when it has been specified, in the context of the particular application, what action is required with the possible error conditions can error-handling be properly included in the design.

The formal specification, if written in an appropriate specification language such as Goguens OBJ (for reference, see bibliography at end of book), can be used to provide a prototype of the required program. The prototype is used only to demonstrate *what* the program will do and does not reflect the operational characteristics such as speed of response or volume of data catered for. These characteristics are important in the design of the final program.

8.3 Data structure design

The problem analysis may not at first yield all the structures which will be needed in the solution. There may be auxiliary data structures needed to provide the required operations.

Suppose, for example, that the problem is to take a list of integers and produce an output list sorted into ascending order. The data structures involved are two lists of integers. They both contain exactly the same entries, but the desired output list is in order. This is a specification of the problem but it does not show how to solve it. For a solution we must determine *how* the operations are to be carried out.

It is possible to design a sort operation on the list without any auxiliary data structures, as was done in the bubble sort in chapter 1. The analysis of this method shows it to be inefficient, but the real question to be asked is whether it is acceptable in the context of the application. The golden rule is: *Keep it simple*.

If the method is unacceptably inefficient, alternative methods, or the use of additional structures, can be examined. Introducing a binary tree as an auxiliary structure with its operations of building the tree and printing it provides a more efficient solution.

A good programmer must be able to design good data structures. Time must be spend on deciding what is the appropriate structure to use.

As already stated, the starting point is to analyse the problem to identify the data, which the program will have to process, and find its inherent structure. Think in terms of abstract data structures at this stage, rather than being concerned with implementation details. The structures that we have examined in the previous chapters will be adequate for most programs.

The next stage is to design the algorithm for the program using a top-down approach. Make use of the primitive operations of the abstract data types and again keep implementation details out of the design.

Once an algorithm has been produced, examine the use made of the primitive operations to determine how often they are performed. Knowing this and being aware of the size of the data structures, try to select an implementation which will provide efficient algorithms for the primitive operations used. If there are clashes between different implementations because of operations requiring different accessing methods, give preference to those operations which are performed most frequently. Remember to consider efficiency in the context of the given problem.

This may well be an iterative process. If you find it impossible to select an appropriate implementation, it will be necessary to reconsider the algorithm design, or to consider additional data structures to support the operations.

8.4 Internal data structure or external file?

For a program that processes a batch of data, the initial data is likely to be held on an external file and after processing the updated values would be written to an external file. However, intermediate structures, required by the program, could well be held in main store or externally. The following paragraphs identify some of the various factors which need to be considered when deciding where the data should be held.

8.4.1 Volume

If a program is processing a large volume of data, then a file held on backing store is usually more appropriate. The majority of standard commercial computing operations fall into this category. The actual cost of providing a computer with a large main store, to hold data, is seldom justifiable. The majority of commercial operating systems provide paging or virtual memory, where a disc is used to back-up main store. However, if an attempt is made to hold large volumes of data in main store, the overhead of the paging mechanism, swapping data from main memory to disc, is likely to seriously reduce the speed of the system.

8.4.2 Response time

Data held in main store can be immediately accessed. If the overriding requirement, for a particular application, is instant access to data, then an internal data structure should be employed. Some operating systems allow the programmer to set up a logical disc in main store, allowing instant access to filed data. Alternatively, a large buffer area can be declared in main store so that the need for disc access is rare. In such cases response time can be dramatically improved. Response time can dictate which type of file to use − that is, fast response implies a direct access file.

8.4.3 Permanent or temporary storage?

If data is to be stored permanently, a copy of it must be held in an external file. Modern semiconductor memory will lose data if there is a power cut, for example, so at the very least a back-up copy of the data should be stored in a file. Whether or not the data is normally held in main store will be decided by considering other factors.

A temporary file or data structure, created by a program to hold intermediate results, is unlikely to require backing-up if by re-running the program it can be re-created. Such considerations as volume of data and overall speed of program execution will decide where the data is stored.

8.4.4 Shared access

If more than one user requires simultaneous access to the data, it is normal practice to store that data in an external file. The memory management layer of any operating system will, normally, prevent users from accessing data held in another user's main store area. Routines to allow shared access can be written. FORTRAN programs can share data by means of COMMON data blocks held in system area of main store. However, the normal procedure is to store shared data in a file. If a user wishes to update a particular record, it can be locked, preventing other users from accessing it, until the updating is complete.

8.4.5 Language facilities

The target programming language, in which your program is to be coded, will have a major influence on whether or not you will use internal data structures or external files. A language such as Pascal offers a wide range of internal data structures, but provides few file processing facilities. If the target language is COBOL, the file processing facilities are extensive, the internal data structures limited. As a result COBOL programmers write more programs using random access files than do Pascal programmers. A Pascal programmer may well make use of a simple database package, such as IMAGE (discussed in chapter 11) to provide the file processing facilities not provided by the language. The application should have a major influence on the target language, however the reality of the situation (available compilers on the computer system, interfacing to existing programs, etc.), often limits the programmer's choice.

8.5 Summary

The overall design of data structures and/or files is likely to be a compromise, having taken due regard of all the factors involved. The initial algorithm design should use abstract data structures so that changes necessary because of implementation details are apparent, and appropriate decisions can be made.

9 Database Management Systems

9.1 Introduction

Databases have developed as organisations have attempted to make fuller
use of the information held on their computers. Technological advances have
resulted in development staff salaries becoming a major part of software development budgets. A properly designed database management system can
dramatically improve development staff productivity.

Originally, application programs would have their own file set. A logical
development of this was the integrated file system where one file can be
accessed by several programs. For example, accounting systems are normally
integrated file systems, where the files (or ledgers) can be accessed by several
different programs. Such integrated file systems tend to reflect an organisation's departmental structure, there being accounts systems, stock control
systems, etc. Often the questions management require to be answered before
they can successfully run the business need the assessment of information from
several departmental areas. By collecting all organisational data within one file
and using sophisticated access methods, a database is created. Such a system
should allow managers to access the information they require.

The first real databases were developed in the middle 1960s in the US
aerospace industry. By the early 1970s large organisations were attempting to
set up single databases to hold all their data. Because of human limitations, as
much as technical problems, such an approach was unrealistic. The current
approach is to hold the organisational data in several databases with clearly
defined interfaces.

9.2 Limitations of conventional filing systems

The traditional development of file-based applications has resulted in serious
limitations in the final software.

The first problem is uncontrolled redundancy. As different applications have
been developed with their own files, the same piece of information is likely to
be held in several different files. If this information is to be updated, it is likely
that the same data will have to be input to different programs to update all
the occurrences. Related to redundancy is the problem of inconsistency. If some

occurrences are not updated, different systems will have different values for the same data item.

A file processing system tends to be inflexible. While it can easily produce the standard output for which it was designed, it cannot respond rapidly to a request for a new or revised format. Even though the file may contain the details required by the user, it may be difficult to produce the information in a reasonable form without writing a special program to interrogate the file.

Every organisation requires standard procedures and methods so that it may operate effectively. Using conventional filing systems it is difficult to enforce standards because both system design and operation are decentralised. With different applications using different names and formats for the same data item, this makes sharing of data impractical.

Using conventional files a programmer is responsible for both the file and the algorithm design. The task of file design is repeated for each application developed. If file designing is removed, the programmer's productivity, in terms of number of lines of usable code produced, will increase. Related to this is program maintenance. If the physical characteristics of the data files are embedded within the programs code, any modifications made to the files will result in alterations to the program's code. Therefore, conventional filing systems may result in low programmer productivity and excessive program maintenance levels.

9.3 What is a database?

Often the word 'database' is used to refer to any large collection of data. Specialised database texts tend to have stricter definitions. A *database* must be organised so that it can serve the data requirements of different applications. The term relates to the physically stored data and software required to enable users to access the data. The Database Management System (DBMS) provides this interface between the users and the physical data. It is the users of the system who dictate the form of the database.

If a database is to be robust (that is, if it does not have to be redesigned each time a new application is added), an attempt has to be made to find some natural relationships between those data items which it holds. To achieve the physical implementation of such relationships it may be necessary to use complex data structures. The process of normalisation, discussed in chapter 10, is a means by which a data model can be developed which is easily transferable into a form acceptable to most general database systems.

9.4 DBMS software

The Database Management System (DBMS) software allows users to create their database. It handles all data requests, usually providing concurrent access

to several database users. It also has the capability to recover or restore the
database from back-up copies and logs of database activity. User access is
normally either by means of a special-purpose query language or by the use
of procedures in a high-level language such as Pascal or COBOL.

A DBMS should allow the user to create a database which overcomes many
of the limitations of conventional filing systems. As data is now centralised it
can be placed under the control of one person, or section, which can enforce
standards. This function is called *Database Administration*. It is now the responsi-
bility of the database administrator to ensure that data is held in an acceptable
form, releasing the programmer from his file design obligations.

Redundancy of data can be controlled. It is possible to store a particular
data item once, and allow different programs access to it via the DBMS software. To improve the efficiency of operation it may be that two copies of a
data item are held, for example as a key and non-keyed entry. However, a
definite decision is made to allow redundancy, as opposed to the *ad hoc*
appearance of it within conventional filing systems.

The DBMS provides the user with on-line access to the database. Usually
they provide a query facility so that 'special' questions can be asked without
having to resort to the writing of a program for a one-off run.

9.5 Conceptual, logical and physical models

The process of generating a working database involves the creation of three
separate models: the conceptual model, the logical model and the physical
model.

The conceptual model is based on our perception of the organisational area
or problem which is being examined. The term can be applied to an informal
model which can consist of reports in use, documentation produced by fact
finding, and so on. The term can also be applied to a more formal model which
shows data items and their relationships but is independent of any particular
DBMS implementation. Applying structured design techniques, for example, to
an informal conceptual model will have the effect of formalising the representation.

The logical model is derived from the conceptual model and is a formal
representation describing data items and their structural relationships. It takes
into account the DBMS which will be employed to create the database, so any
limitations imposed by the particular DBMS implementation will be reflected
in the logical model. For certain implementations, the term *schema* is used to
describe the formal definition of the database, which is written in a well-defined
data description language. The schema is the complete logical view of the data.
If only part of the data is examined, the term *subschema* is applied.

The final stage is to translate the logical schema into the physical database.
The physical model is the actual implementation of the database consisting of

the data files with supporting software. The translation process, from logical schema to physical model is performed by the DBMS software.

9.6 Database terminology

Data analysis is the process by which data from the 'real world' is examined in order to formulate the conceptual model. Data analysis identifies entities, attributes, relationships (or relations) and access methods.

An *entity* is a conceptual model representation of an object in the real world. For example, a hospital administration system is likely to have entities of PATIENT, DOCTOR, WARD, NURSE, PRESCRIPTION, etc.

The properties possessed by an entity are called its *attributes*. For example, the entity PATIENT could have attributes of: patient number, surname, initials, age, home address. The key field which uniquely defines a particular occurrence of an entity is called its *identifying attribute*. For example, considering the suggested attributes for the entity PATIENT, it is probable that the patient number is all that is required to identify a particular patient. The entity PATIENT would be shown as follows:

PATIENT (Patient-no,Surname,Initials,Age,Home-address)

Patient number is underlined to show that it is the identifying attribute. It may be necessary to use more than one attribute to identify a particular occurrence of an entity. For example, an entity PRESCRIPTION could have attributes of: patient number, doctor number, date, drug, dosage. To identify a particular 'prescription', assuming that more than one doctor can prescribe for a patient, the identifying attributes would be: patient number, doctor number and date.

In which case PRESCRIPTION would be defined as

PRESCRIPTION (Patient-no,Doctor-no,Date,Drug,Dosage)

Entities may be associated by *relations*. Chapter 7, section 7.4, introduced the idea of relations showing links between entities, or nodes. The entity PRESCRIPTION is likely to be 'related' to the entity PATIENT. A particular PATIENT will be prescribed 'many' PRESCRIPTIONs. Figure 9.1 shows the representation of the three main relational types. A 'many' relation is shown by a double arrow head.

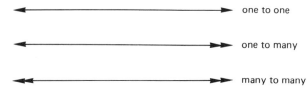

Figure 9.1 Diagram to represent the degree of entity relationships.

Let us consider the example of an invoice which has several lines, each line ordering a different item. Then the INVOICE can refer to several ORDER-ITEMs and the relationship between these entities can be diagrammatically represented as in figure 9.2.

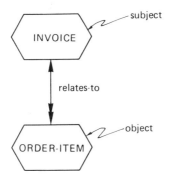

Figure 9.2   Entity diagram: INVOICE 'relates-to' ORDER-ITEMs.

The diagram defines that an INVOICE 'relates to' ORDER-ITEMs. The relationship is described by a verb, while INVOICE is the subject of the relationship, and ORDER-ITEM its object. By convention, in a 'one-to-many' relationship the subject of the relation is the entity at the 'one' end of the relationship. That is, in this example, INVOICE. The diagram (figure 9.2) translates into the expression INVOICE 'Relates to' ORDER-ITEMs. 'Relates to' is the name of the relation. Notice that in the diagram the object entity box shows ORDER-ITEM; the plural is implied by the double arrow head.

If a SUPPLIER supplies many PARTs, and a PART can be supplied by many SUPPLIERs, then a 'many-to-many' relationship exists between SUPPLIER and PART as shown in figure 9.3. By convention the subject is SUPPLIER, the entity at the top of the relation, and PART, the entity at the bottom, is the object of the relationship 'supply'.

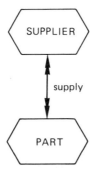

Figure 9.3   Entity diagram: SUPPLIERs 'supply' PARTs.

If the degree of the relationship is not yet clear, no arrow head is shown. For example, figure 9.4 shows a relationship 'leased by' between the entities CUSTOMER and PROPERTY.

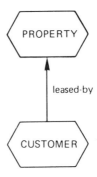

Figure 9.4   Entity diagram: PROPERTY 'leased-by' CUSTOMER (or CUSTOMERs).

It states that a CUSTOMER leases a single PROPERTY, but the relationship between PROPERTY and CUSTOMER is not known. It could be that this database is used by an estate agent who only goes for long-term leasing of property. In that case the relationship would be one to one. However, an estate agent in a holiday area could have the PROPERTY leased to many CUSTOMERs during the season for which it is available. In this case the relation is one to many. It could be that the letting price of a particular PROPERTY was too high, so no CUSTOMERs leased it; therefore in this case 'many' may include this zero case.

In this section, two representations have been introduced. Firstly, an entity has been shown as a collection of attributes, unique occurrences being defined by means of identifying attribute(s). Secondly, entity diagrams show the relationships between entities. A formal conceptual model could well use both of these representations to define data item relationships.

9.7 Summary

A database can be seen as an attempt to overcome some of the limitations imposed by conventional filing systems. It is the database management which allows the user to create and maintain a database system. The database is a physical implementation of an information or data model. Entity relationship diagrams are one means of formally expressing a data model.

The following three chapters consider databases and their design in further depth. Chapter 10 examines the process of database design, without regard to any particular database management system. Chapter 11 looks at changes which may be required if a network database is to be used, while chapter 12 repeats the process for a relational database.

10 Database Design

10.1 Introduction

In order to design a database for a particular application, initially the relevant elements of the 'real world' information have to be identified. This first stage is called *conceptual modelling*. A conceptual model serves two main purposes. Firstly, it describes the data in a form that users and computer specialists can discuss so that the implications of the design can be identified. Secondly, the conceptual model is the starting point for the construction of the logical model.

10.2 Conceptual models

Data analysis is the term applied to the analysis of information and its use. The final formal version of the conceptual model marks the end of the data analysis phase. The entity diagrams introduced in the final section of chapter 9 are a useful method of presenting part of a conceptual model. Data analysis is very much an iterative process, where each iteration should attempt to get closer to an acceptable design. A design is developed and then reviewed. Defects in the design are identified and the initial model is altered and reviewed.

As part of the process of data analysis, *functional analysis* can be performed. This is concerned with both data and processes within a functional area (for example, sales) of an organisation. The end result of functional analysis is a local conceptual data model: 'local' as it relates to only part of an organisation's information processing. Often functional analysis will be performed first and the local data models merged to form the global conceptual data model which represents the structure of all the information examined within an organisation.

10.3 To develop a data model diagram

The following example relates to a simplified view of the operation of a cinema chain.

The cinemas operated by a company are split into film groups. A film group shows a particular film programme. A manager is allocated to control several cinemas in a region. This regional grouping consists of cinemas from different film groups. The net receipts from a particular film programme are recorded on an individual cinema basis.

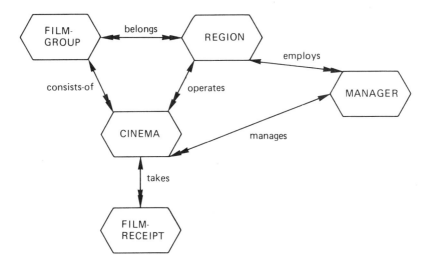

Figure 10.1   Cinema conceptual data model.

Figure 10.1 shows a possible conceptual data model diagram to represent this information. It assumes information will be held about the following entities: FILM-GROUP, REGION, MANAGER, CINEMA, FILM-RECEIPT. All relationships joining the entities are named, with one-to-many relationships being drawn down the page, where possible.

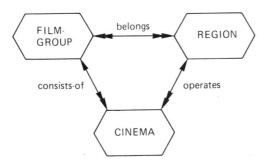

Figure 10.2   Entities: FILM-GROUP, REGION and CINEMA.

Often it is possible to link two entities in more than one way. Figure 10.2 shows three possible relationships between the entities FILM-GROUP, REGION and CINEMA. The relationship 'belongs', between the entities FILM-GROUP and REGION, is many to many, FILM-GROUP has CINEMAs belonging to many REGIONs while REGION has CINEMAs from more than one FILM-GROUP. The remaining two relationships 'consists of' and 'operates' are both one to many. A CINEMA is only in one FILM-GROUP and a single REGION, although there are many CINEMAs in each FILM-GROUP and REGION. One of these relationships may be redundant if it can be obtained from the other two. Assuming that the only link between a REGION and a FILM-GROUP is through CINEMAs which belong to both a particular REGION and a particular FILM-GROUP, the relationship 'belongs' can be removed. Many DBMSs are unable to represent many-to-many relationships directly, so the final version of the diagram could not have the 'belongs' relationship.

Figure 10.3 shows a similar situation between the entities REGION, MANAGER and CINEMA.

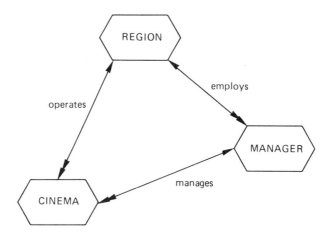

Figure 10.3 Entities: REGION, MANAGER and CINEMA.

Here all three relationships are one to many, so at first inspection it may appear that it is likely to make little difference to the actual implementation of the database which one is removed. In practice, if all CINEMAs in a REGION are managed by MANAGERs employed by that REGION, the REGION to CINEMA link can be perceived as being via the MANAGER and hence the 'operates' relationship can be removed. Figure 10.4 shows the final version of this data model. It is essential to check that, when removing a relationship, the remaining relationships can provide all the necessary links between the entities. For example, in figure 10.3 it is not possible to remove the relationship 'manages' as it would no longer be possible to identify which MANAGER is responsible for a particular CINEMA.

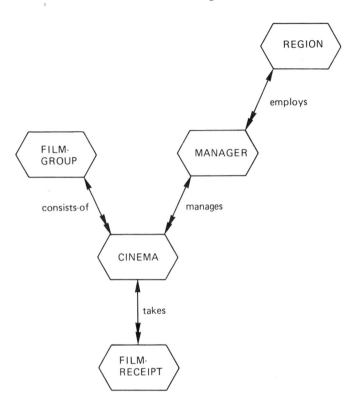

Figure 10.4   Modified cinema conceptual data model.

Only entities about which information is to be stored should form part of the data model. There could be an entity **FILM-PROGRAMME**, for example. However our model assumes that film programme is held as an attribute of an existing entity, perhaps **FILM-RECEIPT**.

Besides identifying entities, data analysis collects the attributes (or properties) of the entities which are to be stored. So the entity CINEMA could have the following attributes:

    CINEMA (Cinema-no, Cinema-name, Address, Manager-no, Film-group)

Often the initial entities chosen will not result in a workable database implementation. During data analysis entities may be split into further entities. For example, to remove many-to-many relationships it could be necessary to create new entities. The process of normalisation, discussed at the end of this chapter, uses the entity's attributes and their interrelationships to modify the data model, resulting in a robust model less likely to require future changes.

10.4 Functional analysis approach to conceptual modelling

Functional analysis tends to be a more practical approach to adopt when looking at any non-trivial information system. In this section we will use an example to build up local conceptual models, and finally merge them to create the global conceptual model. We will consider only entities and their relationships, although if such analysis was being performed in a real situation, attributes would also be identified.

This example relates to the operation of an express coach company. Three different functional views of its operations will be considered. Let us first consider the functional area of timetabling.

A coach company operates a number of routes, where a route consists of one or more stages. A stage is a non-stop journey between two towns, and can be a part of many routes. Many departures serve each route daily. Figure 10.5 illustrates a possible data model to represent this example.

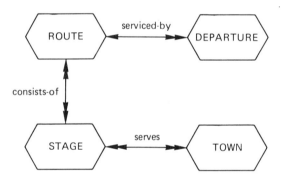

Figure 10.5   Timetable local conceptual data model.

The entity coach company is not included. It would only be necessary if the model was to represent more than one coach operator. The relationship 'serves', between the entities STAGE and TOWN, is a many-to-two relationship as a STAGE has an origin and a destination TOWN. However, it is simply represented as a many-to-many relationship.

Reservation view of the coach company's operations is slightly different. A passenger makes a reservation for a journey from one town to another, to travel on a particular departure which is identified by time and a date. Each departure is invariably operated by a particular coach type with a known seating plan. Figure 10.6 shows a possible data model to represent these entities.

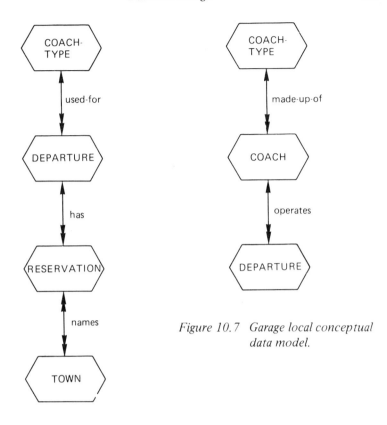

Figure 10.7 Garage local conceptual data model.

Figure 10.6 Reservation local conceptual data model.

Finally, we will consider a garage view of the company's operations.

Each coach operated by the company is of a given type. Every coach is scheduled for a number of departures each day. Figure 10.7 gives the garage local data model.

If we consider that figures 10.5, 10.6 and 10.7 adequately define the three functional areas which are to be represented by our model, then the global data model will be achieved by merging these three related local models. Figure 10.8 shows a possible global conceptual model. There may be redundant relationships in this data model. For example, the relationship 'made-up-of' between COACH-TYPE and COACH could be obtained from 'used-for' between COACH-TYPE and DEPARTURE, and 'operates' between COACH and DEPARTURE. We are told that in this example all coaches are allocated to DEPARTUREs, but it would be more realistic if on certain days a coach was unallocated, for example if it was to be serviced. If the link 'made-up-of' was removed, unallocated coaches would be removed from our model.

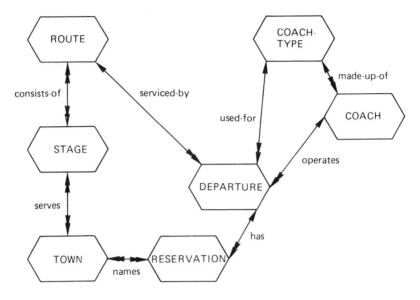

Figure 10.8   Coach company global conceptual data model.

The three many-to-many relationships between ROUTE and STAGE, STAGE and TOWN, and RESERVATION and TOWN, are likely to cause problems when an attempt is made to convert the conceptual model into a logical model. While from figure 10.8 it appears that there is an alternative path between the two entities ROUTE and STAGE (via DEPARTURE, RESERVATION and TOWN) we would no longer know which STAGEs were on which ROUTEs if 'consists-of' were removed.

While it is important to simplify the global conceptual model, care must be taken to ensure that necessary relationships are not lost. Even with this simplified view of the coach company's operations, the process of functional analysis, followed by merging of the local data models, can identify areas in which more information is required before a final model can be constructed. For example, is there any other entity which could provide a link between ROUTE and STAGE? It is possible to use the conceptual model diagram as a means of discussing with user departments their view of their data requirements. Such discussions should lead to more accurate conceptual data models.

10.5 Normalisation

The technique of normalisation was developed by Codd (IBM) to transfer conceptual data models into a form acceptable to relational databases. However, a technique which considers the interrelationships of entities and their attributes is a powerful tool for use in any form of data analysis. It can act as a check on the original data analyses, as well as ensuring that the data model is more flexible. That is, it will easily respond to future changes.

Normalisation is a three-stage process. Figure 10.9 outlines the stages involved. Entities have to be converted into their third normal form, normally written as 3NF, by way of two intermediate states, namely first normal form (1NF) and second normal form (2NF). One effect of normalisation is to regroup the attributes of the entities such that the relationships between the resulting entities are clearly shown.

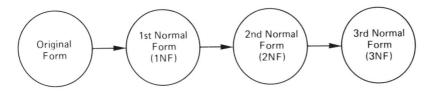

Figure 10.9   The stages of the normalisation process.

10.5.1 To generate 1NF entities

Consider the following example. A local authority with several branch libraries wishes to maintain details of stocked books. It is assumed that each book has a unique title and a single author, but many copies of the more popular titles will be stocked at any branch. The entity BRANCH could be written as

> BRANCH (Branch-no, Branch-address, (Title,
> Author, Publisher, No-of-copies))

The innermost bracket of 'Title, Author, Publisher, No-of-copies' is known as a *repeating group*. For a given occurrence of Branch-no there will be many Titles. To transfer BRANCH into its first normal form, repeating groups have to be removed.

> BRANCH-1 (Branch-no, Branch-address)

> STOCK-1 (Branch-no, Title, Author, Publisher, No-of-copies)

The '1' after the entity name is to show that it is in first normal form (1NF). The repeating group has become a new entity; however, to maintain its link with the outer bracket entity (BRANCH), the original identifying attribute of Branch-no becomes an attribute of STOCK-1. The original entity BRANCH has been converted into two new entities BRANCH-1 and STOCK-1.

The first step, therefore, in the normalisation process is to remove the repeating group(s). The identifying attribute of the original entity becomes an attribute of the new entity. In this example the original entity's identifier (Branch-no) became part of the new entity's (STOCK-1) identifying attributes, because the same title will be found in several libraries. However, if an occurrence of the new entity can be identified without use of this 'outer' attribute, the identifying attribute of the original entity becomes a non-identifying attribute of the new entity.

Let us consider a further example. A computer consultancy keeps details of its clients and contracts. A contract refers to a single client, but any client may have several contracts. Members of staff are assigned to individual contracts. The entity CLIENT could be written as

CLIENT (Client-no, Name, Location, (Contract-no,
                    Estimated-cost, Completion-date,
                        (Staff-no, Staff-name,
                            Staff-location)))

In this entity we have two sets of repeating attributes. A client can have several contracts, and on each contract several staff can work. Obviously, if we had performed data analysis effectively, other entities would have been identified. However, normalisation will provide the necessary entities. To convert CLIENT to 1NF we remove the repeating groups, and make the entity identifier of the original entity an attribute of the new entity. Firstly, we remove the outer set of inner brackets:

CLIENT-1 (Client-no, Name, Location)

CONTRACT (Contract-no, Client-no, Estimated-cost,
            Completion-date, (Staff-no,
                Staff-name, Staff-location))

The entity CONTRACT uses only Contract-no to identify an occurrence of the entity, as it is assumed each Contract-no is unique. Client-no is carried over from the original entity CLIENT, but is now treated as an ordinary attribute. To complete this first stage of the normalisation process, the entity CONTRACT has to be converted into 1NF:

CLIENT-1 (Client-no, Name, Location)

CONTRACT-1 (Contract-no, Client-no, Estimated-cost,
                            Completion-date)

STAFF-1 (Staff-no, Contract-no, Staff-name, Staff-location)

It has been assumed that Contract-no uniquely identifies occurrences of the entity CONTRACT-1. The entity STAFF-1 has two identifying attributes, Staff-no and Contract-no. It is assumed that a member of staff may work on more than one contract at any time. This being the case, both Staff-no and Contract-no are needed to identify all possible occurrences of the entity STAFF-1.

The original entity CLIENT has now been normalised into three new entities CLIENT-1, CONTRACT-1, STAFF-1.

10.5.2 To generate 2NF entities

Only entities which have more than one identifying attribute are involved in the transformation from first to second normal forms. If we return to the library example the entity STOCK-1 has two identifying attributes:

STOCK-1 (Branch-no, Title, Author, Publisher, No-of-copies)

To convert this entity into second normal form, every non-identifying attribute is examined to see if it depends on all or only part of the identifying attributes. Author and Publisher only depend on Title, while No-of-copies depends on both the Branch-no and Title. Figure 10.10 illustrates this.

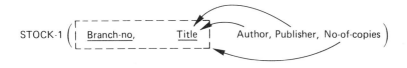

STOCK-1 (| Branch-no, Title | Author, Publisher, No-of-copies)

Figure 10.10   STOCK-1 functional dependencies.

This leads to a 2NF representation of

STOCK-2 (Branch-no, Title, No-of-copies)

BOOK-2 (Title, Author, Publisher)

Therefore the complete second normal form representation of library **BRANCH** is

BRANCH-2 (Branch-no. Branch-address)

STOCK-2 (Branch-no, Title, No-of-copies)

BOOK-2 (Title, Author, Publisher)

BRANCH-1, as it only has one identifying attribute, is already in second normal form.

This second stage of normalisation is to ensure that non-identifying attributes depend on all of the identifying attributes within an entity. The term *functional dependency* is used to describe the fact that an attribute depends on another attribute. For example, for the entity STOCK-1, the attribute No-of-copies is functionally dependent on both the attributes Branch-no and Title.

If we consider our other example with 1NF entities of CLIENT-1, CONTRACT-1 and STAFF-1, as both CLIENT-1 and CONTRACT-1 have a single identifying attribute, their 2NF is the same as their first.

CLIENT-2 (Client-no, Name, Location)

CONTRACT-2 (Contract-no, Client-no, Estimated-Cost,
Completion-date)

STAFF-1 has two identifying attributes, and figure 10.11 shows their relationship with the other attributes.

Figure 10.11   STAFF-1 functional dependencies.

Obviously, the Staff-name only depends on the Staff-no. It is assumed that the Staff-location does not vary with contract. The data analyst would have to ensure that this was the case before converting the entity STAFF-1 into 2NF. Based on these assumptions STAFF-1 becomes

> STAFF-2 (Staff-no, Staff-name, Staff-location)
>
> ASSIGNMENT-2 (Staff-no, Contract-no)

Therefore, this example gives four entities in 2NF, namely

> CLIENT-2 (Client-no, Name, Location)
>
> CONTRACT-2 (Contract-no, Client-no, Estimated-cost, Completion-date)
>
> STAFF-2 (Staff-no, Staff-name, Staff-location)
>
> ASSIGNMENT-2 (Staff-no, Contract-no)

10.5.3 To generate 3NF entities

The third step of normalisation is involved in examining the functional dependencies of the non-identifying attributes of an entity. If one of these attributes implies another one, they are said to be *transitively dependent*.

For example, if in our computer consultancy example it was decided to add an account manager who was responsible for a clients account, the entity CLIENT-2 would be rewritten as

> CLIENT-2 (Client-no, Name, Location, Man-no, Man-name, Man-location)

That is, the entity CLIENT-2 now has attributes of Man-no (account manager's number), Man-name (account manager's name), and Man-location (account manager's location). These three new attributes are unaffected by the previous two stages of normalisation. That is, they are not a repeating group (1NF) or attributes of an entity with more than one identifying attribute (2NF). Figure 10.12 shows the functional dependencies between the non-identifying attributes.

CLIENT-2 (Client-no, Name, Location, Man-no, Man-name, Man-location)

Figure 10.12   CLIENT-2 functional dependencies.

The attribute Man-no uniquely defines Man-name and Man-location, so to transform CLIENT-2 into 3NF the attributes Man-name and Man-location are removed into a new entity.

CLIENT-3 (Client-no, Name, Location, Man-no)

MANAGER-3 (Man-no, Man-name, Man-location)

The example based on the library resulted in three 2NF entities, STOCK-2, BOOK-2 and BRANCH-3. None of these entities has non-identifying attributes which are functionally dependent on other non-identifying attributes.

The third normal form of our two examples is, therefore

(i)   CLIENT-3 (Client-no, Name, Location, Man-no)

MANAGER-3 (Man-no, Man-name, Man-location)

CONTRACT-3 (Contract-no, Client-no, Estimated-cost,
                                            Completion-date)

STAFF-3 (Staff-no, Staff-name, Staff-location)

ASSIGNMENT-3 (Staff-no, Contract-no)

(ii)   BRANCH-3 (Branch-no, Branch-address)

STOCK-3 (Branch-no, Title, No-of-copies)

BOOK-3 (Title, Author, Publisher)

10.5.4 To represent 3NF entities as data models

By examining the third normal form entities, it is possible to draw the corresponding data model diagrams. Figure 10.13 shows the library data model diagram.

The relationships are derived from the attributes of the entities. A relationship exists between two entities if they share one or more common attributes. If the normalisation process has been performed correctly one would expect that any relation would be of degree 1 to 1, or 1 to many. If a 'shared' attribute uniquely identifies an entity, then that entity will be at the '1' end of the relation. BRANCH-3 is identified by Branch-no. STOCK-3 is identified by both Branch-no and Title. Therefore, for a given Branch-no there is a single occurrence of the entity BRANCH-3. However, there can be many occurrences

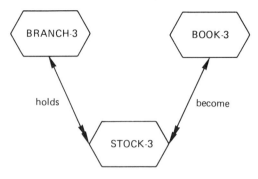

Figure 10.13   Library conceptual data model.

of the entity STOCK-3 for a given Branch-no, resulting in the one-to-many relationship. The relationship between BOOK-3 and STOCK-3 is found using similar reasoning.

Figure 10.14 is a data model of our consultancy example. Both the MANAGER-3 to CLIENT-3 relationship 'looks-after' and the CLIENT-3 to CONTRACT-3 relationship 'takes-out' are 1 to many. Here the degree of the relationship is shown by looking at common attributes between each pair of entities. Man-no is the identifying attribute of MANAGER-3, but a non-identifying attribute of CLIENT-3. Therefore, a single manager number

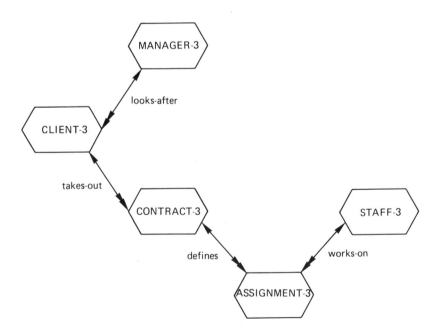

Figure 10.14   Computer consultancy conceptual data model.

(Man-no) uniquely defines an occurrence of MANAGER-3, but several CLIENT-3 occurrences could have the same value for Man-no. The same logic is behind the CLIENT-3 to CONTRACT-3 link where Client-no is the common attribute.

By examining the 3NF entities, it is possible to construct data model diagrams. If the normalisation process has been performed correctly, there should be no many to many relationships. Figure 10.14, showing the computer consultancy model, has CONTRACT-3 and STAFF-3 linked via ASSIGNMENT-3. The direct link between CONTRACT-3 and STAFF-3 is many to many, as a contract employs many staff and each staff member can work on many contracts. The intermediate entity of ASSIGNMENT appeared when the entities were transformed to 2NF, removing the many-to-many relationship.

In general, if two entities share identifying attributes and for one of these entities the shared attributes form all of its key, that entity will be at the '1' end of the relation.

10.5.5 Normalisation example

In this section we will work through a further normalisation example, generating its 1NF, 2NF and 3NF entities. Finally a data model showing how these entities are related will be constructed.

A medical practice keeps patient records as part of a repeat prescription system. The following PATIENT entity shows the attributes held:

PATIENT (Patient-no, Name, Age, Address, (Drug, Date,
Dosage, Doctor, Secretary))

Each doctor has his own medical secretary who prepares the prescription for him to sign.

To convert this entity to 1NF, remove the repeating group.

PATIENT-1 (Patient-no, Name, Age, Address)

PRESCRIPTION-1 (Patient-no, Date, Drug, Dosage, Doctor,
Secretary)

By assuming that an occurrence of PRESCRIPTION-1 can be identified by the two attributes Patient-no and Date, it is implied that only one repeat prescription is allowed per patient, per day and that a single drug is specified.

As PATIENT-1 has only a single identifying attribute it is already in 2NF. Figure 10.15 shows the functional dependencies for the entity PRESCRIPTION-1.

We are assuming that any Doctor in the practice can sign the prescription. If only the patient's own doctor is permitted to sign the prescription, both Doctor and Secretary would only depend on Patient-no, and in 2NF a new entity would be generated. From the diagram it can be seen that all the non-identifying attributes depend on the full key, therefore PRESCRIPTION-1 is already in 2NF. Hence the 2NF form is

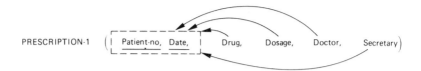

Figure 10.15   PRESCRIPTION-1 functional dependencies.

PATIENT-2 (Patient-no, Name, Age, Address)

PRESCRIPTION-2 (Patient-no, Date, Drug, Dosage, Doctor,
                                                    Secretary)

To convert to third normal form (3NF) non-identifying attributes have to be considered. For PATIENT-2, all the non-identifying attributes depend on the identifying attribute directly. In PRESCRIPTION-2 there are possible links between the non-identifying attributes Drug, Dosage and Doctor, Secretary. If patients were always prescribed the same dosage for a drug, then Drug would imply Dosage. This is unlikely as dosage may vary for a given drug. As the Doctor has one Secretary, the attribute Doctor will imply a given value of Secretary. Therefore 3NF gives

PATIENT-3 (Patient-no, Name, Age, Address)

PRESCRIPTION-3 (Patient-no, Date, Drug, Dosage, Doctor)

DOCTOR-3 (Doctor, Secretary)

The relationship between these entities is shown in figure 10.16.

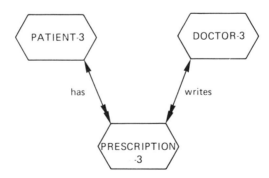

Figure 10.16   Repeat prescription conceptual data model.

10.5.6 Further normal forms

In certain situations, third normal form does not separate the data into suitable entities. An alternative to third normal form, called *Boyce/Codd normal form*, has been developed to deal with the inadequacies of 3NF. Fourth and fifth normal forms have also been defined. For most purposes a model in third normal form will result in a flexible database being built. Discussion of these higher forms will be found in any specialised database text.

10.6 Summary

In this chapter we have examined one approach to data analysis in order to formulate conceptual data models. The powerful combination of entity data model diagrams, backed up by normalisation will ensure, in the majority of cases, that the final model can be translated into workable logical and ultimately physical models which are flexible to change. The final two chapters examine the process of converting the conceptual model into a logical model, supported by a particular database management system. The major design elements of creating a database are within the development of the conceptual model. The translation from conceptual model to logical model is akin to coding a program for which a precise specification exists.

Exercises

10.1 The following description relates to a simplified view of the operation of a company which distributes a range of wines to customers, who, in general, operate retail outlets in many locations.

View of the order processing section:
    Customers send the company orders for wines. Each order contains requests for quantities of many different wines which are required by one shop.

View of the company warehouse:
    The company has several warehouses, each stocking a range of wines, but each wine is only in one warehouse. A warehouse is sent a picking list which shows the wines to be packed and sent to a particular shop.

View of accounts department:
    The company sends invoices to its customers at the end of each month. Each customer receives one invoice per month, which lists the orders for all his shops.

(a) Draw three local conceptual data models, one for each view stated. Only entities and relationships should be shown.
(b) Draw a global conceptual data model which supports the three local models of part (a). State any assumptions made.
(c) For each relationship in your global data model, describe the meaning and degree in terms of the entities involved.

10.2 An entity CAR_DEPOT is defined as having the following attributes:

CAR_DEPOT (Depot_no. Depot_address, (car_type,
(reg_no, colour, mileage)))

Occurrences of this entity represent information about rental car depots, their addresses and the various cars they have available for hire. Particular details are as follows:
 (i) Any car is assigned to only one depot.
 (ii) Every depot will have several car types available, and several cars of each type.
(iii) Not every car type will be available at every depot.

(a) Normalise the entity CAR_DEPOT to give an equivalent set of entities in third normal form.
(b) Draw a conceptual data model diagram for your solution to (a) showing the entities and relationships involved.
(c) An additional attribute, car_make, is added to the original entity, which becomes

CAR_DEPOT (Depot_no, Depot_address, (car_type, car_make,
(reg_no, colour, mileage)))

Show how this affects the normalisation process of part (a), assuming that the company only has one car make for each car type.

11　Network Database Models

11.1 Introduction

A major influence on database logical design during the 1970s was the CODASYL group, who are responsible for the definition of the COBOL programming language. During the late 1960s, CODASYL extended its area of interest to include all areas where COBOL might be used. The possibility of COBOL accessing a database led to the formation of a group within CODASYL to define a CODASYL database model. The resulting model, which has been updated at intervals, has been implemented by many computer manufacturers and software houses. The CODASYL database is known as a network database model. In this chapter we will examine the major components of this model and see how our conceptual models have to be altered to form CODASYL logical models.

CINCOM Systems developed a limited network database model which formed the basis of their TOTAL database system. Several manufacturers developed systems based on the TOTAL database model, including Hewlett-Packard who produced their IMAGE database system. TOTAL and its derivatives are claimed to be the most popular database systems of the 1970s with up to 40 per cent of the database market. We shall, therefore, also examine the IMAGE database system in this chapter. Although it is far simpler than the CODASYL model, it requires more alterations to our conceptual model to produce an IMAGE logical model.

A *network* is an alternative name for a graph, discussed in chapter 7 of this book. Both the CODASYL and IMAGE models allow only one-to-many relationships between the nodes within their networks. If, during data analysis, the process of normalisation has been applied to the conceptual model, all many-to-many relationships will have already been removed. This simplifies the conversion from a conceptual model to either a CODASYL or IMAGE logical model.

11.2 The CODASYL database model

Figure 11.1 shows the difference in terms employed by CODASYL and our conceptual model. Data items are combined in CODASYL to form a *record*. CODASYL uses rectangular boxes to represent records in its data model diagrams. The same term, *relationships*, is used in both conceptual and CODASYL models.

There is a problem in using the term record, as it can have two distinct meanings. The record type of a CODASYL model equates to an entity of our conceptual model.

CONCEPTUAL MODEL	CODASYL LOGICAL MODEL
Entity Attribute Relationship	Record Data item Relationship

Figure 11.1   Conceptual model and CODASYL data terms.

For example, in figure 11.2 DEPARTMENT is a record type. The second meaning of record is record occurrence. For example, sales, accounts, dispatch could all be record occurrences of the record type DEPARTMENT. Therefore if the term record is used in relation to a CODASYL model, it is necessary to identify whether the meaning is record type or record occurrence.

11.2.1 CODASYL set

A basic building block of this logical model, for representing relationships, is the set. Figure 11.2 shows a CODASYL set.

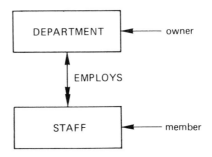

Figure 11.2   CODASYL set EMPLOYS.

The *set owner* is defined as the record at the 'one' end of a relationship, so in our example the record DEPARTMENT owns the set EMPLOYS. The record at the 'many' end of the relationship in a set is called the *member record*. STAFF is the member record of the EMPLOYS set. A *set* is defined as having one or more member record types. Figure 11.3 shows a single relationship USES which has two member record types, STAFF and EQUIPMENT. An alternative method of representing these relationships is shown in figure 11.4. Here the record type DEPARTMENT is the owner of two set types, EMPLOYS and USES.

A member record may belong to one or more set types, as in figure 11.5.

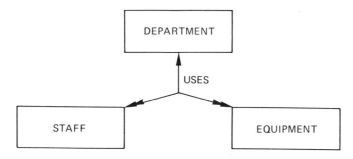

Figure 11.3   Each set type must have one or more member record types.

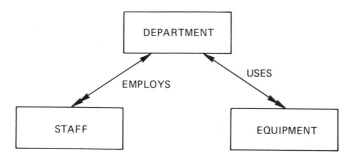

Figure 11.4   A record type may be the owner of one or more set types.

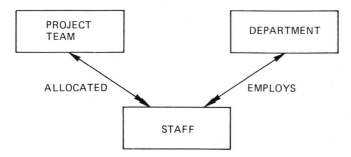

Figure 11.5   A member record type of two set types.

A record type can be a member of one set type and the owner of another, as in figure 11.6. Here PROJECT-TEAM is the member of the WORKED-ON-BY set and the owner of the ALLOCATED set.

As can be seen from these figures, CODASYL sets allow the representation of all the one-to-many relationships likely to be required in our logical models. The term set can refer to a set type or a set occurrence. A *set type* is defined as a named logical collection of one owner record type plus zero, one or more member record types. A *set occurrence* is actual owner records linked to the member records which they own within the set. The figures so far have illustrated set types, however figure 11.10 shows set occurrences of the set types of figure 11.8.

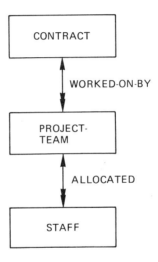

Figure 11.6   A record type being both a member and an owner of set types.

11.2.2 Translation of conceptual models into CODASYL logical models

In chapter 10 we developed a library model which had the following entities in 3NF:

BRANCH-3 (Branch-no, Branch-address)

STOCK-3 (Branch-no, Title, No-of-copies)

BOOK-3 (Title, Author, Publisher)

Figure 11.7 shows the corresponding conceptual model. The conceptual model translates into the CODASYL model of figure 11.8.

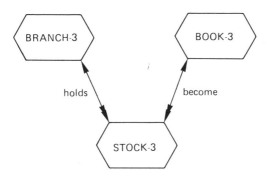

Figure 11.7   Library conceptual data model.

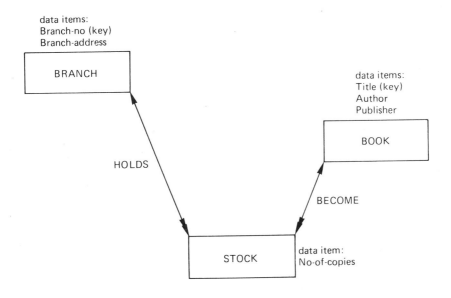

Figure 11.8   Library CODASYL logical data model.

In a CODASYL model it is not necessary to repeat data items in a member record that are already to be found in the owner record within the same set, because they are accessible via the set construct. Therefore the record type STOCK contains the single data item No-of-copies.

The library conceptual model was fairly simple, consisting of only three entities. In chapter 10 we also developed a conceptual model for a computer consultancy which consisted of the following entities:

CLIENT-3 (Client-no, Name, Location, Man-no)

MANAGER-3 (Man-no, Man-name, Man-location)

CONTRACT-3 (Contract-no, Client-no, Estimated-cost,
Completion-date)

STAFF-3 (Staff-no, Staff-name, Staff-location)

ASSIGNMENT-3 (Staff-no, Contract-no)

Figure 10.4 shows the computer consultancy conceptual data model. Figure 11.9 shows the corresponding CODASYL data model. Because the CODASYL model does not require us to repeat data items in the member record which already occur in the owner records of the sets, the record type ASSIGNMENT contains no data items. It is simply acting as a logical link between the record types CONTRACT and STAFF. This empty record is perfectly acceptable to a CODASYL database.

In practice, data analysts often place a data item in such records, as human beings find it difficult to cope with a record which is only a complicated pointer.

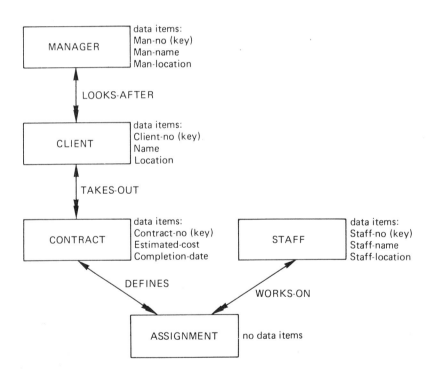

Figure 11.9   Computer consultancy CODASYL logical data model.

In this example there are several data items which might be placed in the ASSIGNMENT record. For example, date of being assigned, days worked to date, charges by staff member to given contract, etc.

11.2.3 Navigation of a CODASYL database

If we wished to find details of a text called 'First Aid', figure 11.10 indicates the relationships that exist within CODASYL sets which allow us to navigate around the database. Each owner record occurrence has its own set of member record occurrences for a given set type. Within the set BECOME all the occurrences of the record type STOCK which refer to this title, that is, belong to this particular BOOK record type, are indicated. Each of these STOCK records will belong to an owner within the HOLDS set.

Therefore, to access details of which branches hold copies of the text 'First Aid', the following steps are involved:

1. Go to the record type BOOK and FIND occurrence with title 'First Aid'.
2. FIND the first member of set BECOME.
3. GET details of No-of-copies.
4. FIND owner in HOLDS set.
5. GET details of Branch.
6. FIND next member in BECOME set.

Steps 3 to 6 are now repeated until there are no more STOCK records which belong to the BOOK 'First Aid' in the BECOME set.

The words FIND and GET used in the previous paragraph are new verbs (or statements) added to COBOL to allow that language to access the database. Many of the software products using the CODASYL model also allow access to the database via other languages.

11.2.4 Implementation of set membership using linked lists

CODASYL databases normally use linked lists to chain together member records which belong to the same owner record, while individual member records are directly linked to their owner record. Therefore a set is likely to be implemented by at least two forms of linked lists. For example, an owner record which has ten member records related to it within a set will be implemented as ten member-to-owner pointers, one in each member record. A single linked list, starting and ending on the owner record, will also link together the ten member records.

In figure 11.10, the BECOME set could be implemented as linked lists. The required occurrence of the record BOOK, 'First Aid', is chained by a linked list which relates together the four record occurrences within the STOCK record type which refer to this text. Finding the next STOCK record occurrence simply involves moving to the next record in this particular linked list. When accessing

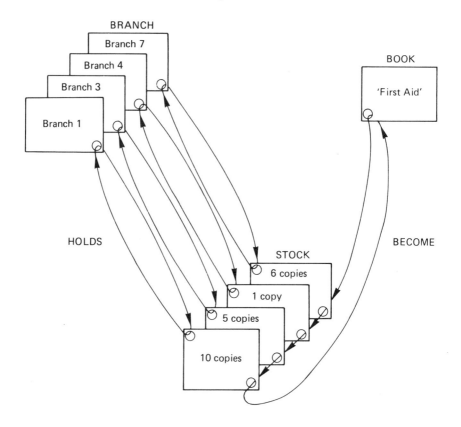

Figure 11.10   Navigating the library CODASYL data model.

the HOLDS set, a pointer within the STOCK record will indicate the BRANCH record required.

Hence, every occurrence of a STOCK record is likely to contain four pointers. These are:

1. A pointer to its owner in the BECOME set.
2. A pointer to the STOCK record which comes after it in the BECOME set.
3. A pointer to its owner in the HOLDS set.
4. A pointer to the STOCK record which comes after it in the HOLDS set.

11.2.5 LOCATION MODE

So far we have been concerned with translating the conceptual data model into a CODASYL logical model. However, some of the terms that have to be defined within a CODASYL schema relate to the physical storage requirements of the physical database. One of the more important of these physical considerations is 'LOCATION MODE'. LOCATION MODE controls the placement of new record occurrences. Where a record is placed obviously affects the ease and speed with which it can be retrieved. The latest guidelines from CODASYL have replaced LOCATION MODE by the 'KEY IS' construction. However, the majority of CODASYL implementations still use LOCATION MODE. The two most commonly used LOCATION MODEs by which a record occurrence can be accessed in a CODASYL database are CALC and VIA.

CALC, short for calculation, is designed to specify a record occurrence which is accessed by means of a hashing algorithm. For example, in the computer consultancy example (figure 11.9) we are likely to want to access the STAFF record by means of a key value, such as staff number. On entering a Staff-no we expect the system to respond by finding the correct occurrence of the STAFF record. So if a record occurrence has a LOCATION MODE of CALC, the record is treated as though it were part of a random access file. As we do not know the order in which the key values will be entered, we use a hashing algorithm to decide the relative positions at which the records are physically stored within the database.

VIA is used when a record is a member of a set and is normally accessed from the corresponding owner record occurrence. The member records will be placed, physically, as close as possible to its associated owner record. For example, in our computer consultancy example (figure 11.9), if we normally go from the CONTRACT record occurrence to the ASSIGNMENT record occurrence, then the ASSIGNMENT record would be defined as having a LOCATION MODE VIA DEFINES (DEFINES being the set in which CONTRACT is the owner record, and ASSIGNMENT is a member record). Use of VIA implies that we cannot access an ASSIGNMENT record directly by a key value. Further, although ASSIGNMENT is the member of two sets, DEFINES and WORKS-ON, it can only be defined as being located VIA one of them. This does not restrict access but the efficiency within the physical model of accessing ASSIGNMENT by way of DEFINES is greater than accessing via WORKS-ON.

11.2.6 Set ORDER

When defining a set in a CODASYL schema, an ORDER clause specifies how new member records are to be added. Member records are logically connected to their owner record by means of a linked list. Figure 11.11 defines the ORDER alternatives.

If ORDER IS SORTED, it is necessary to define a key value from the data items of the member record and to say whether it is to be sorted in ascending or descending order. The system then sorts new records and places them in the appropriate position in the linked list.

The remaining options fall into two categories, those which are done by the system (FIRST and LAST) and those carried out under application program control (NEXT and PRIOR). Figure 11.12 shows a possible occurrence of the

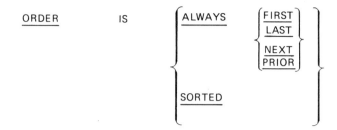

Figure 11.11   CODASYL ORDER clause.

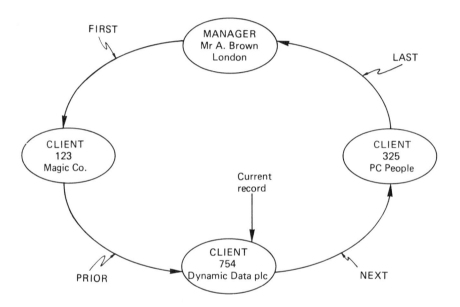

*Figure 11.12   Addition of new occurrences of CLIENT record to LOOK-
AFTER set.*

set LOOKS-AFTER in figure 11.9, where a linked list from an occurrence of
the MANAGER record, for Mr A. Brown, links three occurrences of the CLIENT
record. It is assumed that the current situation is that the user has progressed
down the linked list to the Dynamic Data plc CLIENT record occurrence. If
new records are added as either FIRST or LAST, their position is shown on
figure 11.12. If PRIOR or NEXT is used, the current record being accessed by
the program is identified before placing the new record either side of its position
in the linked list. In figure 11.12 it is assumed that the previous record occurrence
of CLIENT accessed was Dynamic Data plc, so PRIOR and NEXT will be as
indicated.

11.2.7 Membership class

When defining a set member, the description must include a membership class for the record type. The membership class defines how the links between the owner record and member records in a set are initially established and how and when these links can be removed.

When inserting a record occurrence in the database, its links within a set are defined as either AUTOMATIC or MANUAL. If the membership is AUTOMATIC, when a record occurrence is first stored in the database, the system automatically links it into the appropriate set occurrence. A MANUAL membership means an application program has to do the linking, that is it is not automatic.

For example, in figure 11.9 a CONTRACT, when added to the database, is likely to be automatically linked to CLIENT in the TAKES-OUT set. The CONTRACT refers to a known CLIENT. However, the link between MANAGER and CLIENT could be MANUAL. A new CLIENT is added to the database and at a later date a MANAGER is assigned to look after this CLIENT.

There are three options relating to retaining links once they have been established, namely, FIXED, MANDATORY and OPTIONAL. FIXED means that once a record occurrence has been inserted into a set then it must remain linked to that one owner. In figure 11.9, the link between CONTRACT and CLIENT is likely to be FIXED. MANDATORY means the record must remain linked to some owner, but this can be changed. If we assume that once a CLIENT has been assigned MANAGER there must be someone, at all times, to 'look-after' the CLIENT, the link between these entities could be MANDATORY (figure 11.9). OPTIONAL means a record occurrence can be removed from the set but still remain in the database. In figure 11.6 a member of STAFF may not belong to a PROJECT-TEAM at a particular point in time, but so that his details are kept on the database, the retention membership class could be defined as OPTIONAL.

The pointers, which provide the links of the model, are part of the record structure. The IDMS version of the CODASYL model, developed by Cullinane, actually requires the user to define these pointers when setting up the logical schema. For the LOOKS-AFTER set of figure 11.10, the set declaration in figure 11.13 could be used. The MANAGER record has a pointer to the next occurrence of a MANAGER record (NEXT POSITION 1), while the CLIENT record has pointers both to its next occurrence (NEXT POSITION 1) and to its 'owning' MANAGER record occurrence (OWNER POSITION 2).

11.3 The IMAGE database model

The smallest addressable unit of an IMAGE database is a *data item*, a term also used by the CODASYL model. The data items are grouped into data sets, which equate to entities within our conceptual model. Notice that the IMAGE database uses the term 'data set' for what in the CODASYL model would be termed

```
SET NAME LOOKS-AFTER.
ORDER IS NEXT.
MODE IS CHAIN.
OWNER IS MANAGER NEXT POSITION 1.
   MEMBER IS CLIENT
   NEXT POSITION 1
   MANDATORY MANUAL
   OWNER POSITION 2.
```

Figure 11.13   Defining the LOOKS-AFTER set in a CODASYL schema.

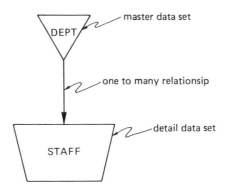

Figure 11.14   IMAGE data sets.

a 'record'. There is no equivalent to the CODASYL set within the IMAGE model. There are two types of data sets provided by IMAGE, master and detail. Figure 11.14 shows a logical model diagram representation of the data set types.

A master data set is always at the 'one' end and the detail data set at the 'many' end of an IMAGE relationship. A detail data set must be linked to at least one master data set, while a master data set can stand alone. A master data set can only be linked to detail data sets, while a detail data set can only be linked to master data sets.

The requirement that detail sets cannot be directly linked imposes a major limitation on the IMAGE data model, namely that it only supports a two-level structure. The model illustrated in figure 11.6, having three levels, could not be directly represented as an IMAGE data model. To overcome this problem one of the entities has to be repeated in the model, as both a master and detail data set. Figure 11.15 shows an IMAGE representation of a three-level structure. The data sets PROJECT-TEAM-1 and PROJECT-TEAM-2 refer to the same entity.

CONTRACT has a one-to-many relationship with PROJECT-TEAM-1. The relationship between PROJECT-TEAM-1 and PROJECT-TEAM-2 will be one to one, an occurrence of PROJECT-TEAM-2 holding the key data item from

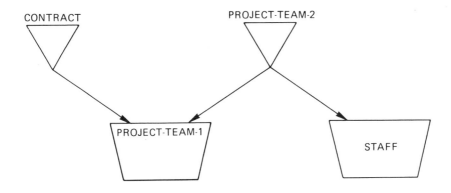

Figure 11.15 IMAGE two-level structure.

the corresponding PROJECT-TEAM-1 occurrence, to provide a one-to-many relationship with the STAFF data set.

A master data set allows access to a particular data set occurrence by means of a key value. It equates to a CODASYL record CALC mode. A detail data set is normally accessed by means of a linked list from a connected master data set, equivalent to a CODASYL record VIA mode.

11.3.1 Translation of conceptual model into IMAGE logical model

The two-level library conceptual model of chapter 10, already converted into a CODASYL model (figure 11.8) can be developed into an IMAGE logical model, as shown in figure 11.16. Unlike the CODASYL model, the key items of the master data sets are repeated in the linked detail data set. That is, the link is provided by repeating one data item in both the master and linked detail data set.

To access data sets within an IMAGE database from an application program, there are very similar commands to CODASYL's 'FIND' links and 'GET' data set occurrences. So the process of finding all details of the book 'First Aid' held within the library database would be logically equivalent to that already shown for the CODASYL logical model.

The computer consultancy conceptual data model of chapter 10 has four levels. It is necessary to convert this into a two-level structure, by means of introducing redundant data sets. Figure 11.17 shows a computer consultancy IMAGE data model.

The data sets CLIENT-2 and CONTRACT-2 repeat a key value of CLIENT-1 and CONTRACT-1 respectively. They act as a link and IMAGE provides automatic master data sets which can be used in such circumstances.

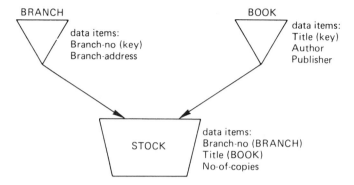

Figure 11.16   Library example IMAGE logical data model.

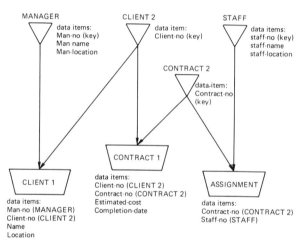

Figure 11.17   Computer consultancy example IMAGE logical data model.

IMAGE master data sets are defined as either automatic or manual. A manual data set has a single key data item, plus optional non-key data items. MANAGER and STAFF data sets in figure 11.17 are manual masters. The values of a manual master data set occurrence have to be entered before linked detail data set occurrences can be added. In figure 11.17 this implies that the MANAGER data set occurrence is already in the database before one adds the values to the linked CLIENT-1 data set occurrence. If a master data set is stand-alone, it must be of type manual.

An automatic master data set has a single data item, its key. It is linked to at least one detail data set. Both CLIENT-2 and CONTRACT-2 data sets in figure 11.17 could be automatic masters. If a new occurrence of the detail data set causes a new key data item to be introduced, a new occurrence of the automatic master data set is 'automatically' generated. Care must be taken to validate data entered in such detail data sets. An invalid entry for Client-no in data set CONTRACT-1 would generate an invalid data set occurrence in CONTRACT-2.

When defining a key item in a master data set an indication of how many detail data sets are linked to this particular master data set is given, allowing the IMAGE DBMS to establish the appropriate number of linked lists. For example, the data set CONTRACT-2 of figure 11.17 would be defined as shown in figure 11.18.

```
NAME: CONTRACT-2::A;
    << Defines Data Set Name & Type >>
ENTRY: CONTRACT-NO (2);
    << Key Data Item, two links      >>
CAPACITY: 40;
    << 40 Occurrences of Data Set
                            Allowed  >>
```

Figure 11.18   Defining the data set CONTRACT-2 in an IMAGE schema.

11.4 Summary

Network databases make extensive use of the data structures discussed earlier. By adjusting the logical and physical characteristics of such a database, it is possible to tune its performance. At present, large efficient databases tend to be network ones. IMAGE (and TOTAL) databases, while able to support large database models, are often found in simpler systems. An IMAGE database often replaces an integrated filing system for an accounts package, for example. By using the database, the programmers are not as involved in file designing and problems of concurrent user access are overcome by the IMAGE DBMS.

Exercises

11.1

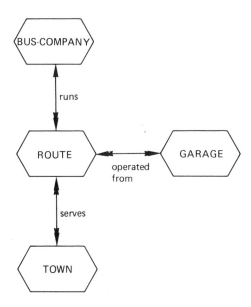

The diagram represents part of a database conceptual model. Show how the entities and their relationships could be held in:
(a) CODASYL logical data model;
(b) IMAGE logical data model.

11.2 As a result of a normalisation exercise, the following third normal form entities, which relate to staff training details, have been found.

> DEPT-3 (Dept-no, Dept-name, Manager)
>
> STAFF-3 (Staff-no, Staff-name, Dept-no)
>
> COURSE-3 (Course-no, Course-name)
>
> ATTENDANCE-3 (Course-no, Staff-no, Date, Grade)

Show how these entities would be represented in both a CODASYL and IMAGE logical data model. Indicate the data items held in each record (or IMAGE data set) and indicate the relationships between entities.

11.3 Figure 11.8 defines a library CODASYL logical data model. Suggest appropriate location mode, set order, and membership class to be used when implementing this model.

11.4 The entity HOTEL is defined as:

> HOTEL (Name, Town, No-of-beds, Manager)

This information relates to a chain of hotels, where the same hotel name is found in several towns. An IMAGE master data set can only have a single key data item. How could this entity be represented in an IMAGE logical data model?

12 Relational Database Models

12.1 Introduction

It is true to say that nearly all the current development work on databases involves relational database systems. Relational databases use a simple logical model which is further removed from the physical implementation than was the case for the network models examined in the previous chapter. A network database requires the user to navigate around the sets, as was illustrated in figure 11.10 for a sample CODASYL model. Often, in a relational database, the user merely defines what is required and the relational database decides how to achieve it. Because of this feature, relational databases are said to provide 'automatic navigation'.

Because the user is further removed from the actual physical database, the DBMS for a relational database has to do more work in translating from the logical to the physical model than would a network DBMS. It could be compared to the difference in compiling a program written in a high-level language to assembling a low-level program. The high-level program is far easier and faster to write than the low-level equivalent. However the resulting machine code from the low-level language is invariably faster, when executed, than that due to the high-level language. The same advantage, and disadvantage, applies to relational databases. Users find it easier to implement a relational database but the resulting physical model is slower in operation than that due to an equivalent network database. This slowness will be less of a problem as technology gives us faster, cheaper machines and at the same time software development costs continue to increase as a result of increasing staff salaries.

12.2 Relational database terminology

A new range of terminology has been introduced for relational database systems. Most of the initial work was performed by E. F. Codd whose normalisation technique we examined in chapter 10. James Martin suggests: "The enthusiasts of relational databases use a vocabulary different from conventional database wording and have a tendency to dress up a basically simple subject in confusing language." While C. J. Date, perhaps one such enthusiast, explains that new terms were necessary so they could be given a precise definition by Codd as he developed the relational database model.

The relational logical model uses two-dimensional tables to represent the database. If normalisation has been performed the resulting entities in third normal form are equivalent to a relational database logical model relation. For example, the entity STOCK-3 in chapter 10 library example was defined as

STOCK-3 (Branch-no, Title, No-of-copies)

This would be a relation in the relational logical model.

Figure 12.1 shows some possible entries for this relation.

Branch-no	Title	No-of-copies
3	Self Help	3
3	Car Care	2
3	Simple Sums	4
4	Self Help	3
4	Simple Sums	2
5	Car Care	1
5	Simple Sums	2
6	Self Help	1

Primary keys — (Branch-no, Title)

tuple — (4 Simple Sums 2)

attribute in defined domain

Figure 12.1   Relation:
STOCK-3 (Branch-no, Title, No-of-copies)

The rows of the relation (or table) are referred to as *tuples*. A tuple is equivalent to a record occurrence in a CODASYL system. A n-tuple consists of n attribute values. For the relation STOCK there are three attribute values, so figure 12.1 is an example of a 3-tuple.

The domain of an attribute is the set of possible values of an attribute for it. For example, the domain for the attribute No-of-copies in STOCK relation is all integers greater than zero.

The identifying attributes of an entity in our conceptual model are called the primary keys. For the relation STOCK the primary keys are Branch-no and Title.

Therefore, the relational database model for the library example would consist of three relations:

BRANCH (Branch-no, Branch-address)

STOCK (Branch-no, Title, No-of-copies)

BOOK (Title, Author, Publisher)

BRANCH is a 2-tuple relation with a primary key of Branch-no. STOCK is a

3-tuple relation with primary keys Branch-no and Title. BOOK is a 3-tuple relation with a primary key of Title.

There is no pre-defined order to the rows (or tuples) of a relation. Each tuple must be uniquely defined by its primary keys, one row cannot duplicate another. Each column contains values relating to the same attribute, and each cell can contain only a single value. Each attribute has a distinct name, and the order of attributes (or columns) is immaterial.

To summarise, the logical model of a relational database consists of a collection of two-dimensional tables called relations. If, as part of data analysis, normalisation has been performed, third normal form entities can be equated to the relations. A logical model based on simple tables represents all relationships implicitly. It is a far simpler model for a user to work with than is a network logical model.

12.3 Relational database operations

In order to manipulate the relations of a relational database, a range of new operations have been defined. Codd originally defined eight such relational algebraic operations. We will examine the six of these operations implemented in existing relational database systems. The operations naturally fall into two groups of three. The first group consists of traditional set operations (union, difference, intersection), while the second group (select, project, join) are special relational operations.

12.3.1 Union, difference, intersection

The three operations of union, difference and intersection are normally used to

(a) add a new tuple to a relation (union),
(b) remove tuples from a relation (difference),
(c) find tuples which are common to two separate relations defined over identical domains (intersection).

For example, the 3-tuple relation CAR is defined as:

CAR (Reg-no, Make, Colour)

Figure 12.2 shows some possible entries in this relation.

The operation

"CAR UNION (A555 LLV, MG, Blue)"

would produce the new relation of figure 12.3, that is, an extra tuple has been added.

Reg-no	Make	Colour
A 123 ABC	Austin	Red
B 533 XYZ	Rover	White
C 112 ADB	Ford	White
B 433 XXB	Peugeot	Black

Figure 12.2 CAR relation.

Reg-no	Make	Colour
A 123 ABC	Austin	Red
B 533 XYZ	Rover	White
C 112 ADB	Ford	White
B 443 XXB	Peugeot	Black
A 555 LLV	MG	Blue

Figure 12.3 CAR UNION (A555 LLV, MG, Blue).

The intersection of two relations *A* and *B*, *A* INTERSECT *B*, is the set of all tuples belonging to both *A* and *B*. For example, if a 3-tuple relation HIRER-CAR is as defined in figure 12.4a, then the result of

"CAR INTERSECT HIRER-CAR"

is as shown in figure 12.4b. Notice that the attributes of CAR and HIRER-CAR do not need to have the same names, but they must be defined over the same domains.

Reg	Manufacturer	Colour
A 123 ABC	Austin	Red
B 443 XXB	Peugeot	Black
C 345 KKF	Rover	Green

Reg-no	Make	Colour
A 123 ABC	Austin	Red
B 443 XXB	Peugeot	Black

(a)   (b)

Figure 12.4 (a) HIRER-CAR. (b) CAR INTERSECT HIRER-CAR.

Reg-no	Make	Colour
B 533 XYZ	Rover	White
C 112 ADB	Ford	White

Figure 12.5 CAR MINUS HIRER-CAR.

The difference of two relations A and B, A MINUS B, is the set of tuples belonging to A and not to B. For example

"CAR MINUS HIRER-CAR"

would give the relation shown in figure 12.5.

12.3.2 Select, project, join

These special relational operators provide more powerful means of manipulating a relational database.

The select operator allows a user to select from a relation those tuples which satisfy a condition. The format can be assumed to be:

SELECT relation-name-1 WHERE condition GIVING relation-name-2

For example

SELECT CAR WHERE Colour≠white GIVING CAR-A

would set up the relation CAR-A with the entries shown in figure 12.6.

Reg-no	Make	Colour
A123 ABC	Austin	Red
B443 XXB	Peugeot	Black

Figure 12.6   CAR-A relation.

Make	Colour
Austin	Red
Rover	White
Ford	White
Peugeot	Black

Figure 12.7   CAR-B relation.

The projection of a relation is that relation formed by extracting only the stated columns from the original relation, removing any redundant tuples. The format can be assumed to be:

PROJECT relation-name-1 OVER (attribute names) GIVING relation-name-2

For example

PROJECT CAR OVER (Make, Colour) GIVING CAR-B

would give the relation shown in figure 12.7. The project operator could simply be used to re-order the columns in a relation. For example

PROJECT CAR OVER (Colour, Make, Reg-no) GIVING CAR-R

would generate a relation CAR-R whose columns were in the reverse order to those of CAR.

The join is an operation on two relations. A common domain exists between the two relations and is used to link tuples of each relation giving one resultant relation which will contain data items from both original relations. A possible format for join is

> JOIN relation-name-1, relation-name-2 GIVING relation-name-3

For example, figure 12.8 shows three relations, REL1, and REL2 being joined to form REL3.

Employee #	Name	Dept #
5421	Smith	007
5533	Jones	010
5677	Brown	012
5794	White	007

REL1

Dept-code	Location
007	Manchester
010	Carlisle
012	York

REL2

Employee #	Name	Dept #	Location
5421	Smith	007	Manchester
5533	Jones	010	Carlisle
5677	Brown	012	York
5794	White	007	Manchester

REL3

Figure 12.8   JOIN REL1, REL2 GIVING REL3.

This form of the JOIN operation assumes the right-most column of the first relation is over the same domain as the left-most column of the second. If this is not the case, by means of the project operation, the relation's columns can be re-ordered. In practice, the JOIN operation is likely to include any necessary projection, so the format becomes:

> JOIN relation-name-1, relation-name-2 EQUATE attribute1,
> attribute2 GIVING relation-name-3

where attribute1 is an attribute of relation-name-1 and attribute2 is an attribute of relation-name-2.

With these six operators (union, difference, intersect, select, project, join) a user can perform all the necessary operations on his relational database. This approach to the manipulation of the database is based upon relational algebra. There is an alternative approach, using relational calculus. The major difference between these two approaches is that in relational calculus you state the properties of the data required rather than give an algorithm for obtaining it. With relational algebra it is necessary to express a sequence of operations to achieve the result. To the non-mathematical, relational calculus is difficult to comprehend, however many query languages are being developed which use relational calculus without exposing the user to the underlying concepts. The two database systems which we will examine in later sections of this chapter are both relational algebra orientated.

12.4 Translation of conceptual model to a logical relational model

As we have already seen, by looking at the library example, provided that the entities of the conceptual model have been normalised into 3NF, the process of converting to the logical model of a relational database is trivial. Each 3NF entity becomes a relation. The attributes repeated across the relations are necessary to provide the implicit linking of the relations.

12.5 Using relational operators to access a database

In section 11.2.3 we saw the outline of processing the library CODASYL model to find details of which libraries stocked copies of the text 'First Aid', and the number of copies each held. To give some comparison of using relational and network databases, we will perform the same operation on a library relational model. The library model consists of three relations:

BRANCH (Branch-no, Branch-address)

STOCK (Branch-no, Title, No-of-copies)

BOOK (Title, Author, Publisher)

For our purposes we only need to consider the relations BRANCH and STOCK.

1. Select those tuples of the relation STOCK which refer to the title 'First Aid'.

   SELECT STOCK WHERE Title="First Aid" GIVING REL1.

   Figure 12.9a shows a possible resultant relation REL1.
2. It is necessary to combine the relation REL1 with BRANCH to get the Branch-address. In order to use the simple form of JOIN it is necessary to re-order REL1 by:

   PROJECT REL1 OVER (Title, No-of-copies, Branch-no) GIVING REL2

   REL2 is shown in figure 12.9b.
3. Finally the relation REL2 and BRANCH can be combined using a JOIN operation:

   JOIN REL2, BRANCH GIVING REL3

   REL3 is shown in figure 12.9c. All necessary details are now held in REL3 and can be outputted.

Branch-no	Title	No-of-copies
1	First Aid	10
3	First Aid	5
4	First Aid	1
7	First Aid	6

(a)

Title	No-of-copies	Branch-no
First Aid	10	1
First Aid	5	3
First Aid	1	4
First Aid	6	7

(b)

Title	No-of-copies	Branch-no	Branch-address
First Aid	10	1	Long Lane
First Aid	5	3	High St
First Aid	1	4	Central Square
First Aid	6	7	East End

(c)

Figure 12.9   (a) REL1. (b) REL2. (c) REL3.

12.6 SQL/DS relational database

SQL/DS is the IBM relational database for use on mainframes using VM/CMS
and DOS/VSE operating systems. It is based on the language SQL (Structured
Query Language) developed by IBM, originally under the name SEQUEL,
which provides commands for the definition of and control of access to a
database and the manipulation of data within it.

A fuller discussion of SQL will be given in the next chapter. For the present
section, we note that there are four data manipulation statements - SELECT,
UPDATE, DELETE, INSERT - which are powerful enough to cover all the basic
operations of relational algebra. SELECT includes elements of 'select', 'project'
and 'join' as defined in section 12.3.2. We can 'select' tuples which satisfy a
given condition and 'project' only some of the attributes to the resulting
relation. Selecting tuples from more than one relation with appropriate conditions performs a 'join' operation. The other relational algebra operators,
'union', 'difference' and 'intersection', defined in section 12.3.1, are also
covered by the four data manipulation commands, making SQL a powerful
data manipulation language.

The relations of the relational model are implemented as tables in the database. SQL allows B-tree indexes to be defined for one or more columns within
the table which support fast access to the data through the column values. The
SELECT commands which retrieve the data do not say how it will be accessed,
but the system makes such decisions based on the available indexes.

IBM used the language SQL for both SQL/DS and DB2. More recently, SQL
has become a standard and been adopted by a number of other vendors for their
database systems, some being based on SQL directly and others providing an
SQL interface. INGRES, from Relational Technology Inc, Oracle from Oracle
Corp, Rdb/SQL from Digital, Informix/SQL from Informix Systems, formerly
Relational Database Systems, and dbaseIV from Ashton Tate are just some of

the products now using SQL. It is interesting to note that INGRES was based on a powerful language called QUEL but now provides an SQL interface as well, bringing it in line with other products. On the other hand, dbaseIV has been developed from earlier versions which were less powerful and did not use SQL. In the next section an overview of dbaseII is given to show how the more primitive version fitted the relational model. It can be contrasted with the features of SQL outlined here and expanded further in chapter 13.

12.7 dBase II database

The dBase II database was originally designed to operate on microcomputers using the CP/M operating system. An extended version of the package, dBase III has been developed for use on IBM PC compatible microcomputers. dBase II has become the microcomputer database standard by which all such new products are judged.

The model employed by dBase II is a two-dimensional table (that is, the relational model), although it uses the terms *record* and *field* to describe the structure when it is initially created (where record equates to tuple, and field equates to attribute in the relational model). The term *file* is used to describe a relation. A major limitation of dBase II is that only two of its 'files' can be used at any one time. The files are called Primary and Secondary.

dBase II has a wide range of commands, and normally operates on a single relation or dBase II file. This emphasis on single relation operation is reflected in the format of the commands used. It does, however, have a JOIN command of the form:

JOIN TO <file> FOR <exp> [FIELDS <list>]

This command creates a new database file by merging records of the Primary and Secondary files for which the 'FOR <exp>' evaluates as a logical True. The FIELDS list allows you to specify fields from both the Primary and Secondary files.

For example, if the Primary file was equivalent to REL1 of figure 12.8, and the Secondary file was REL2, to get REL3 the following dBase II commands would be required:

```
. use rel1          (open file REL1 as Primary)
. select secondary  (move to Secondary file area)
. use rel2          (open file REL2 as Secondary)
. select primary    (return to Primary file area)
. join to rel3 for Dept=Dept-code fields
                    employee, name, dept, location
```

dBase II performs this JOIN operation by accessing the first record in the Primary file and then reading through every record in the Secondary file. Each time the required match is found, a new record is written to the new file. Having read through all records in the Secondary file, the process is repeated for the second record of the Primary file. If there were 50 records in the Primary file and 100 records in the Secondary, in order to process the JOIN 50 × 100 (that is, 5000) records would be accessed. This operation is a combination of the merge and update of serial files which were examined in sections 2.6.2 and 2.6.3.

Any data file can be indexed by several files. Although the actual data file can be accessed via only one index file at a time, the other index files will be automatically updated as records are added, deleted and amended. For example, using the CAR relation of figure 12.3 we could set up three index files based on Reg-no, Make, and Colour by:

```
. use car                    (open file CAR.DBF)
. index on reg-no to regind   (set up REGIND.NDX,
                                    reg-no index)
. index on make to makind     (set up MAKIND.NDX,
                                    make index)
. index on colour to colind   (set up COLIND.NDX,
                                    colour index)
```

To specify that the data file CAR.DBF is to be accessed by means of the Reg-no, while maintaining the Make and Colour indexes, the following form of the USE command is employed:

```
                    . use car index regind, makind, colind
```

The first .NDX file defined after the word index is used when accessing the data file via any index-based command. All .NDX files defined in the USE command will be automatically updated as the data file changes.

While the JOIN command is a slow process, the FIND command, which uses the index files to access particular records, is by comparison rapid. Each .NDX file provides an index on a single field of the linked data file. The .NDX file uses a B-tree structure to provide rapid access to the data file.

12.8 Implementation considerations

A relational database manipulates 'tables' of data. The nature of this processing is sequentially orientated, relations being examined in the order in which they appear within a table. It is easier to process fixed-length records in such a manner. Relational systems which allow variable-length fields may place a reference number in the database record which points to the actual field held elsewhere.

Such a system would be appropriate to hold character data, and the database management system is likely to assign a reference number which reflects the collating sequence of such a character field. This allows the table to be resorted on the character field without having to access the actual variable-length fields indirectly.

The simplicity of relational operations hides their potentially high computer execution costs. Effective use of access structures, and the ability of the database management system to make effective use of those structures it has available to it, are the hallmarks of a good database management system. For example, consider the join operation between two relations. The simplistic approach is to compare each tuple in the first relation with every tuple in the second, as done by dBase II. This can be done by executing a nested loop where the outer loop takes a tuple from the first relation and compares it, in the inner loop, with all the tuples of the second relation. The number of steps involved in this process is the product of the relation sizes of the two relations.

If both relations (or files) are already in the appropriate sequence for the join operation, the process can be performed using a merging algorithm. In this case the number of steps involved will be the sum of the relation sizes of the two relations. If the relations are not already in order they can be pre-sorted before performing the join, or fetched, using either an index or hashed coding, as required.

12.9 Summary

A wide range of different relational database systems is available. Some are comparatively simple, such as dBase II, while others, such as SQL/DS, provide a powerful database management system. The major advantage to the user of relational databases is their comparatively simple logical model which leads to a simple user interface. An important data structure for use with relational systems are B-trees which allow fast access to large data files. Other relational database systems use different file structures; for example, several employ inverted files to provide rapid access to data.

Exercises

12.1 The following relations of a relational database model are used to keep data for a classical record club.

RECORD (Record-no, Orchestra, Title-code)

TITLE (Title-code, Composer, Title-name)

ORDER (Member-no, Month, Record-no)

MEMBER (Member-no, Name, Address)

The order relationships show that each member is expected to order one record each month.

(a) Draw a data model diagram showing the relations between the entities MEMBER, ORDER, RECORD and TITLE.

(b) The following series of commands, written in a simple relational command language, is applied to the relations.

> GET RECORD
>
> SELECT Orchestra = "Halle"
>
> PROJECT Record-no
>
> JOIN ORDER
>
> PROJECT Member-no
>
> JOIN MEMBER
>
> PRINT Name Address

The GET command brings a relation into the system's workspace, while the PRINT command displays the current contents of that workspace. Both SELECT and PROJECT perform their operations on the relation in the workspace. The JOIN operates on the relation in the workspace plus the relation defined in the JOIN command. The JOIN command allows a 'join' to 'either side' of a relation. There is also a KEEP command which copies the current contents of the workspace to a relation. For example, KEEP TEMP copies the contents of the workspace to a relation TEMP. What is the overall purpose of this routine?

(c) Do the existing relations allow for several orchestras to record the same work?

(d) Using commands of the same form as in part (b), write a series of commands which will identify the member-no and name of all members who have ordered a record of a work by the 'Composer' Mussorgsky.

12.2 In section 10.5.5 of chapter 10, the 3NF entities for a repeat prescription database for a medical practice were given. Using the relational operators introduced in section 12.3, state commands to produce the following:

(a) the names and addresses of all patients aged over 60;

(b) the names of all patients who had prescriptions on 20/1/91;

(c) the doctors who gave no prescriptions on 20/1/91 for patients who are aged under 40.

12.3 Show that the union operator is associative. That is

(A UNION B) UNION C

is equivalent to

A UNION (B UNION C) .

Is the difference operator associative?

13 SQL

SQL (Structured Query Language) was first developed by IBM and produced for SQL/DS and DB2 database management systems. It has since been adopted for numerous database packages, including dBase IV, Informix, Oracle and Ingres as a command language for creating and modifying databases, manipulating data within them and controlling user access. Although there is much similarity between the different implementations, there are a few differences. SQL has been adopted as an ISO standard, but unfortunately the standard has certain defects which have led most implementations to include extensions.

A comprehensive description of SQL is beyond the scope of this text. References to texts devoted to SQL are included in the Bibliography at the end of the book. In this chapter the main commands of SQL are introduced, using a simple example of a painting database for illustrations. The aim is to show the correspondence between the relational model and its implementation using SQL.

Throughout this text, the importance of considering a problem at a conceptual level before moving to an implementation has been stressed. With data structures, an abstract view was formed before the data representation was chosen, and before algorithms were designed to produce the operators on the data. With databases, the conceptual model is derived without regard to the exact implementation details, before an implementation is defined. We shall follow this principle by first describing the example problem and giving the conceptual data model for it. Then we shall turn to the SQL commands which are used to implement it. In many ways the SQL hides the implementation details from the user, making it close to the relational model, but there are a few areas of divergence, as we shall. First, a description of the example problem.

A regional centre runs a number of art galleries in which paintings are displayed. A simple database is to be set up holding details of the paintings, artists and galleries. It is to hold the cost of each painting, where it is held and details of the artist. Starting with a single entity with the required data;

> PAINTING (Title, artist name, initials, nationality,
> cost, gallery_name, gallery_address)

we can reduce it to a set of entities in 3NF using the normalisation process described earlier. The result is:

PAINTING (<u>Title</u>, <u>artist name</u>, cost, gallery_name)

GALLERY (<u>gallery name</u>, gallery_address)

ARTIST (<u>artist name</u>, initials, nationality).

The conceptual data model diagram for this is shown in figure 13.1.

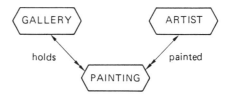

Figure 13.1 Conceptual model diagram for painting database.

In this model, it is assumed that the artist_name is the primary key for the artist entity, that gallery_name is that for the gallery entity, while the painting needs both the title and the artist name.

13.1 Creating the database, tables and indexes

In SQL, commands are given to define the structure of the database. Each database is identified by a name, which is given in a CREATE DATABASE command. The entities are defined as tables, with each attribute defined as a column in the table. A table, then, is given a name, and each attribute declared by giving it a column name and stating its type. Supported data types include:

- CHARACTER strings of stated length;
- INTEGER values;
- SMALLINT, a restricted range of integers;
- DECIMAL, which allow a fixed number of decimal places;
- FLOAT, for floating point values;
- MONEY, for monetary values;
- DATE, for dates.

Not all of these types are supported in the standard, nor in all implementations. In particular, MONEY and DATE are useful types, but can be implemented by other types if they are not available.

Each data type allows a certain set of possible values. There is also a possibility of a column having an unknown value called NULL. When a column is specified it is assumed to allow a null value unless the phrase NOT NULL is stated. NULL values should not be allowed on any column which forms part of the primary key of the table; nor should they be allowed on any column where a value must be given.

Figure 13.2 shows the SQL CREATE commands used to define the database. The name paintingdb is chosen for the database, while the tables are called painting, artist and gallery. The data type MONEY has been used, so is assumed to be supported by the implementation. The only column which allows a NULL value is nationality in the artist table. A NULL value in this column of a particular row would mean that the actual value is unknown.

```
CREATE DATABASE  paintingdb


CREATE TABLE  painting
   ( title          CHAR(20)   NOT NULL,
     artist_name    CHAR(20)   NOT NULL,
     cost           MONEY      NOT NULL,
     gallery_name   CHAR(15)   NOT NULL )

CREATE TABLE  gallery
   ( gallery_name   CHAR(15)   NOT NULL,
     gallery_add1   CHAR(20)   NOT NULL )

CREATE TABLE  artist
   ( artist_name    CHAR(20)   NOT NULL,
     initials       CHAR(4)    NOT NULL,
     nationality    CHAR(10)   )

CREATE UNIQUE INDEX paintingIDX ON painting
                ( title, artist_name )

CREATE UNIQUE INDEX galleryIDX ON gallery
                ( gallery_name )

CREATE UNIQUE INDEX artistIDX ON artist
                ( artist_name )
```

Figure 13.2 SQL commands to create the database.

Unique indexes are defined on the tables for the primary keys to prevent the system allowing rows in the table with duplicate values in the key. This is one area where the implementation is deficient. As Date has argued, the primary key ought to be a feature of the table and its integrity guaranteed by the system. Instead, an index is created for the key and is specified as unique, so that any attempt to add rows with the same key will be trapped as an error. For the gallery and artist tables, the key has just one component attribute, but the key for the painting table has two attributes and the index is created for the pair

(title, artist_name)

Indexes may be created for any number of columns in the table. Usually their purpose is to speed up access to the data using the column value. Each index must be given a name, although it is not used again unless it is to be deleted. The names used for the indexes in figure 13.2 are paintingIDX, galleryIDX and artistIDX.

13.2 Altering the database structure

A database structure can be modified in a number of ways. Extra tables can be added using the CREATE TABLE command, and extra indexes set up using CREATE INDEX or CREATE UNIQUE INDEX. Tables and indexes can be removed using the DROP commands:

DROP TABLE ⟨tablename⟩

and

DROP INDEX ⟨indexname⟩

while the whole database can be removed using the command:

DROP DATABASE ⟨databasename⟩

Dropping a table and creating it again with a modified definition is one way of making changes to a table. An ALTER command is sometimes provided to make such changes easier to perform. For example, a new column in the gallery table for a second address line would be added by the command:

ALTER TABLE gallery
ADD gallery_add2   CHAR(10)

The result is as if the extra column had been declared in the table along with the two already there, as shown in figure 13.3.

```
CREATE TABLE  gallery
  ( gallery_name     CHAR(15)   NOT NULL,
    gallery_add1     CHAR(20)   NOT NULL,
    gallery_add2     CHAR(10) )
```

Figure 13.3   Equivalent definition of ALTERed gallery table.

13.3 Adding, deleting and updating data

Once a database has been defined, data can be added to the tables, deleted from them, retrieved and updated. We shall examine addition, deletion and updating in this section, leaving retrieval for the following section.

13.3.1 Adding data

SQL provides an INSERT command to add a single row to a table. The command names the table and lists the values which form the row. NULL values may be specified in the value list for columns which allow them. For instance, the command

INSERT INTO gallery VALUES
('Spencer', 'Oldham', NULL)

would add the row with 'Spencer' as the gallery name, 'Oldham' as the gallery_add1 value, and NULL as the gallery_add2 value in the modified gallery table.

The command

INSERT INTO artist VALUES ('Lowry', 'LS', 'UK')

would add a row to the artist table with all column values defined.

The indexes associated with the tables are updated automatically when an insert command is performed. Any attempt to add a second row to the artist table with the name 'Lowry' would fail since the index is defined as UNIQUE. Of course, several rows may be added with different artist names which duplicate the values in the other columns. The only unique index defined on this table was for the artist name column, the primary key.

Several rows may be added by giving INSERT commands for each row. SQL does have other commands which permit more than one row to be added at once but we shall not discuss them here.

13.3.2 Deleting data

The DELETE command is used to remove rows from a table. In its simplest form it will remove all the rows, as in the command

DELETE FROM painting

which removes everything from the table painting. Usually the command is used with a WHERE clause to state the conditions used in choosing the rows to delete. The general format is then:

DELETE FROM ⟨tablename⟩ WHERE ⟨condition⟩

The condition can be a simple test on one column of the table, such as

artist_name = 'Lowry'

or a more complex condition, such as one combining two simple tests:

artist_name = 'Lowry' AND gallery_name = 'Spencer'

Only those rows in the table which satisfy the conditions in the WHERE clause are deleted. In the case of the command

> DELETE FROM painting WHERE
> artist_name = 'Lowry' AND gallery_name = 'Spencer'

the rows in the table painting corresponding to all the Lowry paintings held in the Spencer gallery are deleted.

The WHERE clause is used in the DELETE command and in other commands. The conditions can be quite complex, enabling the commands to be very selectively applied. They allow:

- AND, OR and NOT to be used as logical connectors;
- numerical and character data to be compared for:
  - equality and inequality = ⟨ ⟩
  - order relations ⟨ ⟨= ⟩ ⟩=
- columns to be tested for NULL value, such as:
  - nationality IS NULL
  - nationality IS NOT NULL
- pattern matching with wildcards on character data, such as:
  - gallery_name LIKE 'A%'
    - where % matches any character
- columns to be tested against sets of values, such as:
  - artist_name IN ('Lowry', 'Turner', 'Monet')
- subqueries (to be discussed in the next section).

13.3.3 Updating data

The command to alter the values in one or more columns of selected rows of a table is the UPDATE command. Again a WHERE clause is used to state the conditions for selecting the rows to be updated. Suppose that there is a gallery called 'Clayton' which holds several paintings. It is decided to move all the paintings costing more than 1000 from Clayton to Spencer. To reflect this change on the database, the rows in the painting table must be updated. The following command would make the necessary alterations.

> UPDATE painting
> SET gallery_name = 'Spencer'
> WHERE gallery_name = 'Clayton' AND cost > 1000

The SET clause used here names just the one column and gives its new value. All rows selected by the condition in the WHERE clause will have the gallery name changed, but their other column values will be left as they were.

It is possible to alter more than one column value in an UPDATE command. The SET clause can be followed by a list of columns, each with the new value associated with it. The command to alter the initials and nationality of the artist 'Monet' in the table is

UPDATE artist
SET   initials = 'C',
       nationality = 'French'
WHERE artist_name = 'Monet'.

13.4 Retrieving data from one table

The SQL SELECT statement is used to retrieve data from a table. It combines elements of the relational algebra operations via its various options, as we shall show.

13.4.1 Selection

In its simplest form a SELECT command will select all the data from the table, as in the example

SELECT * FROM painting

where the asterisk indicates that all the columns of the table are to be selected. Using a WHERE clause will restrict the rows which are selected to those satisfying the condition. For example:

SELECT * FROM painting
WHERE cost > 1000

In this form the SQL SELECT provides the function of the SELECT statement of relational algebra.

13.4.2 Projections

There is provision in the SQL SELECT to cover the PROJECT of relational algebra. The rows selected from a table can be projected onto a list of their columns by including the column list instead of the asterisk. The command

SELECT title, artist_name, gallery_name
FROM painting
WHERE cost > 1000

will produce a table with three columns: title, artist_name and gallery_name. This is obtained from the painting table by first retrieving the rows which satisfy the condition (cost > 1000), then projecting them onto the three columns. The cost values are omitted from the result. Figure 13.4 shows a sample table, while figure 13.5 shows the result of this SELECT command applied to it.

Title	artist_name	cost	gallery_name
Hawk	Bunter	1020	Spencer
Eiffel Tower	Clifford	925	Spencer
Golden Mile	Clifford	1428	Cheadle
1066	Bunter	2040	Spencer

Figure 13.4 A sample table.

Title	artist_name	gallery_name
Hawk	Bunter	Spencer
Golden Mile	Clifford	Cheadle
1066	Bunter	Spencer

Figure 13.5 Result of SELECT including a projection.

If the SELECT command specifies all the components of the primary key of the table as part of the column list, the resulting rows will also be identified by the key value. In particular, there will be no duplicate rows in the table. However, if the list of columns does not contain the whole of the key, there may be duplicate rows in the resulting table. An example is shown in figure 13.6, which is the result of applying the command

> SELECT gallery_name FROM painting
> WHERE cost > 1000

to the table of figure 13.4.

gallery_name
Spencer
Cheadle
Spencer

Figure 13.6 Result of a SELECT containing duplicate rows.

A variation of the SELECT command can be used to ensure that duplicate rows are removed from the result. It uses the DISTINCT keyword within the SELECT. The command

> SELECT DISTINCT gallery_name FROM painting
> WHERE cost > 1000

will remove all duplicate gallery names. When applied to the table of figure 13.4, it will produce the result as shown in figure 13.7.

Figure 13.7 Result of the SELECT DISTINCT command.

13.4.3 Ordering the rows

All of the SELECT commands mentioned above produce tables as their results with the rows appearing in the order in which they are found. It is possible to specify a particular order for the rows based on the selected column values by including an ORDER BY clause. For instance, the command

> SELECT DISTINCT gallery_name FROM painting
> WHERE cost > 1000
> ORDER BY gallery_name

will produce the rows in ascending order of gallery_name.

13.4.4 Subqueries

The WHERE clause can express a complex condition, as was mentioned in the previous section. It can be used in what is called a *subquery*. This makes use of another SELECT statement as part of the condition. For example, suppose we want to find all paintings by Austrian artists. To find the names of the artists who are Austrian, the following statement can be used:

> SELECT artist_name FROM artist
> WHERE nationality = 'Austrian'

This produces a table of artist names. It can be used as part of the WHERE condition in a SELECT statement which accesses the table painting:

> SELECT * FROM painting
> WHERE artist_name IN (SELECT artist_name
>   FROM artist
>   WHERE nationality = 'Austrian')

It extracts rows from the table painting where the artist name appears in the subquery. The IN operator is used to perform this test on the result of the subquery.

The IN operator and its negation NOT IN are not the only ones available for use with subqueries. ALL and ANY can be used with a relational operator such as $>=$ to test a column value against the result of a subquery. To select the titles of the most costly paintings, we could use the following command:

> SELECT title FROM painting
> WHERE cost $>=$ ALL
>   (SELECT cost FROM painting)

The subquery finds the costs of paintings. The selection condition chooses the rows from the table painting whose cost is greater or equal to all the values in the subquery. It thus selects the paintings which cost the most.

There are also the operators EXISTS and NOT EXISTS which are used to test whether a subquery contains any rows. In the above examples, the subquery has been a separate SELECT which can be performed once and its result used to test each row of the table of the outer SELECT. The subquery

> SELECT cost FROM painting

produces a table of costs, which is then used for each row in the table painting in the condition

> WHERE cost $>=$ ALL (. . .)

To use the EXISTS operator or its negation, the subquery must use conditions which refer to values in the rows of the outer select, so that the subquery itself depends on the particular row. It is known as a *correlated subquery*. As an example of their use, consider the query to find the names of all artists who have no painting at the Spencer gallery. The command

> SELECT artist_name FROM artist
> WHERE NOT EXISTS
> (SELECT * FROM painting
> WHERE gallery_name = 'Spencer'
> AND painting . artist_name = artist . artist_name)

will examine the rows of the artist table, and for each one will form the subquery consisting of all paintings from the Spencer gallery which are by that artist. Notice that the artist_name column appears in the two tables, and the names in the WHERE clause are qualified by the table names to identify which are being referenced. The value of artist . artist_name used in the condition of the subquery is that of the row of the artist table being examined. Thus the subquery is dependent on the particular row. If the subquery produces no entries, there are no paintings in the Spencer gallery for that artist and the artist row is selected for the main query statement. If the subquery produces one or more paintings, the artist row is rejected. The result is a table of artists with no painting in the Spencer gallery.

It is the ability to use subqueries that prompted the use of 'Structured' in the name of SQL. They provide a powerful way of expressing complex queries and cover the relational algebra operators of intersection and difference. SQL also provides a UNION operator to cover the equivalent operator in relational algebra.

13.5 Retrieval from more than one table

Data from more than one table can be retrieved by a SELECT statement which names the tables in its FROM clause. This incorporates the feature of the JOIN operator of relational algebra. The result is a table which combines rows from the named tables. The conditions in the command must define the connections between the tables, as well as any other selection criteria.

For example, to produce a table of painting titles, artist names and artist initials, the two tables painting and artist must be used. The SELECT command takes the form

```
SELECT title, artist . artist_name, initials
FROM    painting, artist
WHERE  painting . artist_name = artist . artist_name
```

Note that because the column artist_name is in both tables, it is necessary to qualify any reference to it in the command. It is not necessary to qualify the other column names by the table names, since they are unique. However, it is permitted.

The join of the painting and artist tables is done on the artist name column. This must be stated explicitly in the WHERE conditions for the join to work correctly. A common error is to omit this condition, which leads to incorrect results. The command

```
SELECT title, artist . artist_name, initials
FROM painting, artist
```

would list each painting title with every artist name and initials.

SELECT commands which join tables must have conditions in the WHERE clause to say how the tables are to be joined. Extra conditions may be stated to make further selections on the joined tables. In fact, SELECT statements which use subqueries, as discussed in the previous section, can be written alternatively as a SELECT joining the tables involved. The subquery example given there selected all paintings for artists whose nationality was Austrian. The following SELECT command produces the same result

```
SELECT painting. * FROM painting, artist
WHERE  painting . artist_name = artist . artist_name
   AND    nationality = 'Austrian'
```

The join links the painting and artist tables on the artist name and selects the rows which have nationality 'Austrian' before projecting onto the columns of the painting table, denoted by painting.*.

13.6 Grouped data

There are additional clauses in the SELECT command which allow it to deal with groups of data, rather than individual rows. The GROUP BY clause names one or more columns in the SELECT and causes the selected rows from the table to be brought into an intermediary 'table' containing the groups. Each group is one row in this 'table', and is formed from all the rows of the original table which have the same values for the GROUP BY columns. The final result of the SELECT is formed by projecting onto the selected columns.

As an example, consider the command:

> SELECT gallery_name FROM painting
> WHERE cost < 1000
> GROUP BY gallery_name

It will produce a list of gallery names which hold paintings whose cost is less than 1000. The GROUP BY clause causes all selected rows with the same gallery name to be grouped together to form one row in the intermediary 'table'. The projection onto the gallery_name is then performed, and the resulting table has no duplicate names. In effect, it is equivalent to a SELECT DISTINCT command.

An added advantage of grouping data is that there are standard functions which can be applied to groups, producing one value for the whole group. They include:

- SUM to sum the values in one column;
- AVG to calculate the average value in a column;
- MIN to find the minimum value in a column;
- MAX to find the maximum value in a column;
- COUNT to count the number of values in a column.

A function can be used to provide a new column in the resulting table of the SELECT by including it in the list of selected columns. For instance

> SELECT gallery_name, SUM(cost)
> FROM painting
> GROUP BY gallery_name

will produce a table of gallery names, each with the sum of the costs of all the paintings held there. The rows of the table painting are grouped by gallery name, so each group will have several individual costs within it. The SUM(cost) function will total these values for each group, calculating the sum associated with that gallery, and this value is used as a new column.

The functions can also be used in selection criteria for the groups. The WHERE clause applies a condition on the original rows used to form the groups. Further conditions are stated in a HAVING clause associated with the GROUP BY clause, and apply to the groups in the intermediary 'table'. The command

        SELECT gallery_name, AVG(cost)
        FROM painting
        WHERE cost > 500
        GROUP BY gallery_name
        HAVING COUNT (∗) > 5

will extract all the rows from the table painting which have a cost greater than 500, group together those with the same gallery name and select the groups with more than 5 individual rows. The asterisk as the argument to the COUNT function means that it is to count the number of rows in the group. The average cost of each group is calculated by the AVG(cost) function, and the values are used as a new column alongside the gallery name in the final result.

The order of applying the clauses in a SELECT should be noted. The rows are first extracted from the tables (FROM clause), then selected according to the WHERE condition, grouped using the GROUP BY clause and further selected on the HAVING condition. Finally, the projection onto the columns named in the SELECT is applied. If an ORDER BY clause is included, it is performed last of all.

13.7 Controlling user access

When a central database is used for a number of different users who have different requirements, it is essential to be able to tailor the data to the differing needs. In this selection, we shall look at two SQL features which provide these facilities: defining views to limit what is seen and granting access privileges to particular users.

13.7.1 Views

A view is a 'virtual table' obtained from the real tables by a SELECT command. Its main use is to tailor the data of a table to the needs of particular users, so that it omits details they are not interested in or should not see. In the example of the table painting, it may be desired to let most users see all the data except for the costs. A view can be created which omits the cost column, as follows:

        CREATE VIEW picture AS
            SELECT title, artist_name, gallery_name
            FROM painting

The view is given the name picture. To the users it looks just like a table, and can be treated as a table in most SQL commands. However, it is not a real table. Its data is obtained from the painting table by performing the SELECT command each time it is accessed. The SELECT command

SELECT * FROM picture WHERE gallery_name = 'Spencer'

uses the view as a table. It retrieves the data relating to the paintings in the Spencer gallery, but does not include the costs, since the virtual table is formed by ignoring the cost column and is not part of the view.

Views can be created for any SELECT statement, not just those which limit the columns of a table. A virtual table of all paintings held at the gallery Spencer would be created by the command:

CREATE VIEW Spencer_pic
AS SELECT * FROM painting
WHERE gallery_name = 'Spencer'

This would contain all four columns of the painting table, but only those rows relating to the gallery 'Spencer'.

Once a view has been created, its definition as a SELECT command will exist until a DROP VIEW command is performed. While it exists, it can be treated as a table, although it is only a virtual table and is only associated with real tables via its SELECT.

13.7.2 Granting privileges

Users of a database are identified by a user name. Individual users can be granted privileges which give them certain permissions to use the SQL commands on the database. Permissions may also be granted to all users by using the keyword PUBLIC instead of a user name.

The GRANT CONNECT command is available to define passwords for a list of users. It has the form

GRANT CONNECT TO ⟨user list⟩
IDENTIFIED BY ⟨passwords⟩

It can be used to set up the password for a new user or to alter the password of an existing user. Some implementations do not use this facility but rely on the operating system to deal with passwords for users.

Specific privileges to permit the use of SQL statements on a table (or view) are allocated by further GRANT commands. They have the form

GRANT ⟨privilege list⟩
ON ⟨table⟩
TO ⟨user list⟩

where ⟨table⟩ is the name of the table or view,

⟨user list⟩ is either a list of user names or the keyword PUBLIC, and
⟨privilege list⟩ is a list of keywords for the privileges

The privileges are any of the following:

- SELECT
- INSERT
- DELETE
- UPDATE ⟨column list⟩
- INDEX
- ALTER
- ALL

and permit use of the corresponding SQL command on the table. INDEX
permits indexes to be created and dropped, while ALL permits all commands.
UPDATE may have a list of columns, stating those which are allowed to be
updated. The default is to allow all columns to be updated.

As an example, the command

GRANT SELECT, UPDATE(cost, gallery_name)
ON painting
TO Codd, Date, Curran

would let all three named users (Codd, Date and Curran) use the SELECT
command on the table painting and UPDATE the columns cost and
gallery_name.

Since the privileges can be granted selectively, a considerable degree of
control of user access to the data is available. Being able to grant access to a
view and not the underlying table adds to this control, since the rows and
columns of a real table can be limited by the view.

13.8 Interactive and host-language access

The original development of SQL was as a language for interactive use. In this
mode, each command is performed as soon as it is entered. Values used in the
commands, such as in the conditions of a SELECT or the new values for an
UPDATE, are constants supplied by the user. Working interactively, the user
can examine the database and find out particular values by appropriate
SELECT commands, and then supply these values to further commands.

Any error in a command is reported to the user at the terminal as soon as it
is found and can be acted on immediately. The user responds to the results of
the commands as they occur.

A SELECT statement produces a table of values as its result. It is displayed
on the terminal screen as the command is performed, or perhaps sent to a
printer. The intention is always that the commands are performed one at a

time, with the results seen before the next command is supplied. There is no need in this mode to pass data between commands.

An alternative mode of use is from a program written in a host language, such as Pascal, C or COBOL. The language is extended to allow the SQL commands to be embedded in the program source code as if they were acceptable language statements. To accommodate this, there must be some variation to the form of the SQL statements and the host language. In particular, there must be ways of defining program variables to match the data types of the columns and rows of the database tables, so that the data can be passed between the program and the database. There is also a need for the program to be able to deal with the rows retrieved by a SELECT statement one by one, since the host programming language will have to deal with the rows one at a time inside a loop.

The concept of a CURSOR was introduced for this purpose. It is a pointer to a row in a table, enabling that row to be accessed. There is an associated command to move the cursor on to the next row and access it, so that the program can step through the rows one by one. The cursor is defined and linked to a particular SELECT statement. An OPEN CURSOR command is used to perform the SELECT and position the cursor in front of its first row. The FETCH command will then retrieve the data from the row into program variables and move the cursor ready to fetch the next row. This is normally done inside a loop which terminates when all the rows have been fetched. The CLOSE CURSOR command is used to release the cursor at the end.

Errors in SQL commands have to be detectable by the program. In particular, a loop which FETCHes rows from a SELECT table will terminate when the FETCH fails to find another row. A simple method of error detection is to have a variable SQLCODE, say, which is set by every SQL command. It is given a zero value for a successful operation, and a non-zero value for an error. The program can test the variable to see if any error has occurred.

An example of the use of SQL commands embedded in a Pascal-like language is given in figure 13.8. Its purpose is to list the titles and artists of all paintings held at a given gallery.

The example is not derived from any particular implementation, but illustrates the typical form of using cursors and embedded SQL. A number of assumptions have been made to keep the example simple. Firstly, it is assumed that the program does not have to name the database it is to use. Secondly, there is no difficulty in distinguishing the program variable names from names in the database, so the value of the variable gallery is used directly in the SQL statement. Thirdly, the READLN can read a whole string of characters (which is non-standard Pascal). Fourthly, the variable SQLCODE is predefined and used to return error codes for the commands and finally, the FETCH command can place the two selected columns into the fields of the record row_data without having to name them individually.

With these assumptions, the example concentrates on the important features of using embedded SQL. The data variables are declared to match the data

```
PROGRAM list_paintings (INPUT, OUTPUT);

(*** The program prompts for the name of a gallery ***)
(*** and uses it in an SQL command to SELECT all   ***)
(*** paintings at that gallery. The titles and     ***)
(*** artists are displayed                         ***)

TYPE   Titles   = PACKED ARRAY[1..30] OF CHAR;
       Names    = PACKED ARRAY[1..20] OF CHAR;
       Galleries= PACKED ARRAY[1..15] OF CHAR;

VAR    row_data = RECORD
                    title : Titles;
                    artist: Names
                    END;

       gallery : Galleries;

BEGIN
WRITELN('Which gallery do you require? ');
READLN( gallery);

WRITELN('Title                          Artist');
WRITELN;

DECLARE rowcur CURSOR FOR
        SELECT title, artist_name FROM painting
        WHERE gallery_name = gallery;

OPEN rowcur;
FETCH rowcur INTO row_data;

WHILE SQLCODE = 0 DO

   BEGIN
   WITH row_data DO
     WRITELN(title, artist);
   FETCH rowcur INTO row_data;
   END;

CLOSE rowcur;
END.
```

Figure 13.8 Sample program using embedded SQL.

types in the database. One variable is used to accept the gallery name at run time and is passed into the SQL command as part of its condition. A cursor, using the name rowcur, is declared for the select, and used to access the rows one by one, fetching them into the program variable row_data to be processed.

13.9 Criticism of SQL

SQL provides commands which cover the full range of operations needed on relational databases. There are, however, a number of criticisms of its current form, voiced notably by Date. A main objection is that it does not have a completely consistent structure to its syntax and semantics. There are several rules which restrict the use of commands in what seems like an *ad hoc* fashion. In fact, the restrictions are often included for implementation reasons, but without the implications being thought through to a more abstract level. They make it more difficult to learn the language properly, since many commands which seem logically correct fail because the rules disallow them.

The definition of the tables makes no reference to the primary keys. Although the primary key is a fundamental concept in the relational model, SQL does not support it directly. Unique indexes have to be set up to ensure the uniqueness of the key values.

Views are treated as tables in most situations, but because they are derived from an underlying SELECT, there are certain restrictions on their use, imposed for implementation reasons. NULL values are another feature which raise problems. Although they are very useful in practice, when they occur in columns involved in arithmetic operators it is not always clear what effect they should have on the results.

These weaknesses, among others, have been identified in SQL. However, the development of the language as a standard may well lead to future improvements which will answer these criticisms.

13.10 Summary

SQL is used on a wide range of relational databases and has been adopted as an international standard. It provides commands to create and modify database tables, but relies on unique indexes to maintain the primary keys.

Data manipulation statements include INSERT to add data to a table, DELETE to remove data and UPDATE to alter the value of one or more columns. Conditions stated in a WHERE clause are used as selection criteria in the DELETE and UPDATE commands.

Data retrieval is done by the SELECT command which also uses the WHERE clause to specify selection criteria. It is a very powerful statement covering the operations of relational algebra. In addition, data can be grouped on one or more columns and standard functions applied to the groups.

Virtual tables are defined as views which are used to tailor the data for particular users. Access to data is controlled by granting privileges to users, or PUBLIC, enabling the use of specified SQL commands on the table or view.

SQL can be used both interactively and by host language using commands embedded in the program source language. Certain changes are needed to accomplish this. Program variables must be able to match the types of data held in the database. There is a mechanism for the program to detect errors in SQL commands and cursors are used with SELECT statements to FETCH the rows one at a time into program variables for processing.

SQL is a powerful query language for relational databases, but has certain weaknesses at present, which may be addressed in future developments.

Exercises

13.1 Write the SQL statements to create the databases, tables and indexes for the two examples given in section 10.5.3 of chapter 10:
  (a) the library database;
  (b) the computer contracts database.

13.2 For the library database defined in exercise **13.1**, write SQL statements to produce the following:
  (a) the number of copies of the book 'First Aid' held by branch number 2;
  (b) the total number of copies of the book 'First Aid' held by all the branches;
  (c) the list, in branch number order, of all branches holding more than one copy of the book 'First Aid';
  (d) the list, in branch number order, of all branches holding any book written by 'A. Robertson';
  (e) the list, in branch number order, of all branches which hold no book by 'A. Robertson'.

13.3 For the computer contracts database defined in exercise **13.1**, write SQL statements to produce the following:
  (a) a list of all staff who have been assigned to some contract for the client number 602;
  (b) the list, in alphabetic order of staff name, of the name and number of all staff together with the number of contracts they are assigned to;
  (c) the list, in manager number order, showing the number and name of all managers together with the total estimated costs of the contracts that each one manages;
  (d) the client(s) associated with the contract(s) with the most expensive estimated cost.

13.4 For the library database defined in exercise **13.1**, write SQL commands to perform the following operations:
  (a) transfer all the books held at branch number 27 to branch 13;
  (b) delete all the stock for the books written by 'R. Hartley'.

13.5 A database of managers' salaries has just one entity:

  SALARY (manager, dept, grade, salary)

where the primary key is the attribute manager and the grade can be A, B or C. There are three usernames set up on the system, one for each of the three grades, called userA, userB and userC. UserA is allowed to see the salary details of managers of grades B and C. UserB is allowed to see salary details of managers of grade C, while userC cannot see any salary details, but can see everything else except the salary column. UserA and userB can also see these details.

(a) Define views for the restricted access to the table needed for the three users.

(b) State the SQL statements which will define the access rights to the views.

13.6 The database paintingdb defined in figure 13.2 has the table artist with the column nationality which allows NULL values. Following the example of figure 13.8, making any additional assumptions as necessary, outline a host-language program which finds all the rows of the artist table with a NULL value in the nationality column, displays them one by one at the terminal, and, for each row, allows the user to enter a new value for the nationality, and updates that row if a new value is given.

14 Fourth Generation Languages

14.1 What is a 4GL?

The name 'fourth generation language' or 4GL has become widely used in recent times, yet there is no precise definition of it. The difficulty is in saying exactly what features are expected in a 4GL, even though the notion of 'fourth generation' is easy to explain.

First generation computer languages are machine codes which use binary patterns for the instructions, data and addresses making up a program. It is possible to write any program in machine code, but it is extremely difficult to do so.

Second generation languages are assembly languages which use mnemonics for the instructions and names for the data. They also allow the structuring of program code into procedures. An assembler is used to translate the source code into equivalent machine code, and will report any errors it finds. Programming in assembly language is significantly easier than using machine code, and programs can be developed much faster. The changes make a significant improvement in programming productivity.

Third generation languages are the familiar high-level languages which were first introduced in the 1950s. They include FORTRAN, COBOL, Pascal and C, among many more. They differ from assembly languages in a number of ways. They are based on statements which refer to data and higher-level operations on the data, rather than basic machine instructions. Thus a calculation such as

$$a := b * c + d * e$$

is a single high-level statement, yet needs many individual low-level instructions to implement. Standard routines handle input and output, so a single statement

$$read(x, y)$$

is used instead of a number of low-level instructions. Later developments improved the facilities of high-level languages considerably by additional data and control structures.

Programming productivity is again significantly improved when compared with assembly languages. The details of the low-level code into which it is compiled is hidden from the programmer. There is some loss of flexibility associated with this since the programmer can use only the facilities provided in the language. Yet particular languages are of general application over a large range of problems. FORTRAN, for example, is suitable for scientific applications, since it supports REAL data and many standard mathematical functions needed in such applications. On the other hand, COBOL is not really suited to this area, but is appropriate for business data processing.

A common feature of third generation languages is that they are procedural. A program is written as a series of steps, which declare the data used and state how it is processed. The design requires the data to be identified, and algorithms to be implemented to perform the operations on the data. The programmer has to code the algorithms in terms of simple input/output and assignment statements and the three control structures: sequences, selections and iterations.

A fourth generation language is expected to rely largely on much higher-level components known as fourth generation tools. It provides the interface to using these tools. The programmer is not expected to define the steps a program needs to perform an operation, but instead defines parameters for the tools which use them to generate an application program. In this way it is non-procedural and differs markedly from third generation languages. It offers a significant increase in productivity, but at the cost of limiting the range of problem which can be tackled.

Fourth generation languages differ from each other in the types of interface that they provide, and the range of tools that they support. It is this which makes it difficult to define precisely what a 4GL is. If the range of problem which can be solved is extremely limited, it is difficult to justify calling it a programming language. But to increase the flexibility and allow a large application range, many more procedural aspects will be introduced, and it will be harder to justify calling it fourth generation.

A database management system, as we have seen, provides the ability to structure data, manipulate it and control access. A query language like SQL is a non-procedural language through which the data can be processed. However, its use interactively does not generate programs. Even if the SQL commands can be saved in a file and used again later, they still have to be used from an interpreter. Its use from a host language using embedded SQL loses much of the non-procedural aspects. To incorporate a DBMS within a 4GL, non-procedural tools must be provided to generate programs which can later be run independently to perform specific tasks on the data.

A full 4GL, in our view, should be based on a database management system and provide ways of generating programs using non-procedural methods wherever possible. It should be very easy to use, so that you do not have to be a professional programmer to use it and so that the programs can be generated significantly more easily than by using third generation languages. Procedural aspects may be included to add flexibility, but should be needed for only exceptional situations.

14.2 4GL environments and 4GL programs

Typically, a 4GL is used interactively with the tools available as options on a menu. We shall call this the 4GL environment. The tools require parameters to tailor them to specific tasks and the interface used to provide the parameters is the 4GL itself. The programs generated by the tools are the 4GL programs. The intention is that they will run independently of the 4GL environment, as stand-alone programs, but there will also be a way of running them from the environment during development.

Although the tools require parameters, there should be sensible defaults, so that the application developer does not have to supply a complete set of values. In particular, certain tools will require very little information to produce a default program. The defaults can be used as rough-and-ready solutions which are later modified to make them more acceptable, leading to the notion of prototyping which will be discussed later.

In the following sections, we shall look at some of the tools which are used within 4GLs. Reports and screen forms are the most important tools for handling data from a database, while the user interface for the programs is controlled by menus. Additional tools include graphics and spreadsheets. As we have already mentioned, 4GLs do vary considerably in the tools that they support and the features they provide for supplying parameters to them. Two packages, INGRES and Informix, will be used to illustrate the tools as they are discussed, and to highlight the different ways in which they are used. INGRES is a single package which has tools to generate applications which run inter-actively and to develop stand-alone programs. Informix uses a different market-ing strategy and has separate packages for interactive development (Informix/ SQL) and generating stand-alone programs (Informix/4GL).

14.3 Reports

A report is a formatted list of data values, usually extracted from a database. It can be produced on the screen, on a printer, or in certain circumstances on a disk file for later processing. Reports can vary considerably in their complexity. The simplest case is to list the data values in columns under suitable headings. More complex reports may have the data sorted into a specific order and separated into groups, with associated totals for chosen columns in each group, or it may go over several pages and require suitable heading and footing lines on each page.

As an example, consider the database table of paintings discussed in the previous chapter. It held the title, artist name, cost and gallery name of all the paintings. Figure 14.1 shows a simple report of data from the table. No specific order has been requested for the data, and so it is produced in a system-chosen order. The headings used for the columns are simply the names of the database

title	artist_name	cost	gallery_name
T1	A	1560	X
T2	B	120	X
T1	B	400	Y
T3	A	110	X
T3	C	2650	Y
T4	C	260	X
T5	A	1328	Y

Figure 14.1 Simple report of paintings.

Report of paintings held by galleries

Gallery	Title	Artist		Cost
X	T1	A		1560
	T2	B		120
	T3	A		110
	T4	C		260
			Total	2050
Y	T1	B		400
	T3	C		2650
	T5	A		1328
			Total	4378

Figure 14.2 A more complex report on the painting data.

columns. In contrast to this, the report shown in figure 14.2 has a page header as well as column headings. The data is sorted into ascending order of title within gallery name and grouped by the gallery. The total cost of the paintings in each gallery is printed after each group. This is a much more complex report, yet is typical of the kind of report needed in practice, and presents the information in a much better way.

Using a third generation language to develop such reports, a programmer would have to design the code structure to produce the individual lines of formatted data in the correct order, and cater for the breaks in the groups, correctly handling the group totals, and for the breaks into pages. As a fourth generation tool, a report generator will produce a report program without such structures having to be designed.

Both INGRES and Informix/SQL provide report generators which can generate the simple report similar to that of figure 14.1 as a default. All that is required is that the table name is supplied to the report generator and the report program will be produced automatically. The report programs are then run from the interactive environment.

Reports similar to that of figure 14.2 can be produced in INGRES, Informix/SQL and as a stand-alone program in the package Informix/4GL. Of course, parameters must be given to define the requirements of the report - in this case, the ordering of the rows, the grouping by gallery, the totalling of the cost column and the page header for the report. The three packages use different ways of specifying these details.

INGRES has a tool called RBF (Report by Forms) which is a menu item in the interactive environment and is the simplest way of stating the requirements for a report. It assumes that the default report specification for the table is the starting point which is edited by information derived from screen forms. The forms are displays shown on the screen which require values to be filled in. The title, column headings and formats are entered on one form. Different forms can be called up to supply additional details, gradually editing the specification into the desired result.

To specify a particular order for the rows of data and indicate the grouping, an Order Column form is used. A sample form is shown in figure 14.3. The columns of the table are listed and the developer can enter the columns used for sorting the data and whether ascending or descending order is wanted. The groups are indicated by control breaks on the column. In the figure, the column gallery_name is the major sort key having the value 1 in the sorting sequence, uses ascending order, and is a break field for the groups. The title is the secondary sort key having a value 2 in the sorting sequence column and again ascending order is required. The other columns are not used for sorting, as indicated by a value 0 in the sorting sequence.

Column name	Sequence	Direction	Break?
title	2	a	n
artist_name	0		
cost	0		
gallery_name	1	a	y

Figure 14.3   INGRES RBF form for Order Columns.

An RBF column options form for each of the columns is used to state additional information about that column. For the example report of figure 14.2, the value of the gallery_name column is printed only once for each group, not in every row, and a total is required for the cost column. The sample forms for the gallery_name and cost columns are shown in figures 14.4 and 14.5 respectively. In the former, the answer 'b' to the question 'When to print values' means 'breaks', that is at the start of each group. The question 'Selection criteria at run time' is to allow run-time requests for values in the column.

None is required in our case, so the answer 'n' is given. The options for aggregate functions are shown by placing x in the appropriate box. Since gallery_name is a character string, the arithmetic functions are not available options on its form. The only option wanted on the cost column is the Sum of the group costs.

```
Column name: gallery_name        Break Column? y
When to print values: b
Selection criteria at run time: n
Enter x to select Aggregation/Break combinations
Aggregate   Over Report   Over Breaks   Over Pages
Count
```

Figure 14.4 INGRES RBF column options form of gallery_name.

```
Column name: cost             Break column? n
Selection criteria at run time: n
Enter x to select Aggregation/Break combinations
Aggregate   Over Report    Over Breaks    Over Pages
Count
Sum                            x
Average
Minimum
Maximum
```

Figure 14.5 INGRES RBF column options form of cost.

The RBF column options forms for the other two columns would state that no selection criteria are needed and no aggregation functions required. The net result would be a report equivalent to that of figure 14.2, though not with exactly the same layout.

Specifying reports by filling in such forms is very easy to do, but there are limitations on how a report can be tailored by this method. To allow greater control of the layout of the report, INGRES does provide a separate method known as the report writer. We shall not discuss the details here, except to say that a text editor is used to enter report definition commands saying what the report should look like. This is the same approach as that used by Informix.

In the package Informix/SQL, a report is specified as lines of text in a file, entered using the standard editor. There are a number of sections, some of them optional, which define the report in a largely non-procedural way. Each begins with a keyword, contains one or more lines specifying requirements for that section and ends with the keyword END. The sections are:

- DATABASE section, to define the database being used;
- DEFINE section, to define any variables or parameters used;
- INPUT section, to allow run-time values to be given;
- OUTPUT section, to define output to a printer;
- SELECT section, where an SQL SELECT statement is used to select the required data;
- FORMAT section, where layout details are defined.

The DEFINE and INPUT sections are optional. If any run-time values are needed, variables must be declared for them in the DEFINE section. The INPUT section would contain the PROMPT commands to display a prompt message and accept the value into the variable. In the example of figure 14.2, no run-time values are needed, so both sections could be omitted.

By default, the report is printed on the terminal screen. The OUTPUT section is used to re-direct the output to a printer and define such details as the page length and required margins. A typical entry in the OUTPUT section is as follows:

```
OUTPUT
    REPORT TO PRINTER
    PAGE LENGTH 60
    TOP MARGIN 2
    LEFT MARGIN 8
END
```

The SELECT section contains the SQL needed to retrieve the required data from the database table. Although our example uses a simple SELECT, complex SELECT statements from one or more tables are possible here. Note that we shall use the ORDER BY clause on the SELECT to obtain the sequencing of the data required.

The FORMAT section is usually divided into a number of subsections dealing with different parts of the report. Each is introduced by a keyword phrase and contains a list of print steps. The subsections are:

- FIRST PAGE HEADER
- PAGE HEADER
- PAGE TRAILER
- BEFORE GROUP OF column
- AFTER GROUP OF column
- ON LAST ROW
- ON EVERY ROW

The header and trailer lines for the pages are stated in the subsections PAGE HEADER and PAGE TRAILER. Any special heading for the first page only is given in the FIRST PAGE HEADER subsection. The subsection BEFORE GROUP OF column is used to specify any group headings before the individual rows of the group are printed, while the AFTER GROUP OF column specifies such things as group total lines. The format of the lines for individual rows is given in the subsection ON EVERY ROW, while any overall totals are stated in the subsection ON LAST ROW.

This method of specifying a report is much more tedious than using the INGRES RBF forms, but has greater flexibility. A report specification for the report of figure 14.2 is given in figure 14.6. This time we do have sufficient control to make the layout exactly as expected.

```
DATABASE paintingdb END

SELECT * FROM painting ORDER BY gallery_name END

FORMAT

   PAGE HEADER
     PRINT "Report of paintings held by galleries"
     PRINT "======================================="
     SKIP 1 LINES
     PRINT "Gallery        Title        Artist        Cost"
     PRINT "--------       -----        ------        ----"

   ON EVERY ROW
     PRINT  column   4, gallery_name CLIPPED,
            column  18, title CLIPPED,
            column  28, artist_name CLIPPED,
            column  39, cost   USING "#####"

   AFTER GROUP OF gallery_name
     PRINT "                                              -----"
     PRINT  COLUMN 31, "Total ",
            GROUP TOTAL OF cost USING "#####"
     PRINT "                                              ====="
     SKIP 1 LINES
END
```

Figure 14.6   Report specification in Informix/SQL.

The PRINT statements are used in the subsections to define the layout of each line, for heading lines, data rows and total lines. Blank lines are created by the SKIP commands. Where more than one command appears in a subsection, they are performed in the sequence shown. The data values from the rows are identified by the column names of the table, while the total figure is calculated by the GROUP TOTAL OF cost function.

Additional features of the Informix/SQL report language permit local variables, assignments and control structures to make it even more flexible. They are more procedural features and consequently make it harder to produce the specification, but they are not needed for most reports.

The reports of INGRES and Informix/SQL are based on data from a database table. The approach adopted in Informix/4GL is to generalise this idea, so that a report is defined like a procedure with parameters through which individual row values are passed. The report procedure is used by a calling routine, a main program, say, which is responsible for obtaining the data and passing it to the report. The data may well come from a database table, but may come from any source. The purpose of the report is to define the structure of the output. Run-time parameters and the selection of the data must be done in the calling routine.

The report definition in Informix/4GL starts with the keyword REPORT followed by the report name and a list of parameters. It is made up of sections, each introduced by a keyword, and ends with END REPORT. The sections are:

- DEFINE section, to define variables and parameters;
- OUTPUT section, to define output on a printer;
- ORDER BY section, to define an ordering of the data;
- FORMAT section, to define the layout.

The FORMAT section is again made up of subsections. This time there can be no reference to database columns, but reference is made to the report parameters instead. Thus, you can group the data on particular parameters and use totals etc. on the groups. Figure 14.7 shows the definition of the report designed to produce the output as figure 14.2. It should be compared with the Informix/ SQL report of figure 14.6.

```
REPORT rep1 (t,a,c,g)

DEFINE  t  CHAR(20), a  CHAR(20), c  MONEY, g  CHAR(15)

ORDER BY g, t

FORMAT
  PAGE HEADER
    PRINT "Report of paintings held by galleries"
    PRINT "===================================="
    SKIP 1 LINES
    PRINT "Gallery          Title        Artist          Cost"
    PRINT "--------         -----        ------          ----"

  ON EVERY ROW
    PRINT   column 4, g CLIPPED, column 18, t CLIPPED,
        column 28, a CLIPPED, column 39, c USING "#####"

  AFTER GROUP OF g
    PRINT "                                          -----"
    PRINT   COLUMN 31 "Total ",
        GROUP SUM(c) USING "#####"
    PRINT "                                          ====="
    SKIP 1 LINES

END REPORT
```

Figure 14.7 Report definition in Informix/4GL.

The calling routine makes use of three statements to use the report. The first step is to use START REPORT rep1, which will identify the report by name and perform any initialisation steps. The individual data values are passed to the report by a command OUTPUT TO REPORT rep1 followed by the values, and the report is finally completed by using FINISH REPORT rep1. The OUTPUT TO REPORT is usually done inside a loop. The general structure is thus:

> START REPORT rep1
>   begin a loop
>
>   OUTPUT TO REPORT rep1 (values)
>
>   end loop
> FINISH REPORT rep1

An example of this is given in figure 14.8, where a main routine is defined to extract the data from the table painting and pass it to the report rep1. The database is defined outside the main routine to make it globally defined. The main program uses variables to match the data columns of the table painting. To access the rows one by one a cursor is defined associated with the SELECT statement on the table. The loop used is a FOREACH loop, which opens the cursor and fetches the rows one by one into the variables. The body of this loop passes the current row values to the report. When the loop is ended, the report is completed. Notice that the SELECT does not order the rows. The report definition itself contains the ORDER BY section to sort the rows into the correct order.

```
DATABASE paintingdb

MAIN

DEFINE   t CHAR(20),
         a CHAR(20),
         c MONEY,
         g CHAR(15)

DECLARE cur CURSOR FOR SELECT * FROM painting

START REPORT rep1

FOREACH cur INTO (t,a,c,g)
   OUTPUT TO REPORT rep1 (t,a,c,g)

END FOREACH

FINISH REPORT rep1

END MAIN
```

Figure 14.8 Informix/4GL Main routine using the report.

The main program is far more procedural than the report specifications in INGRES or Informix/SQL. The greater generality of the report routine is gained at the expense of introducing procedural aspects.

14.4 Screen forms

A screen form is a rectangular region which is used to display field values and text such as titles, instructions and field names. Forms can also be used for data input, where a field location is used to accept a value typed in by the user.

Both INGRES and Informix use screen forms. INGRES allows a form to extend beyond the size of the screen, so that only a portion is visible at a time. Informix/SQL caters for multiple screen forms, but Informix/4GL expects the form to fit on the screen. It will, however, let programs use more than one form, since they have full control over which form is on the screen at any time.

The most common use of a form is with a database table. The form displays the names of the table columns and has fields for the values. It can be used to accept values for the fields to form a new row to be added to the table, to display the values of an existing row, to accept values to update a row, or to accept values to form the basis of a query. Figure 14.9 shows a typical layout of a form associated with the table painting of the database paintingdb. The fields are shown within square brackets and indicate where values are entered or displayed.

```
Painting details
  title:   [                          ]
  artist:  [                          ]
  cost:    [             ]
  gallery: [             ]
```

Figure 14.9   Layout of screen form for table painting.

INGRES automatically generates a form for each table. It can be used as it is or edited using a special editor called VIFRED (VIsual FoRms EDitor). This is a powerful screen-based editor which is designed specially for forms. It lets the developer 'paint' the form on the screen, then save the final result.

Informix/SQL and Informix/4GL can both generate default forms for a table. Each form definition is a text file, so can be modified by a standard text editor. An example is given in figure 14.10. It names the database, and then has a number of lines defining the screen layout with the narrative and field locations shown. The lines appear between brackets { } following the keyword SCREEN. Each field contains a tag number, such as f001, which is defined later in the attributes section. The tables section names the table, whose columns are linked to the field tag numbers in the attributes section.

```
DATABASE paintingdb

SCREEN
{
  Painting details

  title:  [f001                      ]
  artist: [f002                      ]
  cost:   [f003   ]
  gallery:[f004                  ]
}

TABLES  painting

ATTRIBUTES
f001 = painting.title;
f002 = painting.artist_name;
f003 = painting.cost;
f004 = painting.gallery_name;
```

Figure 14.10 Informix form definition file.

INGRES and Informix/SQL provide options to use the forms to query the database. For example, the form of figure 14.9 might be displayed with the fields blank. The user enters a value in one of the columns, say the artist field, and this is used to query the database, searching for all rows in the table which have the given name in the artist_name column. The user can then work through the selected rows, displaying them on the form one by one. The values supplied are, in effect, used as part of the WHERE clause in a SELECT statement.

There are also options to use the form for adding new rows to the table, updating and deleting rows. In these cases the values are accepted into the fields and used as part of INSERT and UPDATE commands.

Informix/4GL makes use of forms from within a program to accept and display data. The program includes commands to OPEN a form, DISPLAY it on the screen, INPUT data from it into program variables, or DISPLAY data values on it from variables. Notice that the form is not used directly with the database table here, but has the fields matched to program variables. This follows the general theme in Informix/4GL of using a procedural program to control the high-level non-procedural features. The program can use SQL commands and cursors to process the database tables, with the values held in program variables. These same variables can be used with forms to interface with the user. An example of using a form for data input is shown in figure 14.11. The form is assumed to be called paint_form, with a definition as in figure 14.10.

The variable p_row is defined to be a record with the same structure as the rows of the table painting. The form is opened with an internal name p_form, and is then displayed on the screen. The data is accepted by the INPUT BY NAME command into the record p_row, and is then added to the table by the

```
DATABASE paintingdb

MAIN

DEFINE  p_row RECORD LIKE painting.*

OPEN FORM p_form FROM "paint_form"
DISPLAY FORM p_form

INPUT BY NAME p_row.*
INSERT INTO painting VALUES (p_row.*)

END MAIN
```

Figure 14.11 Informix/4GL program using a form for input.

SQL INSERT command. The program defines the steps which use the form and SQL commands to use the database.

Application programs using forms can be developed from INGRES with less recourse to procedural statements. Since their use is associated with menus, the topic of the next section, their discussion will be delayed until then.

There are a number of other features of forms which should be mentioned. Form fields can have additional attributes declared for them to control the format of the value displayed, to select such attributes as reverse video, to define validation criteria for the data entered or to declare them as display-only fields, among others. Forms can also be defined to show more than one row of a table at a time, to contain data from more than one table or to have fields not associated with columns of a database table. Forms provide a very flexible method of displaying and accepting values and it is extremely useful to have a tool to generate the code to process a form from a non-procedural description of its layout.

14.5 Menus

A menu is a display of a number of options from which the user makes a selection. It is a very simple way of accepting run-time options, yet is not easy to program in a third generation language. A fourth generation tool which allows a menu to be defined non-procedurally and automatically generates the code to handle it is a significant advantage. All three of the packages INGRES, Informix/SQL and Informix/4GL cater for menus.

In Informix/SQL a main menu can be defined for a database whose options can be to run reports, form queries, SQL procedures, external programs or display another submenu. Since the submenus can offer the same types of options, a hierarchy of menus can be defined. The menus are displayed on the full screen with the options highlighted. The definition of each menu is done by filling in a screen form. The top part of the form defines the menu name and the heading to be displayed. Beneath it the individual options of the menu are defined, one by one, each specifying the text to be displayed for the option, the type of option and the name of the report, form, SQL procedure, program or menu, depending on the type.

When the menu is run the main menu is displayed and the user selects the option required. If this is for a submenu, that submenu is displayed and the user makes a further choice. When the user selects 'exit' from a submenu, the higher-level menu is re-displayed.

Informix/4GL uses ring menus where the options are displayed along the top line of the screen, one of them highlighted, and the second line contains a short explanation of the highlighted option. Additional help on the option is obtained by typing CTRL/W. The remainder of the screen is available for other displays, such as screen forms, so the menu can stay on the screen while other actions occur. A typical menu is shown in figure 14.12 which is to select the level for the program run. It has three options: Artist, Gallery and Exit. The first option is highlighted and its associated text displayed on the line below. The highlight can be moved to the next option by the space bar or cursor movement keys. As it is moved, the text on the second line changes appropriately.

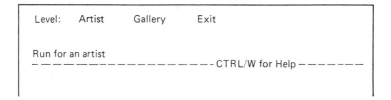

Figure 14.12   Informix/4GL ring menu.

The definition of the menu is by statements in the program. An example is given in figure 14.13. The help file to be used for the help messages is stated in an OPTIONS statement, while the menu is defined by a MENU statement. The menu is given a heading and each option is defined in a COMMAND line which gives the text to be shown in the option, its associated explanation and its help file entry number. Following each COMMAND line is a list of statements to be executed when the option is chosen. In this example, routines are called by the first two options, while the last clears the screen and stops the program. The routines for the options would have to be defined separately.

INGRES makes use of menus as part of its option called ABF (Applications by Forms). In fact it uses what are called *frames* which consist of a form and a menu. The form is displayed on the top part of the screen while the menu options are shown along the bottom. All applications generated by INGRES are based on frames. Indeed, the development environment and the tools are also

```
MAIN
  OPTIONS  HELP FILE "mainhelp"

  MENU "Level"
  COMMAND "Artist"  "Run for an artist" HELP 101
       CALL artistproc()

  COMMAND "Gallery" "Run for a gallery" HELP 102
       CALL galleryproc()

  COMMAND "Exit"  "Exit the program" HELP 103
       CLEAR SCREEN
       EXIT PROGRAM
  END MENU

END MAIN
```

Figure 14.13 Informix/4GL program using a menu.

based on them. An example frame is shown in figure 14.14. To create it the application developer would have to name the form used in it, the menu options, and for each option the actions to be taken. These actions are specified in a language called OSL (Operation Specification Language), which is a high-level procedural language. It has statements to manipulate the database, control the form, perform conditional tests, call procedures and call another frame. A hierarchy of frames can be built up, where the main frame has options which call subframes and so on. In this example, the Artist and Gallery options may have statements to use the form for the input of the name, and then call further frames.

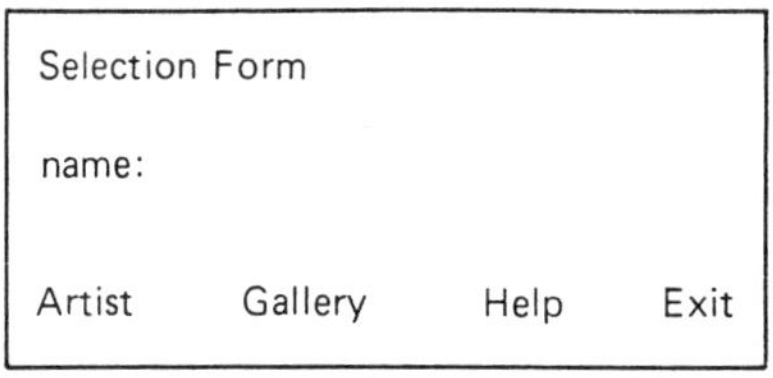

Figure 14.14 Example INGRES frame.

14.6 Additional tools

The fourth generation tools discussed in the previous sections are the most common ones found in 4GLs. There are additional tools which are useful in presenting and processing data derived from a database. In particular, we should mention business graphics and spreadsheets. INGRES supports a graphics tool, but not spreadsheets. Informix supports neither. Oracle, on the other hand does have a spreadsheet. It is likely that as the commercial 4GL packages are developed, additional tools will be added and integrated into the existing environment.

The graphics which INGRES provides will display data in line charts, scatter charts, pie charts or bar charts. Typical examples of line charts and bar charts are shown in figures 14.15 and 14.16. Line charts are often used to show trends, where the figures are associated with particular times, such as monthly sales figures. Scatter charts are similar, but instead of joining the points by line segments only the points are shown, or optionally a single line is fitted to the set of points. Bar charts and pie charts are used to display values from different groups, such as the quarterly sales figures. Pie charts can only show one set of figures, while bar charts are able to show several sets of figures on the same chart.

Figure 14.15   A line chart of monthly sales figures.

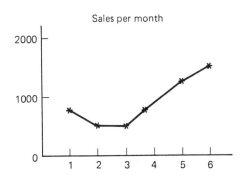

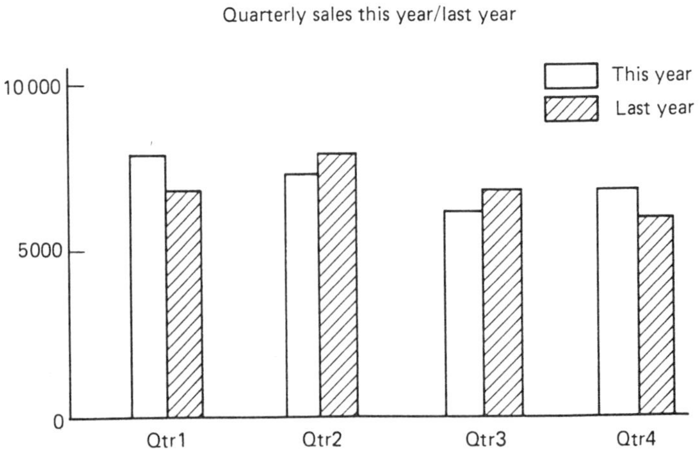

Figure 14.16   A bar chart comparing quarterly sales.

To design the required graph, a special editor called VIGRAPH is provided. The data used is derived from the database, so is assumed to be available in a table with two or three columns. For instance, the data for the bar chart in figure 14.16 would have one column for the labels (Qtr1, Qtr2, Qtr3, Qtr4), one column for the bar heights and one for the year. The whole table of data would have eight rows, two values for each quarter. The process of designing and producing the graphical display is considerably easier than trying to code it in a third generation language.

14.7 Prototyping

In many areas where products other than software are developed, prototypes are used to demonstrate viability and experiment with different options. A prototype is a cut-down version of the desired product, containing certain essential features, but not all. It is cheaper and easier to develop and provides feedback about the development at an early stage. From this feedback, potential problems can be identified early and decisions made about how best to solve them. The main problems are ironed out at the prototype stage and used in the design and implementation of the final product.

The same idea can be applied to software. A prototype version can be developed to provide feedback at an early stage so that problems may be identified and different options evaluated. Again the need is to develop the prototype quickly and at little cost, and 4GLs make this possible with their ability to generate default programs. The ease with which the defaults can be modified and tested is equally important in supporting prototypes.

There are two ways in which prototypes can be used. One is as a throw-away version whose purpose is to investigate certain features of the problem, so that the results can be used in the design of the full solution. The other is as part of an incremental development. The initial prototype is not thrown away, but is gradually modified until it becomes the final product.

For the throw-away versions, a clear understanding of what the prototype is attempting to show should be established before it is built. The results could be examined, and the prototype modified to try alternatives. When all the results are gathered, the decisions can be taken about the design of the final product.

It is not just the developers who are involved in evaluating a prototype. It is often shown to the user who requested the software to confirm that the requirements are properly understood. It helps to establish a better understanding of the problem by both the developers and the user, so that both see more clearly what the product is to do.

For the incremental versions, a proper control of the development is essential. There is a risk that the development will be done without careful design, but by hacking the initial ideas into something which seems to work. When prototype versions are easy to produce and modify, there is a tendency for this approach to be encouraged, but it should be kept in check. The structure of the whole solution should be considered at each stage so that the changes suggested can be properly integrated into the existing solution.

There are many occasions in practice where the precise requirements of a project are not known at the outset, but are changed or clarified as the development is under way. In such situations an incremental approach is needed. A prototype is used to give feedback at as early a stage as possible, allowing the decisions on the requirements to be made.

A 4GL interactive environment gives a simple way of producing prototypes, testing them, modifying them and producing the final product. INGRES is a single integrated package which supports all of these steps. Programs can be developed under the interactive environment, then made into a stand-alone program when the final version has been produced. Informix, on the other hand, is in two packages. Informix/SQL is good for developing prototypes quickly to run under its interactive system, but does not produce separate programs, and has limited features. The other package, Informix/4GL, does result in stand-alone programs, and has powerful features for tailoring the programs to the precise needs. It is highly suitable for producing the final product, but does not produce defaults as easily. To support prototyping, the two Informix packages should be used together, with initial prototypes produced in Informix/SQL, then re-developed under Informix/4GL.

14.8 Summary

Fourth generation languages promise a significant increase in programming productivity over third generation languages. They have fourth generation tools which rely heavily on non-procedural definitions of requirements, and generate the code to implement them automatically.

There are differences between the various commercial 4GL packages in the tools they support and the way they are used. A full 4GL is based on a database management system and provides tools to define processing of the data in a non-procedural way. To increase the flexibility, procedural aspects are also used.

Two packages, INGRES and Informix, were used to illustrate the tools. INGRES is a single package while Informix is marketed in two separate packages, Informix/SQL and Informix/4GL. They show the different ways of providing interfaces to the tools and how this affects the ease of use and the flexibility. In general, to gain greater flexibility, more procedural aspects have to be used.

Reports and screen forms are the most important tools for handling data in a database. Simple defaults can be produced for the data held in one table, or tailored reports and forms can be defined for data possibly derived from more than one table.

Menus can be defined non-procedurally, to provide a simple but effective interface for the application user. Informix treats menus and forms separately, while INGRES uses the concept of a frame which combines a form and a menu as a central building block for its applications.

Additional features include business graphics and spreadsheets. INGRES supports graphics, but not spreadsheets, while Informix supports neither. Spreadsheets are supported in other 4GLs such as Oracle.

The ability to generate and modify programs quickly in a 4GL allows prototypes to be built. They can be used either as throw-away versions or as part of incremental development. They are very useful for obtaining feedback for the user and developer about the proposed project at an early stage, so that a clearer understanding can be gained and better design decisions made.

Exercises

14.1 A database of sales by a company's reps has one entity:

> SALES (<u>rep</u>, area, no-of-sales, sales-value)

where rep is a 10-character name, and area is a 1-character code.
A report is required which lists the sales details by area, with the total number of sales and sales value printed after each area and at the end of the report.
(a) Define the report in Informix/SQL assuming the final totals are produced by functions with the format

> TOTAL OF ⟨column⟩

written in the ON LAST ROW section.
(b) Outline the form entries used by INGRES to define this report.
(c) How would the report in Informix/4GL differ from the answer in part (a)?

14.2 For the artist table in the paintingdb database:
(a) show the layout of the default screen form in Informix;
(b) give the Informix form definition file for this form;
(c) how would you alter the form definition to make the initials appear before the artist name on the form?
(d) write the Informix/4GL program to use this form to input data into the artist table.

14.3 A definition of a menu was shown in figure 14.13.
(a) What would appear on line 2 when the Gallery option is highlighted?
(b) What is the significance of the help file options?
(c) If the artistproc procedure displays a form and alters the menu to show the options:

Add Retrieve Return

write the menu command that this procedure would use, assuming the help file is called arthelp.

Appendix A: Review of Data Types in Pascal

Scalar data types

There are four simple scalar data types in Pascal: INTEGER, REAL, CHAR and BOOLEAN.

Arithmetic operators +, −, * are defined for real and integers data types, with the division operators MOD, DIV (integer division) and / (real division). Standard functions such as SIN, COS, EXP are also provided.

Variables of type CHAR hold a single character value, while Booleans store a value TRUE or FALSE.

Comparison operators allow variables or expressions of compatible types to be compared (for =, < >, <, etc.) to yield a Boolean result. Boolean operators AND, OR, NOT are available to test more complex conditions.

The assignment statement can be used to evaluate an expression involving variables, constants and operators, and store the result in a variable of the appropriate type. Type-checking is performed on all operations and assignments, ensuring that only compatible data types are used. Integer expressions can be assigned to integer or real variables, but real expressions can be assigned only to real variables. Boolean expressions can be assigned to Boolean variables while character expressions can be assigned to CHAR variables.

Defining new scalar data types

The simple data types can be used to build new data types. In Pascal there are the subrange and enumeration types.

(a) Subranges

A new data type which is a subrange of integers or characters can be defined. For example,

```
TYPE

    posinteger = 0 . . maxint; (* positive integers *)
    capitals    = 'A' . . 'Z'; (* capital letters *)
```

249

VAR

(* declare variables of these types *)
i: posinteger;
cap : capitals;

declares the variable i to be a positive integer which is a subrange of the INTEGER data type, and the variable cap to be a capital letter which is a subrange of the data type CHAR.

The main advantages of using subranges are that they show clearly the intended values of the variables and permit more error detection. The internal representation of the subrange may be the same as for the full range, or it may differ. Data items of these types can be used in operations with values from the full range, and any necessary conversions will be done automatically.

(b) Enumeration types

An enumeration type is a list of names of constants which a variable of that type can take. For example, the declaration

TYPE transactionType = (addition, deletion, enquiry, update);

sets up four constants called addition, deletion, enquiry and update. Variables of this type can take any one of these four values.

(c) Ordinal types

The data types INTEGER, CHAR and enumeration types all share the property that there is an underlying order to the values which allows you to determine the successor or predecessor of any particular value. This property is not shared by the data type REAL. The types sharing the property are called ordinal types and are the only ones which can be used as the base type for subranges. Although there may be situations when you would like to use a subrange of REAL values, such a type cannot be defined in Pascal.

Structured data types

Pascal provides three structures to enable data values to be organised: sets, arrays and records.

Sets

In Pascal, a type can be defined as a set of another base type. For instance (assuming the declarations as above), in the statement

IF cap IN ['A' .. 'C' , 'L'] THEN . . .

the set constant ['A' . . 'C' , 'L'] is used in the test to see whether cap is any one of the values 'A', 'B', 'C' or 'L'.

The similar statement

IF i IN ['A' . . 'C' , 'L'] THEN . . .

would be trapped as an error because the variable i is not of the correct type to be compared with the characters in the set.

The base type of the set must be a subrange of an ordinal type, and may be restricted in the number of elements allowed.

Set variables can be declared, and the operators +, * and − used for set union, intersection and difference. Figure A.1 shows a set variable ACCEPTED being declared as a set whose base type is the letters A to Z. It is used in the code to build up the set of characters found on one line of text.

```
(* declarations *)
VAR Accepted : SET OF 'A'..'Z';

(* code *)
Accepted:= [];  (* initialise to empty set *)

WHILE NOT EOLN DO
   BEGIN
   READ(ch);
   IF ch IN ['A'..'Z'] THEN
      BEGIN
      IF ch IN Accepted
      THEN
         WRITELN(' Character already given ')
      ELSE
         BEGIN
         Accepted:=Accepted + [ch];
                      (* add ch to Accepted set *)
         WRITELN(' New character accepted')
         END;
      END
   END;
```

Figure A.1 Set variable declaration and use.

One-dimensional arrays

A one-dimensional array is a block of elements, all of the same base type, each value being identified by a subscript value. The subscript range must be from an ordinal type such as 1 . . 20, −60 . . 43, or 'A' . . 'Z', and is specified as part of the array declaration.

In some situations the array values will be processed element by element. On occasions the whole array will be processed without specifying the elements individually. Pascal allows an array to be copied to another array of exactly the same type using a single assignment statement:

a:=b; (* a and b are arrays of the same type *)
      (* that is, same base type and same subscript range *)

Although it may seem reasonable to compare two arrays of the same type for equality or inequality, this can only be done element by element in Pascal.

Packed arrays of characters

Strings of characters: abstract and concrete views

In abstract, a string of characters is a single data item used to represent a name, address, etc. These data items can sometimes be of varying length. Languages like BASIC and, to some extent, COBOL directly support string data items, but Pascal does not.

To handle strings of characters in Pascal, the data type used is a PACKED ARRAY with base type CHAR. For instance, to hold a string of up to 20 characters, you could declare a type:

TYPE

String20 = PACKED ARRAY [1 .. 20] OF CHAR;

The attribute PACKED is specified to ensure the correct form of internal storage is used.

Processing strings

Individual characters can be accessed as elements of such an array, while the full string can be processed by referring to the array name without subscripts. With the declarations

VAR name1, name2 : String20;

the assignment

name1:=name2;

can be used.

Furthermore, comparisons between strings are allowed, testing for equality, inequality, or any of the order relations which check for alphabetic order, as in

IF (name1 = name2) THEN . . .

IF (name1 < name2) THEN . . .

A major limitation in this implementation is the requirement that the strings be declared of a fixed size and that, for assignments and comparisons, the variables must be of exactly the same type. Little help is provided in handling strings of different lengths. The only remedies are either to pad all strings out to the same length, thereby wasting space, or to process the strings element by element which increases processing times. Conformant array parameters do allow you to write procedures which can process PACKED arrays of CHAR of varying lengths, thus providing a little help with this problem.

Several compilers for Pascal provide extensions to the language to help in this area. Using these extensions makes string processing much simpler, but the price is a loss of portability.

Higher-dimensional arrays

Representing matrices

A two-dimensional array (or matrix) is a grid of elements of the same base type. Each element needs two subscripts to identify it. Often these two subscripts can be regarded as the element's row and column position. We shall treat the first subscript as the row position, the second as the column position.

M

M[1, 1]	M[1, 2]	M[1, 3]
M[2, 1]	M[2, 2]	M[2, 3]
M[3, 1]	. . .	. . .
. . .	. . .	. . .

Processing matrices

As with the one-dimensional case, the array can be processed element by element, or treated as a single unit in an assignment. In addition, it is possible to consider rows or columns as vectors in their own right. In Pascal, you can treat each row as a vector and perform assignments to vectors of the same type. But columns cannot be treated similarly. Figure A.2 shows an example where two rows of a matrix are interchanged. It illustrates how Pascal regards a two-dimensional array as a one-dimensional array of rows which are themselves vectors.

Representing higher-dimensional arrays

Arrays of three dimensions may be defined as a one-dimensional array of matrices, and so on for higher dimensions.

```
(* declarations *)

TYPE
      vector = ARRAY [1..3] OF REAL;
      matrix = ARRAY [1..6] OF vector;

VAR
      M: matrix;    (* 6 rows of 3 entries *)
      c: vector;    (* vector of 3 entries *)
      i,j : 1..6;   (* subscript for rows *)

BEGIN
  .
  .
  .
(* swap row i with row j *)

c:= M[i];          (* save row i *)
M[i]:= M[j];       (* copy row j to row i *)
M[j]:= c;          (* copy original row i to row j *)
  .
  .
```

Figure A.2 Declaration of arrays.

Records

Abstract view

Often a collection of data items, usually containing different values about the same entity, are grouped together into a single unit called a record. The individual items of data are called the fields of the record. For example, customer details may be held in a record containing:

account no.	name	address	tel. no.

The individual fields may be of the same or different types. Some processing will look at the fields individually, while other processing will treat the whole record as a unit.

Concrete representation and processing

In Pascal, the record's fields are defined in its type declaration, while the records themselves are declared as variables of that type. In figure A.3 the records are called CustomerA, CustomerB and CustomerC. The individual fields are referred to as CustomerA.account, CustomerB.account, etc. The WITH statement is used to allow one record name to qualify several references to its fields without its name having to be written in front of each field name.

Where the whole record is accessed as a unit, only the record name is specified.

```
TYPE
        (* declare record type *)

CustomerDetail =
                RECORD
                account : INTEGER;
                name    : PACKED ARRAY [1..15] OF CHAR;
                address : PACKED ARRAY [1..40] OF CHAR;
                telNo   : PACKED ARRAY [1..12] OF CHAR
                END;

VAR

    (* declare three records of this type *)
    CustomerA, CustomerB, CustomerC : CustomerDetail;

BEGIN

    (* read values into fields of CustomerA record
                                    one by one *)
WITH CustomerA DO
    READLN( account, name, address, telNo);
    (* repeat for CustomerB *)
WITH CustomerB DO
    READLN( account, name, address, telNo);

(* compare account fields of records *)
IF (CustomerA.account = CustomerB.account) THEN
    WRITELN(' Same account numbers ')
ELSE
IF (CustomerA.account > CustomerB.account) THEN
    BEGIN (* swap the records *)
    CustomerC := CustomerA;
                            (* save first record *)
    CustomerA := CustomerB;
                    (* copy second record to first *)
    CustomerB := CustomerC;
            (* copy original first record to second *)
    END;
.
.
.
END.
```

Figure A.3 Declaring and processing records.

Appendix B: Text Files in Pascal

A text file is a serial file whose basic component type is character.

Data in a text file is usually arranged in lines, corresponding to the lines on a screen display or a printed page. The end of each line is marked by one or more special characters. For example, the two characters CR (carriage return) and LF (linefeed) could be used. Sent to a screen display they would cause the cursor to be positioned at the start of the next line. On a disc or tape file these characters are stored as components of the file (figure B.1).

Figure B.1 End-of-line markers.

The exact format of the end-of-line markers varies from machine to machine. Programming language features can isolate the programmer from these details by providing ways of writing end-of-line markers, detecting them and skipping over them. The programmer must be aware that special markers are there, but need not know exactly what the markers are.

In Pascal, the two files INPUT and OUTPUT are pre-declared text files. Other text files can be declared as variables of the file type TEXT, as in

VAR reportFile : TEXT;

Some Pascal implementations require the names of all files used in a program to be declared in the program header. A program using three files could use a program header statement of the form

PROGRAM Sales (INPUT,OUTPUT,reportFile);

The file variable name is used inside the program to identify the file. The correspondence between this name and the actual file is done by the operating system in a manner which depends on the system.

A file being used for input must be initialised by the RESET statement, while one being used for output must be initialised by the REWRITE statement. The two pre-declared files are already initialised. The procedures READ and WRITE can be used to process text files. The first parameter to these procedures is the file variable. If omitted, the file INPUT or OUTPUT is assumed.

```
(* declarations *)
VAR   infile, outfile : TEXT;
      ch : CHAR;
       x : REAL;
       i : INTEGER;

(* program body *)
BEGIN

RESET (infile);
          (* prepare file for input *)
REWRITE (outfile);
          (* prepare file for output *)

READ (infile, ch);
          (* read a single character *)
READ (infile, x,i);
      (* read a real value and an integer *)

WRITE (outfile, 'Character was ',ch,
       ' and numbers were ',x,' and ',i);
      (* write text and values to output file *)
```

Figure B.2 Reading and writing values on text files.

Figure B.2 shows how individual characters, real and integer values can be handled by the READ and WRITE procedures. Real and integer data types are said to be compatible with the file component type CHAR. Only values of compatible data types can be read from or written to a text file. The appropriate conversions are carried out as part of the READ or WRITE procedures.

The two Boolean functions, EOF and EOLN, can be used to detect the end-of-file and end-of-line conditions. They return a value TRUE when the file is positioned at the end of file or end of a line. READLN will skip over an end-of-line marker, skipping any preceding characters still unread, while WRITELN will write an end-of-line marker to the output file.

Figure B.3 is an example program which processes a text file character by character. It reads an input text file and copies it to an output text file, including line numbers on each line. Note that although the example uses its own file variable names, the files INPUT and OUTPUT could have been used instead.

```
PROGRAM addnumbers (infile, outfile);
CONST blank=' ';
VAR   infile, outfile : TEXT;
      ch : CHAR;
      lineno : INTEGER;

      (* program to copy a text file and incorporate
                    line numbers *)

BEGIN
RESET (infile);      (* prepare file for input *)
REWRITE (outfile);   (* prepare file for output *)

lineno:=0;

WHILE NOT EOF(infile) DO
    BEGIN
    lineno:=lineno+1;
    WRITE (outfile, lineno:6, blank);
    WHILE (NOT EOF(infile)) AND
                            (NOT EOLN (infile)) DO
        BEGIN
        READ (infile, ch);
                        (* read next character and *)
        WRITE (outfile, ch);
                        (* write it to outfile *)
        END;
    READLN (infile);
                        (* skip end of line marker *)
    WRITELN (outfile);
            (* write end of line marker to output *)
    END;
END.
```

Figure B.3 Processing text files character by character.

Bibliography

In this section, we present a selective bibliography for references to the topics covered in this book, and to material recommended for further reading.

(1) Pascal language texts

The following texts cover the features of Pascal including pointer data types and recursion.

W. Findlay, and D. A. Watt, *Pascal, An Introduction to Methodical Programming*, 2nd edition, Computer Science Press, 1981.

D. M. Munro, *A Crash Course in Pascal*, Edward Arnold, 1985.

I. R. Wilson and A. M. Addyman, *A Practical Introduction to Pascal – with BS6192*, 2nd edition, Macmillan Computer Science Series, 1982.

(2) Data structures

The references on data structures include texts which give a fuller exposition of the material covered in this text, including the topic of AVL-trees referred to in chapter 6.

A. V. Aho, J. E. Hopcroft and J. D. Ullman, *Data Structures and Algorithms*, Addison-Wesley, 1983.

E. Horowitz and S. Sahni, *Fundamentals of Data Structures*, Computer Science Press, 1975.

D. E. Knuth, *The Art of Computer Programming, Vol. 1: Fundamental Algorithms* 2nd edition, Addison-Wesley, 1973.

D. Kruse, *Data Structures and Program Design*, Prentice-Hall, 1984.

A. M. Tenenbaum and M. J. Augenstein, *Data Structures using Pascal*, 2nd edition, Prentice-Hall, 1986.

N. Wirth, *Algorithms + Data Structures = Programs*, Prentice-Hall, 1976.

(3) Program design

Many of the above references cover the program design aspects of data structures. In addition, we give three other references.

D. Coleman, *A Structured Programming Approach to Data*, Macmillan Computer Science Series, 1978.

M. Jackson, *Principles of Program Design*, Academic Press, 1975.

M. J. King and J. P. Pardoe, *Program Design Using JSP – A Practical Introduction*, Macmillan Computer Science Series, 1985.

(4) Abstract data types and formal specifications

Texts dealing with formal specifications and the role of abstract data types using different approaches are:

M. Azmoodeh, *Abstract Data Types and Algorithms*, Macmillan Computer Science Series, 1987.

C. B. Jones, *Software Development, A Rigorous Approach*, Prentice-Hall, 1980.

J. J. Martin, *Data Types and Data Structures*, Prentice-Hall, 1986.

The language OBJ referred to in chapter 8 is specified in

J. Goguen, 'Parameterized Programming', *IEEE Transactions on Software Engineering*, Vol. SE-10, No. 5.

(5) Databases, SQL and 4GLs

Texts providing a more extensive treatment of databases include

A. Abdellatif, J. Le Bihan and M. Limame, *Oracle – A User's Guide*, Macmillan Computer Science Series, 1990.

C. J. Date, 'A Critique of the SQL Database Language', *SIGMOD Record*, Vol. 14, No. 3, 1984.

C. J. Date, *An Introduction to Database Systems, Vol. 1*, 4th edition, Addison-Wesley, 1986.

C. J. Date, *A Guide to the SQL Standard*, Addison-Wesley, 1987.

S. M. Deen, *Principles and Practice of Database Systems*, Macmillan Computer Science Series, 1985.

D. M. Kroenke, *Database Processing*, 2nd edition, SRA, 1983.

E. Lynch, *Understanding SQL*, Macmillan Computer Science Series, 1990.

F. R. McFadden and J. A. Hoffer, *Database Management*, Benjamin–Cummings, 1985.

J. Martin, *Principles of Database Management*, Prentice-Hall, 1976.

J. Martin, *Fourth Generation Languages, Vol. 1*, Prentice-Hall, 1985.

R. F. van der Lans, *Introduction to SQL*, Addison-Wesley, 1988.

Index